NOT QUITE SHAMANS

A VOLUME IN THE SERIES

Culture and Society after Socialism

edited by Bruce Grant and Nancy Ries

A list of titles in this series is available at www.cornellpress.cornell.edu.

Not Quite Shamans

Spirit Worlds and Political Lives in Northern Mongolia

Morten Axel Pedersen

Cornell University Press *Ithaca and London*

First published 2011 by Cornell University Press
First printing, Cornell Paperbacks, 2011

Printed in the United States of America

Library of Congress Cataloging-in-Publication Data

Pedersen, Morten Axel, 1969–
    Not quite shamans : spirit worlds and political lives in northern Mongolia / Morten Axel Pedersen.
        p. cm. — (Culture and society after socialism)
    Includes bibliographical references and index.
    ISBN 978-0-8014-4910-9 (cloth : alk. paper) —
    ISBN 978-0-8014-7620-4 (pbk. : alk. paper)
  1. Shamanism—Political aspects—Mongolia.   2. Post-communism—
Mongolia.   3. Mongolia—Politics and government—1992–   I. Title.
II. Series: Culture and society after socialism.
    BL2370.S5P36 2011
    306.09517'309049—dc22   2010047278

Cloth printing   10 9 8 7 6 5 4 3 2 1

Paperback printing   10 9 8 7 6 5 4 3 2 1

For Kimi

Contents

Acknowledgments

This book has been a long time in the making, and many people have contributed greatly to its completion. First of all, I wish to thank those people from northern Mongolia who allowed me to participate in their lives with such openness, curiosity, and above all hospitality. In particular, I express my heartfelt thanks to the following persons from the Ulaan-Uul district and neighboring towns, villages, and nomadic settlements in Hövsgöl province: Ts. Ganhuyag, G. Dariimaa, G. Ariun-Mörön, G. Ariun-Bayar, G. Ariun-Bold, G. Arvin, R. Terbish, Ts. Enebish, the late T. Tsetsegmaa, G. Enhbayar, P. Battsetseg, Yo. Seseer, H. Maruush, Ch. Bold-Erdene, Ö. Sarantsetseg, Ts. Toljaa, the late S. Davaajii, D. Amar, L. Nyamdalai, Ch. Nyamsüren, Ts. Batsuur', R. Hürel, R. Soslov, S. Baasanjav, R. Enhtuya, L. Bayarmagnai, Ts. Tümen-demberel, Sh. Enh-Amgalan, T. Enhtuya, and A. Otgonbayar, Mr. Sanjid, Mr. Dorj-Palam, Mr. Bashish, and the late L. Nadmid.

The final form of this book has been much influenced by the comments and critique received from a number of readers along the way. Above all, I express my deep sense of appreciation to Caroline Humphrey, who supervised the doctoral research on which this book is partly based. Her work sets a standard for anthropological scholarship on both the postsocialist world and Inner Asia, and its lasting influence on my own work is obvious. I also thank my second Ph.D. supervisor, David Sneath, a scholar whose prodigious knowledge of Mongolian history and society is exceeded only by his clarity of thought; and the members of my viva voce committee, Roberte Hamayon and Marilyn Strathern, whose respective contributions to the field of anthropology have also been formative for my argument, albeit in very different ways. At Cornell University Press I thank John Ackerman, Susan Barnett, Ange Romeo-Hall, and Amanda Heller, the copyeditor. A big thank you also goes to Peter Geschiere, who as a reader for the Press offered a generous, learned, and constructive response. Finally, I am enormously grateful to the two series editors, Bruce Grant and Nancy Ries, whose support, encouragement, and suggestions have been truly invaluable and instrumental in the making of this book.

Four anthropologist friends, alongside some of whom I have carried out ethnographic fieldwork in northern Asia, deserve special mention for their lasting and pervasive influence on my thinking: Martin Holbraad, Lars Højer, Morten Nielsen, and Rane Willerslev. In addition, I thank the following scholars for stimulating discussions, critical questions, comments on drafts, recommendations about literature, and much more: Christopher Atwood, Anders Blok, Ole Bruun, Nils Bubandt, Uradyn Bulag, Mikkel Bunkenborg, Matei Candea, Gregory Delaplace, Philippe Descola, Hildegaard Diemberger, Yves Dorémieux, Rebecca Empson, Esther Fihl, Jerome Game, Tine Gammeltoft, Giovanni da Gol, Signe Gundersen, Agnieszka Halemba, Judith Hangartner, Kirsten Hastrup, Heiko Henkel, Leo Howe, Steven Hugh-Jones, A. Hürelbaatar, Tim Ingold, Casper Bruun Jensen, Peter Kirby, Regnar Kristensen, Heonik Kwon, Gaëlle Lacaze, James Leach, Laurent Legrain, Michael Mahrt, Mandühai Buyandelger, Peter Marsh, Ida Sofie Matzen, Latetia Merli, Carlos Mondragon, Nasanbayar, Ida Nicolaisen, Ton Otto, Adam Reed, Andreas Roebstorff, Cecilie Rubow, Amira Salmon, Steven Sangren, Michael Scott, Finn Sivert-Nielsen, Vera Skvirskaja, Inger Sjørslev, Nikolai Ssorin-Chaikov, Carla Stang, Andrea Stockl, Katie Swancutt, Bjørn Thomassen, Anna Tsing, Terence Turner, Martijn van Beek, Henrik Vigh, Ricardo Vitale, Piers Vitebsky, Eduardo Viveiros de Castro, Roy Wagner, Sari Wastell, Britt Winthereik, Alan Wheeler, and Susan Whyte. Thanks go also to Bayar-Mandah Gaunt, Bayarmaa Khalzaa, Tim Morris, and Uranchimeg for linguistic assistance, to Laurent Legrain and Latetia Merli for permission to use images, and to Ann Dunbar-Nobes, Dina Dineva, Steen Kelsaa, and Ea Rasmussen for helping to prepare the manuscript, the index, and the illustrations for publication.

The moral support and practical assistance I received, in Denmark, Britain, and Mongolia, from family, friends, and colleagues have been invaluable. In addition to my wife, Kimiko, to whom this book is dedicated, and my mother, Ellen, the other person without whose enduring love and relentless support this book would not have been written, I extend my warm thanks to Bjørn Bedsted, Christel Braa, Alistair Carr, Nikola Dimitrov, the late Klaus Ferdinand, Jerome Game, Rolf Gilberg, Jens Rune Gissel, Michael Haslund-Christensen, Søren Haslund-Christensen, Mette Holm, Pie and Hans Meulenkamp, Tim Morris, Dastan Nigamet, Bulgan Nyama, the late Else Olsen, Armen Papazian, Libby Peachey, Leif F. Pedersen, Poul Pedersen, Jóse Rodriguez, Pierre Yves Tessier, Søren Sattrup, Torben Vestergård, and Camilla With Aasager.

Several scholars from the Mongolian National University in Ulaanbaatar offered much-appreciated assistance with matters both scholarly and practical: Professor Bat-Ireedüi, Professor Chuluunbaatar, and especially Professor S. Dulam and his son, Professor D. Bumochir, who accompanied me on a memorable trip to northern Mongolia in 2000. I also express my gratitude to my Ulaanbaatar friends, whose hospitality, knowledge, and assistance I have so often benefited from: Jenia Boikov and his family; B. Otgonchimeg and her family; N. Tungalag and her family, including Burmaa; as well as Ch. Chuluunbat, K. Bayarmaa, and Dastan Nigamet. A special thanks to my Mongolian brother Jenia, who, in his unique capacity as friend, research assistant, and urban nomad, has accompanied me on several trips to northern Mongolia.

My research would never have been completed had it not been for the generous support of the following institutions: the Danish Research Academy, His Royal Highness Crown Prince Frederik's Grant for Scientific Expeditions, Her Majesty the Queen of Denmark Margrethe's and Prince Henrik's Fund, King Christian 5th's Fund, Knud Rasmussen Fondet, and Mindefondet, all in Denmark; as well as the William Wyse Fund, King's College, and the Arts and Humanities Research Board in the UK.

Finally, I thank Koninklijke Brill NV for permission to use part of my article "Tame from Within: Landscapes of the Religious Imagination among the Darxads of Northern Mongolia," from *The Mongolia-Tibet Interface: Opening New Research Terrains in Inner Asia,* ed. Uradyn Bulag and Hildegard Diemberger (Leiden: Brill, 2007), 175–96, in chapter 3. I also thank Taylor and Francis Books for permission to use part of my essay "Talismans of Thought: Shamanist Ontologies and Extended Cognition in Northern Mongolia," from *Thinking through Things: Theorizing Artefacts Ethnographically,* ed. Amira Henare, Martin Holbraad, and Sari Wastell (London: Routledge, 2007), 141–66, in chapter 4.

Note on Transliteration and Translation

It is difficult to choose a system for the transliteration of Mongolian terms, since there are several competing conventions, none of which provides any proper standard. In this book I follow the convention adopted by Caroline Pegg (2001) in the transliteration of Outer Mongolian words from Cyrillic. Mongolian terms appearing in citations from other texts remain in their original form, unless typographical reasons have made this impossible. Following convention, I have spelled well-known Mongolian names (such as Genghis Khan) in the form most commonly used in the English-speaking world. Following David Sneath (2000), I refrain from using Mongolian plurals to avoid the multiplication of terms in the text, unless these have been easy to adopt and figure prominently in the book (as in the case of *ongod,* the plural of *ongon,* or shamanic spirit). All translations, unless otherwise stated, are my own.

NOT QUITE SHAMANS

Introduction

As the 1990s drew to a close in the northern Mongolian outpost of Ulaan-Uul (Red Mountain), households often spent the evenings in a state of constant alert. Older children equipped with binoculars were stationed on rooftops to monitor the movements of *agsan* persons. Any trace of alcohol was eradicated from the home. The old and the very young were put to bed early, beneath the family altar. If possible, male relatives or friends were mobilized from other households. In some cases homes were temporarily abandoned for preventive reasons. People, mothers in particular, were tense and found it hard to sleep.

The term *agsan*—which is also used to describe fiery-tempered horses that are particularly difficult to break in—refers to a disturbing condition of drunken rage that was said to afflict a growing number of people in northern Mongolia at the time. The person struck by *agsan* quickly loses control over himself (it is primarily a male phenomenon) and screams, cries, and aims punches in all directions. Angry words may be uttered, but they are made incomprehensible by intermittent sobs and growls resembling those of a shaman possessed by an animal spirit. Indeed, *agsan* persons are said to flit rapidly in and out of different states of consciousness. Anyone may become an object of their drunken violence, whether friend or foe, man or woman, but usually *agsan* is directed toward other male targets, who may well be *agsan* themselves. In these situations, terrible fights invariably erupt.

Agsan persons are believed not to know what they are doing. "Their souls leave them," people say. For the same reason, a person afflicted with *agsan* cannot be reasoned with; only physical intervention will do. It was not uncommon during my time in Ulaan-Uul for people to tie up intoxicated men with ropes and leave them until they had calmed down, often a matter of hours. Sometimes, however, there were not enough people around to do this, or those present were "only" women and children (or anthropologists). In such cases, the target of the drunken rage (such as the anthropologist) would make a dramatic escape while other people struggled to hold the *agsan* person back, only to become targets themselves. Occasionally entire households were forced into rushed evacuations, jumping the fence into a neighbor's compound and abandoning their home to groups of drunken youths. The next morning they would return to find that their home had been ransacked "as if a mad bear had been there," in the words of one housewife.

It is important to emphasize that I am not talking about rare incidents. The persistent flow of gossip involving new cases of *agsan* testified to this: A young guy was stabbed yesterday. Another man beat up his wife, again. Last week, outside the cultural center, someone slammed a rock into the head of one of the policemen; his condition is poor. And so on. Indeed, in the late 1990s Ulaan-Uul was notorious for its drunken violence. A former police officer from the regional capital told me how surprised he had been by the number and severity of crimes in "such a small place." Many locals concurred. "Our village," a doctor remarked with a characteristic mixture of pride and despair, "is the most alcoholic, most violent, and most impoverished in the entire country."

With the sudden, unexpected, and dramatic collapse of state socialism in 1990, drunkenness, unemployment, and violence became part of everyday life in northern Mongolia, especially in isolated and impoverished communities like Ulaan-Uul, which were left shell-shocked by the dramatic effects of the so-called transition from state socialism and a planned economy to liberal democracy and market capitalism. Faced with an escalating economic crisis and rapidly collapsing state institutions, many households in Ulaan-Uul reverted to a nearly cashless economy based on nomadic pastoralism, but also on supplementary sources of income such as petty trading, hunting, and berry picking. In district centers the situation was particularly bad, as the majority of households muddled through with only a handful of animals, various odd jobs, and perhaps a tiny pension.

As elsewhere in postsocialist Mongolia, the rising poverty, alcoholism, and violence in Ulaan-Uul was widely associated with "the age of the market" (*zah zeeliin üye*). The standard complaint went as follows: "Back during socialism, there were jobs for everyone, and the state was strong. Now, with democracy [*ardchilal*] and the market [*zah zeel*], the politicians have all become thieves and the policemen have all turned lazy, many young women have left to work or study in the city, and the young men have nothing to do. There is too much vodka and too little work around here. So *agsan* is everywhere." Another common complaint was that both national and regional governments were neglecting remote districts like Ulaan-Uul. The drivers and traders were grumbling that the road to the regional capital was not being maintained, and there was general agreement that the local district administration was not receiving adequate funds to pay salaries, let alone maintain the health clinic, the kindergarten, and the school.

At first glance, what we are seeing here is a familiar postsocialist scenario, in which the combination of rapidly increasing unemployment and ever more desperate hardship and poverty, together with escalating mistrust of the state institutions, creates a spiral of violence, alcoholism, and mounting social and political tension. This indeed was my own preliminary conclusion after my first few weeks in Ulaan-Uul. Much as anthropologists have reported from many other formerly state socialist contexts (Anderson 2000; Berdahl, Bunzl, and Lampland 2000; Burawoy and Verdery 1999; Humphrey 1998, 2002; Nazpary 2002; Rethmann 2000; Ries 1997; Ssorin-Chaikov 2003; Verdery 1996, 2003; Yurchak 2006), notions of "democracy," "the market," and "transition" in Ulaan-Uul were not just associated with specific political changes and economic policies such as liberal democracy and structural reform, but were seen as harbingers of a total societal and cultural upheaval.

My tentative interpretation at this early stage was that the perceived rise in *agsan* was indicative of a general sense of "violent chaos"—to borrow Joma Nazpary's apt term from his urban ethnography of postsocialist Kazakhstan (2002). According to Nazpary's neo-Marxist analysis, former communist countries such as Kazakhstan (and, presumably, Mongolia) fell victim in the 1990s to a "chaotic mode of domination," an unruly, and unholy, alliance between different hegemonic actors on the national as well as the international level, which rested on a largely tacit agreement about the usefulness for the powers that be of constant but opaque reform and permanent but vaguely promised change. The result was that the majority of people in Kazakhstan found themselves increasingly dispossessed by this strategically generated "chaos" (*bardak*). In place of the society and the economy they had once felt part of, they now sensed "a total void which permeate[d] all aspects of life....The breakdown of social trust and the sudden emergence of the random and invisible logic of the market forces accompanied by the alienated and alienating greed for accumulation of capital, bolstered by the enormous use of force, create[d] the experience of a very ontological disruption" (Nazpary 2002, 4).

In many ways, northern Mongolia in the late 1990s—especially a remote and poor place like Ulaan-Uul—was a model case of postsocialist chaos in Nazpary's sense. Particularly during the spring of 1999, when what little was left of the old socialist welfare state essentially ceased to exist as Ulaan-Uul's teachers and policemen went on strike or simply refused to work after months of unpaid wages, an unnerving sense of disintegration spread to nearly all levels of social life. Individuals and households that had hitherto been mostly spared from episodes of drunken violence and other social problems seemingly associated with "the age of the market" suddenly found themselves to be both subjects and objects, perpetrators and victims, of *agsan* and other uncontrollable forces (such as "the shamanic disease," or *udha*), whose opaque nature and mysterious origin could not easily be accounted for by more straightforward socioeconomic explanations. It was during this same period that, on a number of occasions, *agsan* men tried to extort goods from me by threatening to beat me up. Soon, like the members of my host family, I learned to navigate the dusty village streets along certain routes so as to avoid hot spots where thirsty hordes of unemployed youths congregated, just as I learned to buy my supplies of *arhi* (vodka) and cigarettes from a few trusted shop owners I knew would not betray me even if faced with the risk of being beaten up. For, as my host told me, "it is perfectly fine to lie to someone who is *agsan*, for he is not fully human!"

Remarks such as these made me realize that quintessentially postsocialist phenomena like *agsan* were not simply understood by people in Ulaan-Uul as being caused by rising unemployment and the neoliberal downsizing of the state. Therefore, conventional frames for anthropological explanations like Nazpary's could account for only one side of the coin. For many people in Ulaan-Uul, it was not clear whether the deteriorating conditions of their own and other people's lives were caused by restless shamanic spirits or by runaway market forces, nor did they always distinguish between the two. The only thing that was clear was that the chaos and misery, but also the hope, that were so characteristic of the time were conditioned by invisible and unpredictable forces that took the same labile, amorphous, and capricious shapes that often characterize the spirit worlds of Mongolian and other Inner Asian shamanic contexts.

In its interweaving between shamanism and violence, between the invisible powers of the spirits and the no less opaque forces of postsocialist transition, and between an entrenched feeling of powerlessness and an equally ingrained sense of humor, the *agsan* figure, and people's responses to it, captures the main theme of this book. In being the instrument of occult forces whose manifestation is beyond his control, the *agsan* person is like a shaman, but not quite. Like the shamans who used to be so plentiful in Ulaan-Uul (or so people like to say), he embodies potent nonhuman forces. But whereas shamans can decide when and for what purpose they lose their minds and allow nonhuman beings to take up temporary residence in their bodies, *agsan* persons and other potential shamans resemble newborn children, inexperienced hunters who offend the spirit masters of the game, or the targets of mischievous jokes and malicious slander: their souls are all too easily lured away.

In the most general terms, then, this is a book about shamanism. Or, more precisely, it is a study of shamanism without shamans. Based on nearly three years' fieldwork in Mongolia between 1995 and 2001, it explores what happened to a remote community at the heart of Inner Asia whose occult experts fell victim to the political purges of the 1930s, and whose transition to liberal capitalism allowed—and perhaps demanded—a renewal of occult sensibilities. At the same time, it is a theoretical experiment. As an account of recent political, economic, and cultural transformations in Mongolia through the defamiliarizing prism of shamans and the lack of them, it is an attempt to write about postsocialism, and shamanism, in a new way. The result is an ethnography of a community that sees itself as incurably labile; a chronicle of selves and bodies changing uncontrollably in the face of occult forces that take the form of spirits, the market, and democracy.

Shamanism without Shamans

I first arrived in Ulaan-Uul in July 1998 with the objective of investigating the different powers of, and different relations between, human and nonhuman "owners" (*ezed*) in the Darhad Mongolian landscape (Humphrey 1995; Pedersen 2009; Sneath 2000). From earlier visits to northern Mongolia—as a student of anthropology, I had spent several months in the region in 1995–96 and during the summer of 1997—I had a hunch that concepts of the land might be interrelated with concepts of authority so that the power of different human persons was homologous with the power of different nonhuman persons (spirits, wild animals). This suggested a kind of totemic logic in Lévi-Strauss's sense (1962), where the different powers of humans were similar to differences in nonhuman agents' power (Pedersen 2001). I also expected to find shamans playing a key role in—perhaps even be at the very heart of—this spiritual economy, as they certainly did in most of the literature on Mongolian shamanism as well as in several studies of shamans from elsewhere in Inner Asia (Holmberg 1989; Mumford 1989; Samuel 1993).

Indeed, Darhad shamanism, along with Darhad cultural traditions more generally, had been the subject of significant scholarly interest among Mongolian, Soviet, Hungarian, and French ethnographers since the early twentieth century.[1] Yet only a few attempts had been made to connect these findings

---

1. Studies of Darhad shamanism include Badamhatan (1986, 157–94); Diószegi (1961, 1963); Dulam (1992); Dulam and Even (1994); Even (1988–89, 110–74); Pegg 2001; Pürev (1993, 1999);

to well-known anthropological studies of Mongolian shamanism (notably Hamayon 1990; Humphrey 1996), let alone to draw comparisons with key studies of shamanism from elsewhere in the world (such as Atkinson 1989; Kendall 1985; Taussig 1987; Tsing 1993; and Vitebsky 1993).[2] I found this ironic, as the English word "shaman" is derived from the Tungus-Manchurian term *saman*, which, according to Mircea Eliade's classic treatise, denotes the very ur-form of shamanism (1964). Given the cultural and geographic proximity between northern Mongolia's Darhads and the Evenki peoples of southern Siberia, this seemed to suggest that to study Darhad shamanism would, in a sense, amount to studying the mother of all shamanisms, if one understands this to mean the particular form taken by this seemingly inexhaustible subject of anthropological inquiry among a small indigenous people in the heart of Asia.

Rather excited by this prospect, I was more than a little disappointed when, upon my arrival in Ulaan-Uul, people told me that there were no "genuine shamans" (*jinhene böö*) to be found in their community. The problem was not simply that shamans were considered less powerful than in "the old days" (as in Denmark, where I live, people might say that summers are not as pleasant, or young people not as polite, or universities not as independent "as they used to be"). It was that those persons who did call themselves shamans (*böö*) were accused of being "fake shamans" (*hudal böö*), who, as my new hosts complained on the very first day, "have no clue what they are doing, apart from wanting our money."

Indeed, contrary to what many foreign and local scholars (along with many non-Darhad Mongolians) believe, Mongolia was home to only a handful of Darhad shamans in the late 1990s. While shamans did practice unofficially throughout the socialist period, and although Mongolia as a whole underwent a significant spiritual revival after the ban on public religious activities was lifted in 1990, people lamented that "by then, all the real shamans were

---

and Sandschejew (1930, 41–65). The literature on Darhad society and history more generally consists of expedition reports, detailed ethnographic descriptions of artifacts of Darhad folklore (songs, prayers, and invocations), and ethnological speculations about the origins of Darhad culture (Badamhatan 1980, 1986; Diószegi 1961, 1963; Dulam 1992; Dulam and Even 1994; Even 1988–89; Potanin 1983; Pürev 1993, 1999, 2004, 2008; and Sandschejew 1930). In addition to these (to different degrees and in different terms) relatively dated studies, a new body of ethnographic scholarship is emerging, my own work included, which may be described as more up-to-date in empirical and theoretical terms (Hangartner 2006, forthcoming; Lacaze 1996, 2000; Legrain 2007, 2008a, 2008b; and Pegg 2001).

2. In addition to the well-known work by Hamayon (notably 1990, 1993, 1994) and Humphrey (notably 1995, 1996, 2007), published works in English on contemporary Mongolian shamanism include Buyandelger (1999, 2007); Empson (2006, 2011); Kristensen (2007); Merli (2006); Pedersen (2001, 2007a); and Swancutt (2006, 2007).

gone."[3] For many if not most people I met, this represented a real loss, even if there were also those who did not care, and a few who were clearly pleased by it. ("What do we need these freaks for anyway?" a driver once asked me.)

Ironically, the shaman deficit was particularly pronounced in the traditional Darhad heartland around the Ulaan-Uul and Renchinlhümbe districts, where, I was repeatedly told over the following days and weeks, there simply were no "genuine shamans" to be found. As if to compensate for the lack of "genuine shamans," the Ulaan-Uul community was instead full of people who were "like shamans" (*böö shig*)—a troublesome group of restless, vodka-loving, and violently disposed men in their twenties, thirties, and forties, who seemed to be permanently stuck in the process of becoming shamans. The problem with these incomplete or potential shamans, as I call them (apart from the fact that they were after one's money), was that they attracted the restless souls of dead shamans and living animals without being able to control them. Frequently subject to *agsan,* and universally feared for their unpredictable, extreme, and downright "crazy" (*galzuu*) behavior, these young—and sometimes not so young—fellows (they were all men) were considered, by themselves and by others, to be stalled in the process of becoming shamans because of a politically generated lack of senior shamans to teach them how to tame the spirits of which these "half-shamans" (*hagas böö*) were the driverless vehicles.

It was these incomplete or potential shamans, and the fears and resentments of others toward them, that came to be the focus of my work, and it was because of this involuntary thematic reorientation from whole shamans to half-shamans that I became genuinely interested in questions pertaining to the so-called transition from state socialism to liberal capitalism. Until this point I had, a little naïvely perhaps, imagined that socialism would simply be one context among others in my study of contemporary Darhad shamanism. But more than anywhere else, it was in the amorphous bodies—and the labile minds—of Ulaan-Uul's *agsan*-prone half-shamans that the imbrication of shamanism and postsocialism in Mongolia in the late 1990s manifested itself most vividly.

My argument in this book is based on the ethnographic premise that the half-shamans served as a sort of gathering point for all the multifarious

---

3. Such negative comparisons with the past are common across the postsocialist world. As Balzer notes, "nostalgia is currently rife in Siberia for the pre-Soviet days when powerful shamans, in control of a panoply of spirits traveling across multiple layers of the universe, could cure patients during deeply dramatic and transforming, community-wide séances" (2006, 78). See also Halemba (2006) and Højer (2009) for two highly perceptive accounts of the individual and collective agency (as opposed to passivity) generated by the perceived loss of cultural knowledge in the Inner Asian context.

effects and affects of postsocialist transition in northern Mongolia in the late 1990s. Above all, what people found to be the annoying presence and dangerous proliferation of incomplete shamans in their communities fueled the sense that with the advent of the age of the market, occult forces that had been kept at bay during the socialist period were suddenly interfering uncontrollably and unpredictably in their lives.

Thus, one of the most pervasive sensibilities in the Ulaan-Uul community in the late 1990s was a menacing sense that far too many spirits were on the loose, and that far too little shamanic knowledge and skill were available to rein in this occult excess. Tellingly, no such sense (or fear) of shamanic overdrive was associated with the socialist period. In spite of, or perhaps because of, the de facto ban on occult practices during socialism, the spirits did not seem bothered by the lack of attention and mostly left people alone. This is not to say that the spirits were not there, or that some of them (such as the souls of dead shamans) were not interfering in the lives of certain people, in particular those descended from families with shamans. But it is clear that, as far as the Ulaan-Uul community as a collectivity was concerned—the district, the collective farm, and the government and party institutions that used to define it as a state socialist political and economic unit—the spirits were not felt to play a prominent role in people's lives.

But then, beginning in 1990, people in northern Mongolia witnessed a veritable ontological meltdown, as the once immutable institutions of the socialist welfare state (such as infrastructure, health services, and education) gradually crumbled to dust. As indicated by the proliferation of *agsan* and other instances of loss of control over body and soul, this slow but relentless breakdown of the world as people had known it was not conceived of as merely a transition from one political and economic system to another. Rather, with the advent of the so-called transition, people found themselves exposed to a violent intrusion of invisible forces, energies, and substances, which, during seventy years of socialism, had hovered only in the shadowy margins of self, household, community, and nation. As one man said, it was as if all sorts of uninvited guests had crashed the gates of his *hashaa* (compound), forcing him to engage with all sorts of spiritual entities he had never quite believed in (*itgeegüi*), let alone shown any real interest in knowing about (*medeh*).

It is my central contention that what people took to be the annoying presence and dangerous transgressions of the potential shamans brought together in one figure this double sensation of spiritual excess and postsocialist chaos. In the labile minds and amorphous bodies of these personae, "global" problems of late capitalism, neoliberal governance, and post-authoritarian democracy intersected with "local" concerns about failing state institutions, political oppression, and spiritual loss. On the one hand, the lack of a strong state and viable economic institutions was perceived to have given rise to the disturbing state of total rupture that was commonly known as transition. On the other hand, the lack of "genuine" shamans meant that the creative potential of this cosmic turmoil could not be contained and harnessed in the way it ought to be. The people of Ulaan-Uul were left to deal with a generation of potential shamans, who, so to speak, were an anachronistic residue, a perverse solidification of long-gone socialist politics.

In short, people in northern Mongolia found themselves in a paradoxical situation: most if not all the shamans had disappeared, but the spirits—and the complex assemblage of ideas, practices, and artifacts associated with these occult entities—had come back. This book is about that paradox; it examines the nature and efficacy of shamanic agency in a postsocialist context in which there is plenty of shamanism but hardly any shamans.

At the Edge of Empire

But what is the historical trajectory of local, regional, and global conditions and developments that has led to this state of shamanism without shamans? Might there be something distinctly Mongolian, or distinctly shamanic, about this postsocialist predicament that calls for a rethinking of existing theories about the interweaving of spirit worlds and political lives in postcolonial contexts? Only after having addressed these questions will I be able to return to the issue of people's lives in transition and flesh out the central message of my argument about shamanic agency in northern Mongolia after socialism.

For as long as anyone can remember, the Darhad homeland (*nutag*) has been one of the most remote and impoverished places in Mongolia, if not Inner Asia as a whole. Located west of the Hövsgöl Nuur, Mongolia's biggest freshwater lake, southeast of the Tuvinian Autonomous Republic and southwest of the Buryat Autonomous Region of Russia, the Shishged Depression—or Darhad Depression, as it is also called—is geographically sealed off from the outside world, virtually encapsulated by the Sayan Mountains and the Hordil Sar'dag Mountains (2,500–3,500 meters elevation).[4] Only a single dirt road leads into the Shishged (as I call it from now on),

---

4. Of a total area of 20,000 square kilometers, only about one-third of the Shishged is suitable for Mongolian-style nomadic pastoralism. The remaining two-thirds is *taiga*: coniferous forest, interrupted by streams and rivers, and occasional stretches of bog. The Shishged Depression proper—a pancake-flat basin (1,200–1,400 m.)—consists of grassland that is extremely well watered, as it is crisscrossed by rivers, lakes, and marshes.

and this sometimes closes in the winter because of excessive snowfall. Indeed the climate in the Shishged is harsh even by Mongolian standards. In January the temperature at times plummets below minus 50 degrees centigrade (approximately 58 degrees below zero Fahrenheit), but more typical winter temperatures hover between minus 30 and minus 44 degrees (from minus 22 to minus 47 degrees Fahrenheit). During the short but intense summer, by contrast, the daytime temperature may reach 35 degrees centigrade (95 degrees Fahrenheit), and it can be very humid with frequent thunderstorms.

With a population of more than ten thousand Darhads in its three districts (*sum*), the Shishged is the only place in Mongolia where Darhad people are, and have for centuries been, in the majority.[5] The region is also home to a much-studied group of Tuvinian reindeer herders, the so-called Tsaatang or Duha (Badamhatan 1962; Kristensen 2007; Pedersen 2009, 2009; Wheeler 1999, 2000); a relatively limited number of Halh Mongols, otherwise by far the dominant ethnic group in Mongolia; an obscure population of several hundred so-called Urianhai Darhads; as well as various individuals from other ethnicities, including Kazaks and Chinese.[6] According to Christopher Atwood, in 1989 the Darhad were the most rural of Mongolia's ethnic groups, with 61.5 percent collective herders, 10.1 percent white-collar employees, and 28.4 percent workers or employees of state farms; by contrast, the national averages were 27.8 percent, 21.4 percent, and 50.6 percent, respectively (Atwood 2004, 132). There is nothing new about this picture. For centuries if not millennia, the Shishged region and its indigenous inhabitants have been known as a destitute, barbarian, and shamanic backwater whose fate was always to hover at the edge of civilization. Indeed, since the rise of the Mongol Empire in the thirteenth century if not before, social life in the Shishged seems to have fluctuated between periods of political, cultural, and religious integration when the region was incorporated into large-scale Eurasian polities, and periods of political, cultural, and religious fragmentation when it was not governed by any single sovereign but subject instead to ever-shifting

5. Thousands of Darhads live in Mongolia's three largest and most industrialized cities, Ulaanbaatar, Erdenet, and Darhan, as well as Mörön, the Hövsgöl regional capital.

6. Urianhai Darhads, who seem to be concentrated in Ulaan-Uul's two westernmost *bags*, have an ambiguous ethnic status in the Shishged. While quite a few people spoke of them as "not really Darhads but Urianhai," they themselves claim (with some justification) that they constitute the most traditional group in Ulaan-Uul. Unlike their Darhad peers, most Urianhai I met subcribed to a clan (*ovog*) and were able to claim common ancestry with other Turkic-speaking groups in Hövsgöl, including not just their Duha neighbors but also the Arig and Üüriin Urianhai living east of Lake Hövsgöl. Still, it should be emphasized that very few of the Urianhai Darhads I met spoke any Tuvinian language; all of them lived in Mongolian-style yurts; and there was a high level of intermarriage between them and other groups in the area.

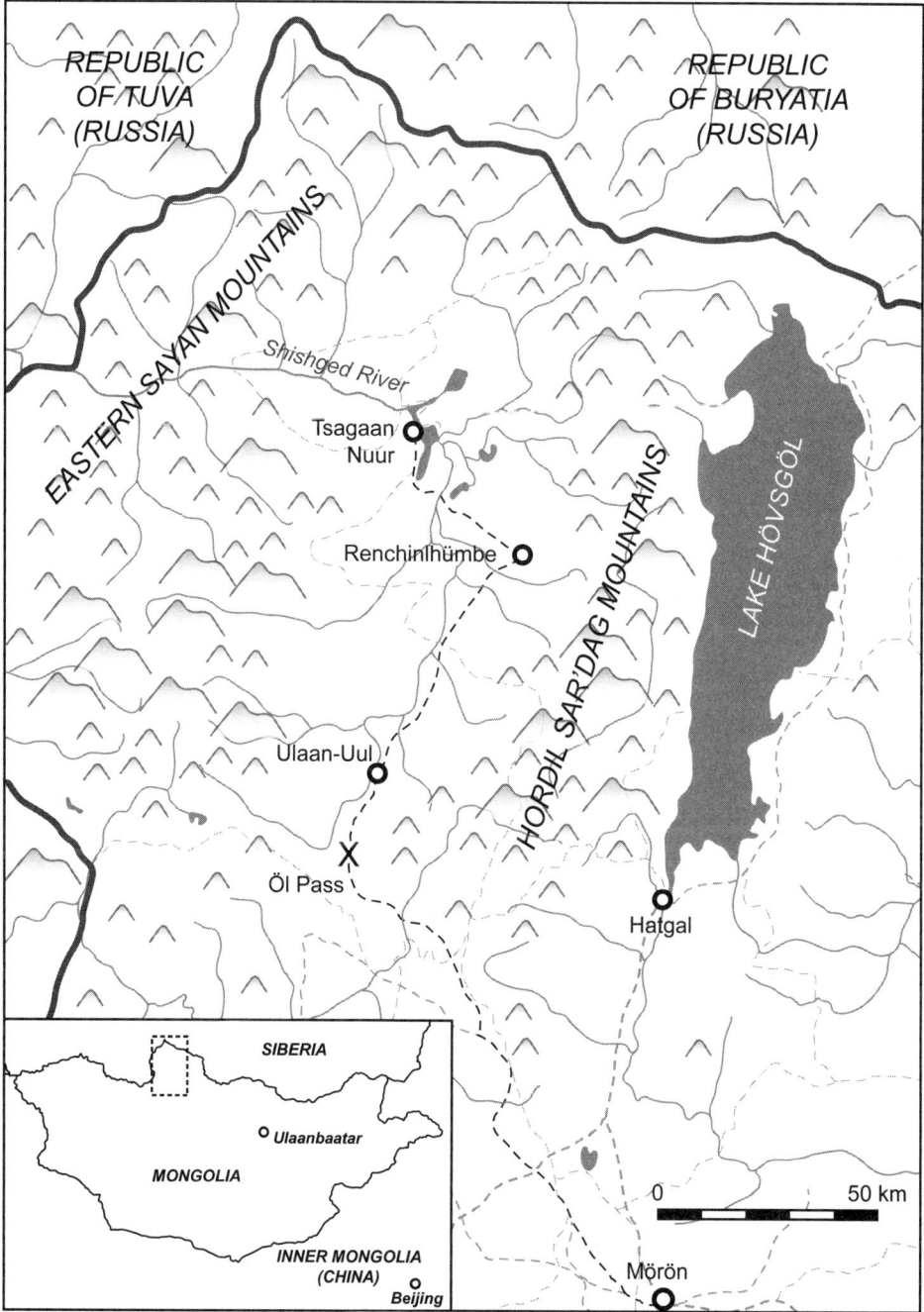

Figure 1. The Shishged Depression. Map drawn by Ea Rasmussen

alliances and feuds between various tribes and their chiefs (Christian 1998; Sinor 1990; Sneath 2007; Vainshtein 1980).

When Genghis Khan was enthroned in 1206, the Shishged was inhabited by so-called forest-peoples (*oin irged*), a patronizing term used by rulers of the central Mongolian plains to describe those they considered to be savage hunters and reindeer breeders of the north. It was at this key moment in Mongolian history that Huduha Beki, an Oirat leader, having submitted to Genghis Khan after his defeat on the battlefield, guided Genghis's eldest son, Jochi, to the Shishged and ordered his *tümen* ("thousands," an ancient military unit) to submit to the new khan (Cleaves 1982, 173). In doing so, Huduha Beki secured the survival of the Oirats as a tribe, while other opponents of Genghis such as the Tatars and the Merkits were annihilated down to the last man (Ratchnevsky 1991; Morgan 1986). More specifically, Huduha's alliance with Genghis Khan ensured that the Shishged, which until then had been dominated by Turkic peoples, would henceforth be part of the Mongolian cultural zone (Badamhatan 1980, 21–22).

With the disintegration of the Mongol Empire in 1368, northern Mongolia entered a tumultuous period about which very little is known. It is reasonable to assume, however, that for nearly four hundred years, until the final defeat of the Jungar (Oirat) federation by the Qing or Manchu Empire in 1757, the Shishged was caught in endlessly shifting alliances and antagonisms between different polities. "Political life," as Charles Bawden puts it, "had degenerated into a centrifugal free-for-all in which each leader tried to get as much freedom of action as he could, at the expense of his fellow nobles" (1986, 40). Certainly these were unhappy times for Mongolia's nobility, but they were in all likelihood even harder for those people who did not belong, or were not subject, to any such human master (*ezen*). For long periods the peoples of the Shishged seem to have been "without masters" (*ezengüi*) in this sense; and especially toward the end of this unhappy period of Mongolian history, this remote region seems to have been a political no-man's-land (or perhaps we could say an every-man's-land), where several polities, including the rising empires of tsarist Russia and Qing China, exercised power by offering protection and extracting taxes in what might be called the Great Game of Inner Asia.

In the mid-eighteenth century, the Shishged entered a period of unusual political stability, which lasted until the fall of the Qing Empire in 1911. During this time the Shishged was home to the so-called Darhad Ih Shav' (Darhad Great Ecclesiastical Estate), which belonged to the wider estate of the Jebtsundamba Khutuktu, the leading incarnate lama, or in the popular parlance, the Living Buddha of Mongolia's Buddhists. It was the Darhad Ih Shav' that defined Darhads as a population of Buddhist disciples (*shabinar*) corresponding to an ecclesiastical territory (*shav'*) and administrative office (*shabi yamen*), and it was this political-religious estate that firmly established Buddhism in the Shishged.

Thus the ethnic group known as "the Darhad people" (*Darhad yastan*), the geographical place named the Darhad (or Shishged) Depression (Darhadyn Hotgor), and indeed the occult orientation sometimes referred to as the Darhad shamanic faith (*Darhadyn böö mörgöl*) were all shaped by complex political processes on the fringes of the Qing Empire from the late seventeenth to the early twentieth century.

The shamanic tradition described by the (mostly Buryat) Russian explorers and ethnographers who came to the Shishged in the first half of the twentieth century resembled those of Daur Mongolian and Buryat Mongolian contemporaries. Sandwiched between the Russian and Qing empires, in areas that had always been located at the edge of polities, all three societies were marked by the absence of local nobility, and for that reason clan elders and male shamans played a central political role (Hamayon 1990; Humphrey 1996). But whereas Buddhism never gained a proper foothold among the Daur or the western Buryats, it certainly did in the Shishged. In addition to the "submission of the shamanic institution to clan law" (Hamayon 1994, 83)—which was common in Mongolian societies—the Darhad shamans were also made subject to the "ecclesiastical laws" of the Buddhist estate of the Darhad Ih Shav'.

This did not come about without a fight. Darhad lore is full of narratives about the conflicts between Buddhist lamas and local shamans at the time. In fact, as the French scholar Dominique Even notes, it is quite "paradoxical" that "the Darkhad region, [as a] stronghold of shamanist traditions[,] ... was controlled by the Buddhist church" (1991, 200). The famous Buryat Mongolian scholar and revolutionary Zhamtsarano, who traveled in the Shishged in the late 1920s, was also surprised. "The Darhads," he observed, "have a blossoming monastery with more than 1,000 lamas." Yet to his clear amazement, at the same time "shamanism is widely practiced" (1979, 16; for similar observations, see Sandschejew 1930). Nevertheless, the presence in the Shishged of the country's biggest Buddhist ecclesiastical estate did have the effect of pushing the shamans and their occult objects of worship farther toward and into the forest. Thus, the abodes of most Darhad shamanic spirits (*ongod*) are today found in or around the edge of the taiga, while the region's flat steppe zone is dominated by Buddhist (or Buddhist-influenced) spiritual entities such as mountain spirits (*gazryn ezed*).

Small wonder, then, that one detects a deeply felt polarity between the attraction of the forest and that of the plains among many Darhads, for whom the Shishged taiga seems to be associated with a centrifugal movement of "shamanic" dispersal, whereas the Shishged plains are conversely associated with a centripetal movement of "Buddhist" unification. Indeed, trying to hold the taiga at bay and yet never quite succeeding is in some general sense what being a "Darhad person" (*Darhad hün*) is all about. Many people told me, if not always in exactly the same words, "If we are not vigilant, we risk being sucked back into the taiga, from where we originally came."

There is an element of truth to statements like these. As some people in Ulaan-Uul liked to emphasize (although the majority preferred to keep quiet about it), Darhads originate from a heterogeneous mix of cultural, linguistic, and political groups, only some of whom were considered (and considered themselves) Mongolian. The rest were Tuvinian, Turkic, and possibly even Tungus "forest peoples," who specialized in hunting and reindeer breeding (Badamhatan 1986, 24–25, 41–63). This muddled origin of "the Darhad people" is presumably reflected in the toponyms, legends, and cultic sites of more than thirty Darhad clans (*ovog*) (Badamhatan 1986; Diószegi 1961, 1963; Even 1988–89). Marie-Dominique Even claimed that Darhads "have kept alive their clan identity" (1991, 200). It is my clear impression, however, that "the Darhad clan system" (if indeed there ever was any such thing) has, for all intents and purposes, ceased to exist. With the noteworthy exception of shamanic rituals in which the old clans are always mentioned in the invocation of spirits, the clans today seem to be essentially defunct. Certainly most people I met in the Shishged did not claim any clan identity, nor did clans play any prominent role in daily life in the Ulaan-Uul community. Instead, most statuses to which people subscribed were of state socialist origin.

The Socialist Period

During the early decades of the twentieth century, in a development that was closely bound up with the concurrent social and political turmoil in China and Russia, Mongolia underwent two revolutions: the nationalist revolution of 1911 and the communist/nationalist revolution of 1921. The first revolution was instigated by an alliance of Mongolian nobles and lamas who took advantage of the fall of the Qing to proclaim the theocracy of Mongolia, with the eighth Jebtsundamba Khutuktu as its "Holy Emperor" (Bogd Khan). Over the next decade, Mongolia was subjected to a number of modern reforms, including the establishment of the first (secular) school in the capital, Urga (present-day Ulaanbaatar), and the creation of a national army (trained by Russian officers). For a variety of reasons, however, notably internal strife and the fact that the new state was never recognized by any foreign power apart from Tibet, it was also a period characterized by increasing political instability and great economic hardship. This sparked new patterns of migration, including a growing influx of ethnic Chinese (which had been banned under the Qing) and increasing internal migration across its ever more porous *aimag* and banner (*hoshuu*) borders (Bawden 1986, 187–205).

While the turmoil certainly left its mark on the Shishged—notably when a White Russian warlord, the "Mad Baron" von Ungern-Sternberg, crossed into northern Mongolia with his soldiers in late 1920—life seems to have continued along the path instituted by the Darhad Ih Shav'. Indeed this was the peak of Buddhist power in Mongolia generally and in the Shishged in particular. As Bawden notes, the "church became more and more of a state within a state, supported not only by the contribution of the Shabi, but by a large slice of the state budget too" (1986, 190). The increasing clout of the lamas after Mongolian independence may also explain why several migrant groups were incorporated into the Ih Shav' during these years, presumably as a result of a desperate escape from the still more impossible taxes levied on them by their nearly bankrupt lords.

From 1919 to 1920 Mongolia's independence was gradually lost to China again, only to be regained, in theory, when the Jebtsundamba Khutuktu was reinstated after the Mad Baron's occupation of Urga in early 1921. These developments inspired a recently formed revolutionary movement, which was critical of the alliance between the Mongolian church and the brutal Ungern-Sternberg, to hold the meeting that became known as the first congress of the Mongolian People's (Revolutionary) Party and to proclaim a provisional government in March of that year. By this time the original core of military men and petty officials, having secured Soviet acceptance and eventually tutelage, had gathered a tiny resistance force and set up headquarters on the Mongolian-Russian border. That spring the rebel army, numbering perhaps only a few hundred soldiers, successfully battled much larger contingents of Chinese soldiers and eventually, with substantial military assistance from the Soviet Union, von Ungern-Sternberg's White Russian forces. In early June, General Damdin Sukhbaatar, the famous revolutionary hero, liberated the capital and over the following months routed all foreign troops from the country, except for the Red Army, which would remain until the early 1990s in an advisory role, and which for long periods maintained a substantial military presence, to quell so-called domestic counter-revolutionary threats and in response to the increasingly strained relationship between the Soviet Union and Communist China. With this the second revolution was complete.

Such was the train of events that by 1925 had made Mongolia the world's second communist country, tying its fate so closely to the destiny of its northern neighbor that many Western observers would henceforth call it a "satellite" of the USSR. Indeed, after the proclamation of the People's Republic and the adoption of a new constitution in 1925 (the last Jebtsundamba Khutuktu had died the previous year), Mongolia was subjected to a range of Soviet-inspired reforms, which, over the next two decades, would eradicate the dominant position of the Buddhist church, the aristocratic lords, and the largely foreign (Chinese) traders. Despite these changes, progress toward the creation of a modern, secular socialist state with a centralized economy remained difficult. Indeed, as Bawden notes, a "less promising field for the development of a socialist society along Marxist lines than Mongolia in the year 1921 can hardly be imagined. It was the antithesis of the industrial society in which the proletariat would be the vanguard of the revolution" (1986, 243).

The Shishged was a case in point. While a "general administrator of the Darhads" was appointed by the government in 1921, and new administrative units of local government were established in the same year, the administration and offices of the Darhad Ih Shav' apparently remained in place until 1925, when "the Great Shabi was named Delger [Ih Uul] province, with its territory confined to the Darhad lands and neighboring [Hövsgöl] banners. All connections to monastic estates were abolished" (Atwood 2004, 211).[7] That same year the first party cells were set up in the Shishged, followed by, as in much of the country, not always wholehearted and often haphazard attempts at socialist reform through the voluntary pooling of herds and the opening of state shops, health centers, and schools. Nevertheless, Garma Sandschejew reported after visiting the Shishged in 1927, people "are not keen on the new system." They "do not trust the local government and accuse it of bad practice" and expressed the "wish that the Bogd Khan would return." In fact, he further noted, people had only "very hazy ideas" of what was happening in Russia and the rest of Mongolia. Some even thought that Mongolia was "becoming part of the Soviet Union because both had the same kind of revolution" (Sandschejew 1931, 35).

As in the USSR, this failure to revolutionize rural livelihoods and sensibilities only led the party to speed up the pace of reform. From 1929 to 1932, in what later became known as "the swing to the left," its leaders attempted to jumpstart the Mongolian leap to communism by launching a full-scale attack on "cruel feudalists, shrewd lamas, greedy Chinese traders, and foreign capitalists and generals" (Atwood 2004, 329). Among other things, this entailed forced confiscation of livestock to form obligatory herder communes, random destruction of religious artifacts, and imposition of massive taxes on all non-state bodies and institutions such as the Buddhist church and the trade houses.

---

7. Delger Ih Uul province was short-lived. In 1928 both Darhads and Urianhais were briefly attached to Arhangai province, only to be united with other political units to form Hövsgöl province in 1931 (Atwood 2004, 132; Badamhatan 1986, 35).

In the early 1930s, in what many Darhads today call the Holy War (Shambalyn Dain), catastrophic losses of livestock, combined with the general brutality of the leftist campaign, sparked nationwide unrest. Soon, serious uprisings if not outright civil war broke out in several parts of the country, including southern Hövsgöl, where a monastery became the center of a major revolt. Eventually the rulers were forced to call in the army in order to remain in power. The so-called New Turn Policy, apparently instituted on direct orders from Stalin himself, rolled back many of the economic and cultural reforms. A brief period of political calm from 1932 to 1936 was followed by yet another onslaught of nationwide turmoil with the advent of the so-called Great Purges in 1937. Over the next two years the Communist Party and the Mongolian government, under the dictatorial rule of Marshal Khorloogiin Choibalsan (known as the "Mongolian Stalin"), used the not fully unfounded fears of a Japanese-sponsored conspiracy to set up a "pan-Mongolian" state in Inner Asia. This was in fact a pretext for inviting the Soviet Red Army to assist in a short-lived but brutal reign of terror. In addition to "destroying almost an entire revolutionary generation in Mongolia[,]...open[ing] the way for a new generation of Soviet-educated, and often Russian-married officials" (Atwood 2004, 209–10), the Great Purge also witnessed the final showdown between the communists and the Buddhist church.

Between autumn 1937 and spring 1939, around 25,000 so-called counter-revolutionaries (*esergüü hümüüs*) were executed, and 5,000 or more, mostly lamas, were imprisoned for ten-year terms (Kaplonski 2004). During the same period, the Buddhist church was fully divested of its by then considerably weakened wealth and influence. Of the approximately seven hundred monasteries, large and small, which had been scattered across the Mongolian countryside in the early 1930s, only a handful remained at the end of the decade. The rest were demolished, often down to the last brick or piece of wood, which found new uses in the construction of collective farms. Meanwhile, the party burned sutras and other holy artifacts in great public bonfires intended to eradicate Buddhism from the face of the earth.

The Shishged suffered its toll of destruction. In 1938 its three main monasteries were burned to the ground, and the lamas, who even at this point apparently numbered more than one thousand (Badamhatan 1986, 36), were killed, imprisoned, or in the case of the youngest and poorest, forced into secular education or jobs. I have not been able to retrieve any official data on the purges of lamas (or shamans, for that matter), but I was told by an elderly survivor who used to be a *bandi* (neophyte lama) in one of the Shishged monasteries that more than ninety people were "taken away by the army," mostly high- or mid-ranking lamas. Presumably the majority of the captives were either shot or left to rot in prison, for only a handful managed to return, sometimes after ten years or more, always to the great shock of their relatives, who had thought them dead (Pedersen 2006b).

Although Choibalsan remained in power until his death in 1952, the Second World War was a watershed in the modern history of Mongolia. The intensity of political repression decreased as the country became embroiled in the war, both in an active military sense (several battles were fought between Mongolian-Russian and Japanese forces) and in a more passive sense (for example, herders were asked to supply the Red Army with meat and other animal products). It was not until the 1950s that the nature of rural life started to undergo significant changes. Indeed, it can be argued that not until the postwar years did social life in northern Mongolia become fundamentally and irreversibly transformed through the institutionalization of a planned economy. This was, as various people's stories about the time also convey, the point of no return.

Among the many radical changes instigated by the Mongolian communists in the course of their nearly seventy-year reign, the introduction of the collective farms (*hödöö aj ahuin negdel*, or *negdel* for short) from 1955 to 1959 stands out as the reform with the most pervasive and wide-ranging consequences. As Bawden points out, it "is worth noting that Mongol writers...usually speak of the collectivization of the herders, not of the herds, thus emphasizing that what [had] been attempted [was] more of a social revolution than a mere transformation of farming methods" (1986, 398). In contrast to what had happened during the ill-fated "left turn" some decades back, this time Mongolia's rulers produced a more comprehensive and coherent plan for "proletarianizing" the rural population through a subtle (and sometimes not so subtle) combination of sticks and carrots. While no one was purged, and there seem to have been few cases of violent resistance, a clear message was conveyed to the herders: you may either volunteer to join the new *negdels* and their offer of superior pastures, transport, distribution, and technical as well as veterinary assistance, or you may remain outside our community (*hamt olon*) and muddle through, subjected as you will be to ever-growing production targets while receiving zero assistance, unlike your collectivized nomadic peers. The message quickly sank in. By 1959 more than 99 percent of adults in rural Mongolia had joined a *negdel* (membership started at age sixteen), and most of the country's livestock, numbering 23 million, had been collectivized too, though herders were allowed to retain ownership of a portion of their former herds for their own purposes (Bawden 1986, 394–404).

Take the example of the Shishged. In 1956 two collective farms were opened there: the Happy Life Negdel (Jargalant Am'dral Negdel) in Ulaan-Uul and the Golden Valley Negdel in Renchinlhümbe. (In 1985 a state farm specializing in reindeer breeding, hunting, and fishing was established in Tsagaan Nuur.)[8] For the next thirty-five years or so, these state socialist institutions, along with various government and public welfare bodies associated with the district centers (schools, kindergartens, medical centers, cultural clubs, and so on) organized practically all aspects of social life.[9] People were pooled into herding teams (*suur'*), comprising two to five households (*ail*), in principle if not always in practice nonrelated. They were responsible, and held accountable, for breeding a single type of livestock—in the Shishged mostly cattle—and for meeting centrally planned production quotas. At the same time, each *ail* belonged to one of a handful of brigades (*bag*), which were subsumed under each rural district (*sum*). Each administrative layer had its own government and party cell, thus replicating the dual political structure familiar from other state socialist contexts.[10]

In the decades that followed, the *negdels* extended their sway over people's lives to such an extent that they were at times conflated with the districts whose territory—and to a large extent whose population—they shared. In Ole Bruun's words, it was

> the most complex community ever built on the steppe....Health and educational standards were vastly improved, veterinary service had advanced both animal and human health, and economic security was secured through stable salaries, motorized assistance when moving the camp, emergency fodder supplies for animals in hard winters, and collective restocking....The cultural center offered theatre, music and dance performances by traveling troupes, public balls, dance lessons, and political meetings. (2006; 14–15; see also Bawden 1986, 401–2)

Indeed, to judge from what people told me about life during the heyday of the *negdel* (1957–1990), it is difficult to point to any corner of a person's life, whether public or private, official or nonofficial, that was not in some way or another influenced by the (omni)presence of these institutions. This was the case even where this influence was mainly prohibitive (as in the banning of informal barter between individuals, households, and even *negdels*) or downright destructive (as in the case of the spirits and other occult matters,

---

8. In fact three collective farms were established in 1956 and 1957, but were then merged into one collective farm in 1958.

9. Although temporary schools had operated in Ulaan-Uul since the 1920s, in 1940 a school with boarding facilities was built in the district center.

10. For more on the history of the Shishged collective farms, see Badamhatan (1986, 34–40) and Pürev (1980).

which people found it hard to talk or even think about as the lamas and shamans disappeared). Perhaps even more than their Siberian counterparts (see Humphrey 1998), in the last decades of socialism the *negdels* of northern Mongolia represented the fulfillment of the modernist dream of a totally organized community. More than in any other society the world has known, these were at least in theory the perfect total social institutions in Émile Durkheim's sense.

The Age of the Market

The political and economic changes that brought state socialism in Mongolia to its knees were radical but largely peaceful. Following its predictable (if reluctant) adaptation to the Soviet reforms instigated by Mikhail Gorbachev beginning in 1985, the Mongolian People's Revolutionary Party saw the first direct challenge to its authority and legitimacy on December 10, 1989. While the consequences were dramatic enough, what took place over the following months could hardly be called a revolution. In contrast to the situation in some eastern European countries, the people who first challenged communist rule in Mongolia belonged, with a few notable exceptions, to Ulaanbaatar's young elite, who had graduated from Russian schools and universities, and whose parents (and often grandparents) enjoyed high positions in state and party. Soon what had begun as a polite display of posters on International Human Rights Day calling for further reform in the spirit of perestroika (*öörchlön baiguulalt*) and glasnost (*il tod baidal*) turned into a full-blown opposition consisting of several newly established political parties. The three most important were the National Progressive Party, the Mongolian Democratic Party (which later morphed into the Mongolian National Democratic Party, but through all its different incarnations has always been the key political platform for Mongolian ultraliberalists and free marketers), and the Mongolian Social Democratic Party (representing a more centrist position in line with European social democratic parties).

By early May 1990, after months of political instability in which the communist rulers tried, with little success, to rein in the Mongolian Democratic Union (as the alliance of reformists called itself) through a combination of mostly moderate containment measures, and during which the new opposition organized rallies (also mostly peaceful, though one left several protesters wounded and one dead), the communist government tried to gather support from trade unions, students, and the wider population. When the opposition eventually resorted to increasingly desperate means such as hunger strikes, the government gave in. Following constitutional change and the adoption of a multiparty system, democratic parliamentary elections were held. To the surprise of the new opposition and many other urbanites, the now re-formed Mongolian People's Revolutionary Party won comfortably. Recognizing the need for national unity in the face of an economic crisis generated by the sudden termination of subsidies from and favorable trade agreements with the USSR and other Comecon countries (which, according to some estimates, accounted for up to one-third of Mongolia's GDP in the 1980s), a number of opposition politicians were invited to participate in the new government. Suddenly, to the surprise of the foreign observers, politicians, and organizations (including NGOs and missionaries) that begun flowing into Mongolia, a new democratic state had emerged in Asia.

The effects of the deteriorating macroeconomic situation were as dramatic as they were swift. In the words of Morris Rossabi, author of one of the most comprehensive accounts of the events of the early 1990s:

> Mongolia's former communist partners now demanded payment in hard currency.... This... led to shortages of fuel, materials, and spare parts.... Factories closed, leading to the first serious levels of unemployment since the advent of the communist state. In the urban areas, such staples as sugar and butter were unavailable, and meat, rice and matches... were rationed. The countryside had meat and dairy products but could often not obtain flour, sugar, candy, and other goods. (2005, 35)

My own accounts from northern Mongolia during these early days speak of a growing sense of confusion and uncertainty, but also a vague but still pervasive sense of freedom and opportunity, as many people sought alternative ways of obtaining goods and income (for instance, by taking up trading), while a small minority became actively involved in politics, setting up local branches and organizing committees for the new parties, or revitalizing the old one.

Despite the fact that the government was largely made up of ex-communists, their approach to the economic crisis might as well have been borrowed from a textbook on neoliberal reform—and in fact, to some degree this was precisely the case.[11] In compliance with the "advice" of international consultants and donors such as the World Bank, the International Monetary Fund, and the Asian Development Bank, and with the enthusiastic support of many Mongolian businesspeople and leading members of the opposition, over the

---

11. Rossabi reports that although Davaadorjiin Ganbold, minister of the economy and first deputy minister, admitted that "he had a 'limited exposure to market economics,' he [sought] to implement an economic program that, 'he recalls proudly,' was exactly according to Milton Friedman's ideology" (2005, 43)

next several years the country embarked on a process of economic liberalization, which later was praised by major proponents of "structural adjustment" as one of the most successful (read: radical) examples of "shock therapy." Like similar policies implemented in eastern and central Europe, as well as much of sub-Saharan Africa, this approach involved a combination of fiscal and decentralizing measures, including

> liberalization of prices and elimination of government subsidies, a balanced government budget, privatization of state assets and of banking, local money linked to a convertible currency, tight credit policies to preclude what [was] considered to be the great evil of inflation, and elimination or reduction of restrictions on foreign trade. Private entrepreneurs would replace government-managed industries, and the planned economy would be dismantled.... [This] would require the government to scale back on what the donor agencies believed to be overly generous social welfare entitlements. (Rossabi 2005, 37–38).

It is certainly telling that in the early 1990s, leaders of the National Democratic Party seriously considered erecting a statue of Milton Friedman in central Ulaanbaatar, at the former site of a Stalin memorial (Rossabi 2005, 82).

In northern Mongolia, the first cracks in the firmament of planned production had appeared in the late 1980s and soon grew wider than anyone could have imagined, let alone predicted. While people in Ulaan-Uul told me that they had followed the dramatic events in Ulaanbaatar closely—or at least as closely as the party's tight control over the media at the time permitted—their most pressing concern clearly was how to deal with the impinging social and economic consequences of "political changes that...were so swift that people [in the countryside] could only react spontaneously" (Bruun 2006, 1).

With the implementation of these and other neoliberal reforms in late 1990, the raison d'être of the collective farms was essentially demolished, and within two years these hitherto dominant institutions had ceased to play any significant role in rural Mongolian life. (Although many *negdels* turned themselves into companies, most closed within a few years, and the few that did survive were so small that they mattered little in the larger picture.) Ulaan-Uul was no exception. In keeping with the government's wish to "privatize everything as fast as possible," as one former leader recalled, first the herds and then other common assets (vehicles, equipment, buildings) from the Happy Life *negdel* were distributed among its several thousand members according to a shareholder procedure, which was later rumored to have favored households belonging to the local elite, many of whose members had also been in charge during the socialist period.

As an example of the murky privatization of the collective farms, consider the dozen or so jeeps and trucks that used to belong to the Happy Life *negdel,* most of which, for practical reasons, were usually parked near the homes of whichever drivers would be on duty the next day. Apparently, one morning in the early 1990s, most drivers woke to discover that overnight they had become the owner of their own vehicle; a few, however, were left with nothing, simply because, they were informed (or so I was told), "it so happened" that the privatization had not taken place during their shift! Although the rationale behind this story may have been more just—or more sinister—than the pure randomness conveyed here, the fact that such stories were so prevalent in northern Mongolia during the late 1990s points to the lack of transparency, if not arrogance and corruption, surrounding the early years of Mongolia's transition to the age of the market.[12]

While the mid-1990s saw a certain slowdown in the intensity of shock therapy, and soon the shops were overflowing with goods (many imported from China by "suitcase traders"), most Mongolian households, rural or urban, continued their seemingly irreversible slide toward poverty. Like so many others in the postsocialist world, they faced the paradox of having access to goods they had never dreamed of, but without any chance of buying them (Verdery 1996). While there were still opportunities galore, or at least so it appeared to the men and women who borrowed huge sums of dollars from private moneylenders to open a stall at a market or a restaurant (often with very limited success), there was a sense that the first wild days of capitalism were giving way to something quite different.

This emerging, rather less hopeful version of the "age of the market" was marked by the incompetence of politicians, the corruption of state officials, and increasing social, economic, and even cultural divisions between rich and poor, country and city. More and more households came to realize that they were not going to be rich after all. Indeed, they were going to stay quite poor, and would have to work harder than ever if they didn't want to find themselves having to beg for food from relatives and friends so as not to starve.

Undoubtedly this mounting dissatisfaction was instrumental in bringing about postsocialist Mongolia's first real change in government since 1990. Until 1996, all elected governments had come from the Revolutionary Party.

12. As elsewhere in rural Mongolia, shares (*huv'*) in formerly state-owned assets were distributed to all members of households, children included. Many shares soon became worthless, however, as firms went bankrupt, while the few that did represent a stake in an economically (which is to say politically) viable company often ended up in the hands of the elite. In the end, as one man joked, "the only value of these shares was as papers for rolling cigarettes—but even for this purpose they weren't any good: the Bibles handed out by the Christians [missionaries] are of superior quality!" (see also Potkanski 1993; Rossabi 2005; and Sneath 2002).

But in the wake of its relatively narrow victory in that year's parliamentary elections, the Democratic Union now had its first shot at running the country. According to the majority of accounts, the new government failed spectacularly. In an attempt to speed up what it considered the painful but necessary transformation to a pure market economy, officials cut taxes, tariffs, and other fiscal regulations. One result was that many cashmere producers went bankrupt as raw wool was bought up and exported across the border to be processed by Chinese companies. At the same time, deregulation of the financial sector led to a proliferation of banks, several of which also went bankrupt or had to be bailed out owing to widespread defaults on loans that, as rumor had it, had originated with shady, vodka-lubricated backroom deals among a self-serving elite of politicians, bureaucrats, tycoons, and other big people (*tomchuud*) and bosses (*bossuud*).

The result was a new onslaught of serious economic—and eventually political—crisis and instability, akin to the chaos of the early 1990s. This time, though, it was arguably the people living in the countryside who suffered the most. This reversed the relative economic disadvantage of urban life, which earlier in the decade had forced many townspeople to migrate to the countryside to become pastoralists (Bruun and Odgaard 1996; Humphrey and Sneath 1999). Faced with an accelerating deficit, the government responded "by first removing 103,000 pensioners from the rolls.…It also rejected pay increases for state medical and educational personnel. The government, with limited resources, did not adequately provide even for the military and other essential personnel.…[D]esperate for funds, the government then resorted to leasing space in state buildings" (Rossabi 2005, 76). The effects were, as one might expect, devastating: "Prices of consumer goods rose 32.6 percent and inflation increased 66 percent in the first four months of Democratic Union rule.…At the same time, real income declined by 30 percent.…Unemployment was conservatively estimated at 20 percent of the population" (Rossabi 2005, 77).

This was the scene when I arrived in Ulaan-Uul in 1998. Since my earlier visits in 1995, the standard of living had clearly deteriorated owing to a combination of the rising cost of energy (firewood), transport (jeep lifts), and flour (noodles being the key supplement to the nomadic diet), on the one hand, and recurring natural disasters (*zud*) on the other. Yet, unlike many other places in rural Mongolia, the Shishged as a whole had experienced no loss of population during the late 1990s; if anything, the population had grown slightly in Ulaan-Uul and neighboring Renchinlhümbe,[13] despite the

---

13. According to local officials, the total out-migration from Hövsgöl province in 1995–2000 was 5,337. In contrast to this general trend, in the period from 1994 to 1998 the population of the Ulaan-Uul district grew from 3,396 to 3,643. Because of its limited amount of good pastureland,

fact that this region of northern Mongolia was at least as hard hit by the economic crisis as the rest of the country (Sneath 2002; Sürenjav 1998). Indeed, I know of several households that had to rely almost entirely on kin and neighbors for food.

In 1997 nearly three-quarters of the 3,500-plus inhabitants of the Ulaan-Uul district (*sum*) were registered in one of its five rural subdistricts (*bag*); that is, they were classified as full-time pastoralists (*malchid*). For the large majority of these countryside households (*ail*)—and for quite a few village households too—animal husbandry was the primary form of livelihood, and in many cases their only source of income (though pensions for the elderly—women past the retirement age of fifty-five and men at sixty—were another key source of cash for many *ails*). People in the Shishged bred (and still do breed) several of the five kinds of livestock commonly associated with Mongolian nomads: horses, cattle, sheep, goats, and camels. What distinguishes the Shishged pastoralists, or at least the wealthier ones, is that their annual migrations are longer than those of most nomads living on the mountain plains of central Mongolia.[14] Because the snowfall is often too deep to allow the livestock to graze, pastoralists with herds over a certain size generally need to migrate to snow-free pastures to the southeast if their animals are to survive the winter and spring.[15] Such migrations require not only the right transportation (such as bull carts or trucks) but also rights to the land. Indeed, as noted earlier, without access to snow-free winter pastures, it was feared that the Shishged pastoralists might revert to a more "Siberian" economy based on hunting and reindeer breeding, as had happened earlier in the region's history (Potapov 1964; Vainshtein 1980).

Although nomadic (and for most village households seminomadic) pastoralism was the leading form of livelihood in the late 1990s, people also engaged in other "primary" or "informal" economic activities, if by this we understand any source of income that does not involve formal employment, public or private. These were, in order of what I estimate to be their

---

however, and also because of a crisis in the Duha reindeer breeding economy, Tsagaan Nuur, the northernmost Shishged district, saw its population drop in the 1990s.

14. As a rule, Darhad nomads spend the summer by one of the many rivers of the Shishged Depression, while winters are spent in the hills sheltered from the north winds. This pattern is comparable to that found in most regions of central Mongolia, which tend to be relatively well watered. The composition of their herds calls to mind other forest-steppe regions, where there is an overrepresentation of horses and cattle (cows, yaks, and the hybrid *hainag*) and an underrepresentation of goats and especially camels, in contrast to the mix in the semiarid grasslands and deserts that tend to dominate elsewhere in Mongolia.

15. Before the socialist revolution, apparently some Shishged nomads made annual migrations of 250 kilometers, following a north-south trajectory associated with the Gobi Desert (Badamhatan 1986, 27).

importance, hunting (mainly for fur from various types of predators, deer, and rodents, including sable, but also organs and antlers for the Chinese market), petty trading (basically trading nomad goods for goods from China at the provincial market), foraging (for berries, nuts, mushrooms, and plants or flowers used in folk medicine), and all manner of odd jobs for wealthy locals, who might need assistance, say, in moving camp, or visitors from outside, such as foreign tourists on horseback expeditions.

The remaining one thousand or so people in the Ulaan-Uul district who were not full-time pastoralists were based in the central *bag*, a thinly populated, barren-looking, but beautifully situated village of fenced courtyards and wooden barns or nomadic yurts (*ger*), a handful of brightly painted official buildings (*sum* administration, border military, health center, kindergarten, and school), some small businesses (mainly shops), and numerous derelict buildings serving as a ghostly reminder of the heyday of socialist modernity. Here, in the windswept and snow-clad (or muddy) alleys of what was affectionately known as "the Center," the inhabitants of the central subdistrict spent the cold period from mid-September to mid-May. For the rest of the year, practically everyone moved to summer camps (*zuslan*), located up to ten kilometers outside the village, close to one of the rivers. For the next four to five months, these semi-sedentaries, as one might call them, cared for their own herds (which were seldom large, typically numbering perhaps a handful of cattle, a dozen of sheep, and a couple of horses) until these were "placed" (*süregt tavih*) with full-time pastoralist *ails*, usually those of relatives, for the rest of the year while the owners returned to the Center.

* * *

My home in Ulaan-Uul consisted of one such semi-sedentary *ail*, comprising a married couple in their late thirties and their three children aged five to thirteen. Unusually, both parents held salaried jobs, and the household was therefore relatively well off, the husband being a warden in the Lake Hövsgöl national park and his wife a teacher at the local primary school, which the children all attended. Their situation differed from that of most *ails* in the village, which survived on only one income or pension or none at all, along with food from their own animals or received from relatives in the countryside, with whom most families in the Center were engaged in informal exchange relations involving a complex flow of goods, people, and services (see Sneath 1993).

As an ethnic Halh who was born in southern Hövsgöl, the husband (*nöhör*) had no family of his own in the Shishged, unlike his Darhad wife (*ehner, avgai*), who had been born in Ulaan-Uul and could count several clusters of relatives (*hamaatan*) in the region. The wife's family history was somewhat

(*Right:* Figure 2. Summer camps along the Shishged River)

Figure 3. Ulaan-Uul district center

unusual: when she was a child, her aunt had adopted her from her mother, an adoptee herself, who had five children with four men without ever getting married. The household maintained especially close contact with the wife's natal mother (*törsön eej*), as well as the household of the wife's elder sister (*egch*) and her Darhad husband (*hürgen*) and that of her younger brother (*düü*) and his Darhad wife (*ber*). Both of these households were also based in the village for the winter and had summer camps close to that of my hosts. The wife's other brother, or *ah*, had settled in a large town in central Mongolia years earlier and played no significant social role in their lives.

As if to compensate for the husband's lack of local kin, and possibly also because the wife's family did not exactly live up to the traditional Mongolian kinship ideal of an unbroken patriline (*yas ündes*) of virilocal, patriarchal households, my hosts maintained a vast network of friends (*naiz*) and acquaintances (*tanil*). Indeed their smallish wooden house (measuring perhaps some thirty square meters), consisting of a bedroom and a kitchen/living space, was one of the most popular spots for socializing in the Center. Anywhere from fifteen to twenty-five visitors would drop in on a daily basis, and all were served tea, bread, and various milk products (*tsagaan idee*), in accordance with nomadic custom (*yos*).

In addition to living with my host family in the village and, during the summer season, in their *zuslan* some three kilometers outside the Center, I also spent several weeks each with two pastoral households, both comprising distant relatives of the wife. This provided me with a knowledge of pastoral life and enabled me to collect countless stories about the landscape and its human and nonhuman residents. In addition, I spent a month traveling the Shishged countryside on horseback, visiting and interviewing a great number of pastoral *ails* accompanied by a local friend, who became an invaluable research assistant. Finally, I spent a few months in the two other Shishged districts of Renchinlhümbe and, especially, Tsagaan Nuur. Here I sought out various people known to possess special knowledge of local history and lore, and it was on these trips that I gathered much of my material about the history of Buddhism in the Shishged, as well as on the more formal and ceremonial aspects of Darhad shamanism.

Back in the village, I gradually came to know a number of local leaders (elders, government officials, businessmen) and occult practitioners (diviners, seers, bonesetters, smiths, and hunters, but no "genuine shamans," whatever that means). In particular, I became very close to one infamous hunter and blacksmith; indeed it was the tragic tale of this man's shamanic forebears and his own troubled life as a "fake shaman" that fully convinced me of the importance of studying shamanism without shamans. Above all, it was my hosts' relationships with their relatives, friends, colleagues, and neighbors, as well as their foes, which provided my basic insights into Ulaan-Uul's troublesome potential shamans and the way in which these quintessentially postsocialist figures symbolized a more general interpenetration of spirit worlds and political life in northern Mongolia in the age of the market.

Occult Economies of What?

It is now more clear how the simultaneous collapse of what was nostalgically remembered as the viable social, political, and economic forms of the *negdel* gave rise to a pervasive sense of postsocialist chaos, crisis, and loss. The lack of an identifiable and recognized class of occult practitioners (shamans and lamas), taken together with the disappearance of enduring and reliable state and government bodies, as well as predictable and trustworthy economic institutions and mechanisms of fiscal redistribution—each in its own way capable of containing the forces of disintegration—was felt to have released unknown and invisible agents of postsocialist transition, from alcoholism and violence to soul loss.

Indeed for many people in Ulaan-Uul, the hardships of transition had been made significantly worse, if not directly precipitated, by the communist repression of occult specialists in the late 1930s. The result was a sort of postsocialist double bind, in which the aftershocks of the consecutive meltdowns of shamanic and socialist institutions came together, like two merging cracks in an erupting earthquake, to produce a general sense of chaos. On the one hand, the disappearance of the socialist state gave rise to a sense of occult excess. On the other hand, the lack of shamans meant that these opaque forces could not be tamed the way they used to be before the communists took over. Consequently, "transition society"—manifested in the form of predatory capitalism, a volatile democracy, a shambolic infrastructure, and runaway corruption—was not simply perceived as representing specific policies pertaining to a market economy and (neo)liberal reform, but was experienced instead as a sign, an index, indeed a portent of an all-encompassing cosmic upheaval, which people in Ulaan-Uul sometimes called "the age of darkness" (*haranhui üye*).

So how do we best analyze this proliferation of things shamanic in postsocialist Mongolia? One solution would be to use the theoretical framework associated with the anthropological literature on "the modernity of witchcraft" (Geschiere 1997) and "occult economies" (Comaroff and Comaroff 1999). This influential strand of anthropological work is concerned with the interweaving, in different postcolonial contexts, of seemingly traditional and esoteric phenomena such as witchcraft, sorcery, and shamanism, on the one hand, with seemingly modern and profane phenomena such as democracy, statecraft, and global capitalism on the other (see, for example, Ashforth 2005; Comaroff and Comaroff 1999; Geschiere 1997; Meyer and Pels 2003; Moore and Sanders 2001; West 2005, 2007; Whitehead and Wright 2004). Instead of being seen as part of a stable and homogeneous cosmological system pertaining to a local community or culture, the occult is understood as a dynamic concept that is continually being molded by wider social, political, and economic processes. For the same reason, the study of occult phenomena has been relaunched as a "fundamental project for an anthropology of the modern world" (Whitehead and Wright 2004, 2). As Jean and John Comaroff put it:

> The pyramid schemes, the epidemic of witchcraft and the killing of those suspected of magical evil, moral panics about the piracy of body parts; all are, alike, symptoms of an occult economy waxing behind the civil surfaces of the "new" South Africa. Drawing on cultural elements with long

indigenous histories, this economy is itself an integral feature of millennial capitalism—that odd fusion of the modern and the postmodern, of hope and hopelessness, of utility and futility, of promise and its perversions. (1999, 283)

This more recent body of work on occult economies and cognate phenomena provides a much-needed, and quite sophisticated, theoretical framework for integrating larger political and economic processes into the anthropological study of the occult, something that was conspicuously absent in classic accounts of magic, witchcraft, shamanism, and other occult phenomena (Eliade 1964; Evans-Pritchard 1976; Tylor 1958). As Peter Geschiere notes about social life in postcolonial sub Saharan Africa: "It is hard to maintain that there is a self-evident opposition between witchcraft and modernity. On the contrary, rumors and practices related to the occult forces abound in the more modern sectors of society...express[ing] a determined effort for signifying politico-economic changes and even gaining control over them" (1997, 3).[16] The same goes for Mongolia. As alluded to earlier, it was hard to distinguish between shamanist and postsocialist aspects of life in Ulaan-Uul during the late 1990s, as if the two belonged to different scales (local/global) and temporalities (tradition/modernity). On the contrary, in postsocialist Mongolia, occult phenomena such as shamanism, magic, and witchcraft constitute an irreducible part of transition, if we understand that term to refer to the chaotic state of total and perpetual change through which social life was perceived to be unfolding in the 1990s.

To provide a sense of the analytical merits but also (inevitably) the limitations of this approach to the anthropological study of occult phenomena, let's take a closer look at Peter Geschiere's acclaimed study *The Modernity of Witchcraft*. In this already classic ethnographic monograph, Geschiere shows how, with the end of one-party rule and economic liberalization in postcolonial Cameroon, witchcraft (*djambe*) became a "key element in discourses of power, despite modern processes of change (or perhaps because of them)" (1997, 7–8). The efficacy of *djambe* hinges on an irreducible ambiguity pertaining to all occult concepts: the fact that they are "related to the accumulation of power but can also serve to undermine it" (16). As the "dark side of kinship" (24), *djambe* thus enables one to "go out" of the body and gain

---

16. As the Comaroffs put it: "The practice of mystical arts in postcolonial Africa, witchcraft among them, does not imply an iteration of, a retreat into, 'tradition.' On the contrary, it is often a mode of producing *new* forms of consciousness.... [W]e do not see this as an isolated, even as an African, phenomenon. In a surging, implosive economy, it is just one element popping up in considerable contexts all over the planet, albeit in a variety of local guises" (1999, 284).

control of and even kill others by "eating" them. Yet this "doubling of one-self" is also very dangerous, for "once it is out, the double is exposed to new dangers: it can fall into ambushes itself" (40–42). In that sense, *djambe* seems to represent a good example of an "occult economy," taken to include all practices that involve "the deployment of magical means for material ends or, more expansively, the conjuring of wealth by resort to inherently mysterious techniques, techniques whose principles of operation are neither transparent nor explicable in conventional terms (Comaroff and Comaroff 1999, 297).

All of this sounds very familiar to the student of Mongolian shamanism. (As we shall see in chapter 3, Darhad persons see themselves as divided into a visible "yellow side" and an invisible "black side.") But how does Geschiere account for the nature of *djambe* in more theoretical terms? On the one hand, he emphasizes that he does not want to deny "the reality of [*djambe*] discourses [by] treating them as pure fantasies"; but on the other hand, he is also "wary of emphasizing too strongly the reality of these beliefs" (21). Geschiere performs this delicate balancing act by conceptualizing *djambe* as a particular kind of cultural discourse: it is "a language that '*signifies*' the modern changes: it *helps one to understand* new inequalities, unexpected and enigmatic as they are, as seen 'from below'; it promises unheard-of chances to enrich oneself; and it can *serve as a guide* to find one's way in the net-works of modern society" (24; emphasis added). The same assumption—that witchcraft is a language that helps people make sense of the world—is made by Harry West in his insightful essay on what he calls ethnographic sorcery in Mozambique: "I slowly came to appreciate that sorcery constituted a language through which the Muedans with whom I worked comprehended and—even more euphemistically—commented upon the workings of power in their midst [and] that if I was to discern how Muedans understood the social, political, and economic transformations they experienced—if I was to uncover their visions of changing times—I would have to learn to language of sorcery" (2007, 11).

This *djambe*-like ambivalence toward the object of one's analysis lies at the heart of most anthropological work on occult phenomena in the postcolonial world—the fact that the ethnographer wants to take seriously the discourse of the occult but not necessarily what this discourse is "about," namely, the occult "itself" (whatever that may mean).[17] Adam Ashforth, who along with

17. With Harry West's 2007 *Ethnographic Sorcery* as the possible exception. Indeed, one of the main points that he makes in it comes close to my own position in this book, namely, that insofar as the people "with whom [we] worked said that…those who articulated visions of sorcery's workings *were* sorcerers; talk about sorcery *was* sorcery; words and deeds were cosubstantial" (59–60), it is not sufficient to treat these as figurative (symbolic) statements, which simply "stand for" something else that is not metaphorical. After all, as he asks with reference to Roy Wagner's

Harry West and Todd Sanders is a key representative of what might be called the second generation of scholars studying occult economies in sub-Saharan Africa, reaches a similar conclusion: "The idea of witchcraft discourse as an idiom expressing other realities…has proved remarkably flexible in the hands of anthropologists.…While this literature has revealed much about African social life, it suffers from the singular defect…of treating statements that Africans clearly intend as literal, or factual, as if they were meant to be metaphorical or figurative" (Ashforth 2005, 114; see also Niehaus 2005).[18]

This ambiguous attitude toward occult discourses and practices essentially looks like a version of the familiar cultural relativist double vision that enables anthropologists to take their informants' "world-views" both too seriously and not seriously enough (Latour 2002). The particular danger with it in the present context is that it risks being translated into a sort of "symbolic-functionalist" analytics, which is in some instances reminiscent of the deterministic, reductionist, and teleological models of some late-nineteenth- and early-twentieth-century social theory. This analytical perspective, it should be emphasized, is less an explicit argument that may be identified in the writings of particular authors such as Geschiere or the Comaroffs and more an implicit agenda that underwrites the entire discourse about occult economies in postcolonial contexts. On this view, occult phenomena, whether rubberized as "witchcraft," "sorcery," or "shamanism," are collective

---

work on symbolism (1981, 1986), "if all discursive engagements with the world are inescapably metaphorical, perhaps the most interesting question is not…whether Muedan sorcerers' imaginings…are metaphors but rather whether metaphors (for that matter, all forms of discourse through which we conceived of our worlds) constitute means of sorcery" (West 2007, 64). If my approach to the analysis of occult phenomena can be said to differ from West's, it is because I do not restrict my study of shamanism in northern Mongolia to "discursive engagements with the world" but instead try to incorporate *anything* imbued with a shamanic ontology, including human bodies and nonhuman materialities.

18. As much as Ashforth and I seem to agree in diagnosing the problem with the literature of occult economies, our preferred solutions are very different. Whereas, for Ashforth, the answer is "simply to set aside [the] conundrums of rationality" (2005, 116) and concentrate on "explicating how questions, doubts—entertained not only by Africans but by all of us—about the possibilities of power and action in the world…can both seem plausible and reasonable" (2005, 121), I am skeptical about the existential universalism that underwrites such seemingly hard-to-disagree-with propositions. While I concur with Ashforth that occult "matters constitute part of the very stuff of politics" (2005, 12) in postsocialist Mongolia, I am not convinced that this state of affairs, there or elsewhere, is caused by "spiritual insecurity" as a "universal feature of human life" (2005, 3). To paraphrase Harri Englund and James Leach's critique of the "meta-narratives of modernity" in much recent anthropology: "The assumption that persons carry 'inalienable humanity' is enough to situate [Ashford's "spiritual insecurity"] perspective in the ethnographic legacy of social scientific discourses on modernity.…Fear there may well be…but we should not presume to know what the fear is about, what its 'real' sources and referents are, however much the social sciences supply us with ideas about modernity and the person" (2000, 229).

representations—or to use a more fashionable term, social imaginaries—within a neo-Marxist (and indeed neo-Durkheimian) model of social reproduction, where some cultural-ideational stuff is metaphorically projected onto some political-economic stuff, or vice versa, in ways that are always in, or against, the interests of the powers that be. Thus, underlying many recent writings on occult phenomena, whatever their theoretical and empirical differences, is a tendency to see these as "symbolic languages" fulfilling certain purposes, such as (1) the mystifying role of concealing hegemonic structures, (2) the counter-hegemonic role of liberating oppressed subjects by exposing and subverting these structures, and (3) an assumed universal human existential need to make sense of the increasing uncertainties brought about by capitalism, globalization, neoliberal reform, and the postcolonial predicament as a whole.

In spite of its many merits, then, a number of analytical blind spots can be identified in the literature on "occult economies" and "the modernity of witchcraft," blind spots that, as we are about to see, become more visible the moment one tries to understand a phenomenon such as shamanism without shamans, which is characterized by a conspicuous *lack* of sense-making and socially reproductive potential in the "symbolic-functionalist" sense I have described.

Impossible Forms

What if "symbolic language" is not a sufficiently adequate way of conceptualizing occult phenomena? And what if occult practices do not, in any clear sense, "serve as a guide" for people? In northern Mongolia, the invisible powers of the spirits and the opaque forces of the market are imbued with similarly labile shapes or (as I like to call them) "impossible forms." Recognizing this basic homology between the "local" forms of shamanic cosmology and the "global" forms of political economy is, I argue, the key to understanding the nature of shamanism without shamans in northern Mongolia after socialism.

As in the "occult economies" of sub-Saharan Africa, an invisible undercurrent of forces was felt to run beneath the surface of everything in Ulaan-Uul during the late 1990s—a proliferating multitude of human and nonhuman agencies set free by the disintegration of the modernist socialist state, made all the more uncontainable by that state's past political purges of the shamans. Yet, I believe, the analogies that people drew between shamanism and postsocialism were not about projecting symbolic meanings from one domain of life onto another (the spirits as metaphors of the market), but about perceiving an isomorphism of form between these two dimensions of the world: the spirits and the market were both variations on one immanent state of transition. On this analysis, shamanism is not so much a symbolic projection of one type of content ("politics" or "economics") onto another type of content ("religion") in someone's ideological and/or existential interest. The claim I am making is subtly different, namely that shamanism *is* the (impossible) form assumed by the world in northern Mongolia after socialism. Shamanism is, so to speak, an ontology of transition.[19]

If the relationship between shamanism and postsocialism is about a similarity of content (as the occult economy crowd would have it), but is also about a shared form, how then do we go about theorizing it? In seeking to answer this question, I bring together disparate strands of theoretical work, ranging from newer anthropological studies on the spectral nature of postcolonial political forms (Hansen and Stepputat 2001; Navaro-Yashin 2002; Taussig 1992) to philosophical studies of play, irony, and laughter (Bateson 2000; Bergson 1999; Kierkegaard 1989), along with influential posthumanist work on nonhuman agents and assemblages (Deleuze 1990, 1994; Deleuze and Guattari 1994, 1999; Latour 1993, 2005) and ethnographically derived theories of "fractal persons" in Melanesia, "multinaturalist cosmologies" in Amazonia, and other recent anthropological experiments using ethnographic data for the construction of "post-plural" analytical concepts (Corzín Jiménez and Willerslev 2007; Henare, Holbraad, and Wastell 2007; Holbraad 2007; 2010; Holbraad and Pedersen 2009b; Pedersen 2007a; Pedersen, Empson, and Humphrey 2007; Strathern 1988, 1998, 2004; Viveiros de Castro 1998a and b, 2004, 2007; Wagner 1977, 1981, 1986).

What unites these disparate bodies of writings is the fact that in spite of their otherwise different areas of inquiry and concern, all share what might be called the same "theoretical object," namely, the ontologies of complex,

---

19. Much energy has been consumed in discussing the pros and cons of the so-called ontological turn within the social and human sciences (see, for instance, Law and Mol 2002; Viveiros de Castro 2004; Henare, Holbraad, and Wastell 2007; Venkatesen 2010). Following Holbraad (2010) in part, in this book "ontology" refers to any theories or concepts of what exists. In that sense it may be distinguished (if only in principle) from "epistemology," which here denotes the knowledge process by which such ontologies (concepts or theories) come into being. Far from referring to "what really really exists" and the "true nature of things," then, the concept of ontology denotes "the set of things whose existence is acknowledged by a particular theory or system of thought: it is in this sense that one speaks of 'the' ontology of a theory, or of a metaphysical system [like shamanism] of having such-a-such an ontology" (Honderich 1995, 634). Crucially, such ontologies are not simply linguistic or mental (ideational) phenomena; on the contrary, as I argue in this book, certain material things (such as shamanic costumes) and certain social forms (such as joking practices) may be said to constitute distinct concepts and theories—and therefore indeed ontologies—in their own right.

capricious, and emergent social forms. The theoretical premise of this book is thus that, precisely because people in northern Mongolia experience the transition as a disintegration of stable religious, political, and economic forms, these theories concerned with the lability and capriciousness of forms offer a useful framework for an account of what it means to live in a world invaded by a multitude of half-baked beings and entities—Ulaan-Uul's potential shamans being a case in point.

Unlike the passive forms of many anthropological and sociological theories, which serve as fixed and therefore "dead" containers of sociocultural content and their purported political-economic context (like, say, many recent invocations of "the global"), the active, living forms studied by anthropologists such as Roy Wagner, Marilyn Strathern, and Eduardo Viveiros de Castro, and by philosophers such as Henri Bergson and Gilles Deleuze, are dynamic assemblages of evolving human and nonhuman life whose dimensions are constantly in the making, and which, for the same reason, cannot be separated from their content, let alone serve as contexts for anything but their own fractal self-differentiation or post-plural self-extension. In Melanesia, the Amazon, and northern Asia, forms are thus not mental or ideological schemata through which some fixed structure of order or symbolic meaning is imposed on an inherently disorderly world of social and material practices (as much so-called critical and constructivist social science would have it) but features of the world in their own right, which must be continually recreated, recalibrated, and reapportioned for the cosmos to assume its correct proportions, and for human and nonhuman lives to unfold at a pace that is suitable to the particular dynamic configuration or continual assembling of their bodies and minds (Hodges 2007; Holbraad and Pedersen 2009a; Nielsen 2009; Viveiros de Castro 2007; Pedersen and Willerslev 2010). Few have captured this nonconventional (that is, non-Euro-American or non-Cartesian) idea of form better than Terence Turner in a recent unpublished paper on Kakapo (Amerindian) cosmology:

> The forms of things…are actually embodied processes of formation, or the potential capacity for them. They contain the agency or force that drives the content of things to assume the specific characteristics and behavioral patterns proper to their species or kind….Forms, in other words, are not to be understood as mere "envelopes" without functional internal relations to their contents.…[T]he form of an entity appears, from the perspective of the process by which it is produced, not only as a final product of the process but as its guiding principle and animating force. In these respects the form of the entity acts as—or in pragmatic terms, *is*—its *spirit*. (Turner, n.d.)

It is precisely this deeply shamanic notion of form that underlies Darhad Mongolian perceptions of what life is like in postsocialist transition. In the Shishged as much as in the Amazon, forms are considered to be alive, to *be* rather than to *have* force—namely, the occult capacity to compel the cosmos to orchestrate itself in a particular way. Yet as we have seen, the problem in northern Mongolia after socialism was that there was a general lack of forms, or, more precisely, a loss of things and entities recognizable as specific and predictable forms, and whose capacities for molding the things of the world could therefore be harnessed for one's own and, perhaps, other people's benefit.

Consider once again Ulaan-Uul's victims of *agsan*, the worst cases of which were considered to be stuck in an endlessly deferred state of being not quite shamans. But does this sense of incompleteness and unfinished metamorphosis ("the shamans are not what they used to be") mean that Darhad social life was less shamanic than it would have been had there been more "real" shamans in the late 1990s? Not necessarily. In fact, my time in Ulaan-Uul left me with the exact opposite impression. It was *because of,* not in spite of, the lack of "genuine" shamans that shamanism (understood in its most general sense as a constellation of occult practices) had grown so strong after socialism—too strong, according to many people. On the one hand, shamanism was understood to constitute an inalienable property or part of who people were. On the other, people were worried about the spirits' growing influence on their lives and voiced concern that they had become stronger since the end of socialism.

To flesh out this apparently paradoxical conclusion—that Ulaan-Uul's half-shamans were, in a sense, more shamanic than the "whole" ones practicing, for instance, in the neighboring Shishged district of Tsagaan Nuur—let us briefly consider one of the gravest problems faced by the incomplete shamans according to themselves and others, namely, their lack of a shamanic costume. My work with shamans in the Tsagaan Nuur district shows that not only is the shamanic gown not completed until it is properly worn, but also the shaman is not complete as a person until he or she possesses this artifact. In that sense the gown has the capacity not simply for inviting but for exorcising spirits as well. For if wearing a costume gives Tsagaan Nuur's shamans the ability to see and be seen by the spirits, they are also enabled *not* to see them—or be seen by them—if they choose *not* to wear one. By contrast, for lack of costumes, Ulaan-Uul's troublesome half-shamans are exposed to spirits all the time, but without being able to see them let alone control them. Above all, this is what renders these persons so feared. They may beat you up in sudden attacks of *agsan*, hurt your soul by casting curses, or create social havoc by telling obscene jokes and "speaking lies."

Throughout Mongolia, Darhads are notorious jokers. Thus they see themselves, and see that others see them, as having a superior sense of humor. In this regard, joking is imbued with an occult agency of its own, as a shadowy potential in people and things. Similarly, people and things are suspected of having an invisible "black" shamanic side. One man told me, "There are two special things about Darhads: our ability to joke and our ability to curse." Here, where crude ethnic stereotypes pertaining to the postsocialist Mongolian nation intersect with little-understood aspects of Darhad shamanic agency, a pristine space of analysis is laid bare. For joking emerges as a way of acting shamanic without being a shaman: it is, so to speak, a vernacular mode of possession.

I hope that these brief glosses of arguments that are spelled out in detail in the course of this book suffice to illustrate how, more than anyone else, the potential shamans—with their missing shamanic costumes and their propensity to joke all the time—are key points of intersection between the book's two overarching themes: shamanism and postsocialism. As "impossible forms"—inherently labile entities that never stand still but exist only in their endless becoming—they, more than anyone else, make visible the invisible forces of transition. To draw out the implications of this insight for the study of postsocialist societies generally, it is useful to contrast the present study of Darhad shamanism in northwestern Mongolia with Manduhai Buyandelger's work on the revival of Buryat shamanism in northeastern Mongolia (1999, 2007).

Like a significant number of Darhads, many Buryats are "convinced that the socialist suppression of religion…eliminated 'real' shamans and that the market economy has produced shamans who are not chosen by their origin species but are motivated by money" (Buyandelger 2007, 133). But there seem to be significant empirical differences between the two cases. Whereas in Ulaan-Uul, people were resigned to living in a community high in shamanism but low on shamans, many Buryats were involved in a continual "search for ever more powerful shamans, who can summon more authentic spirits" (Buyandelger 2007, 128). In that sense, the revival of Darhad and Buryat shamanism, at least around the year 2000, when Buyandelger's and my own work coincided, may represent two contrasting ends of a postsocialist spectrum. Whereas Darhad shamanism assumed the half-cooked form that is the theme of this book, both the number and the status of Buryat shamans have grown since 1990 (Buyandelger 1999, 2007; see also Empson 2006; Swancutt 2006, 2007).

Buyandelger's work on Buryat Mongolian shamanism testifies to the continuing merits of studying occult phenomena by adopting the theoretical approach developed by Geschiere and the Comaroffs, among others. Evidently, in a political and religious context such as the Buryat one where many new shamans are being initiated, and where the different clans have regained much of their presocialist significance, it makes a lot of sense to think of shamanism as "a creative way of dealing with the calamities brought by the changed economy," inasmuch as it can be said to "provid[e] significance to an otherwise hopeless existence on the edge of an impoverished state" (Buyandelger 2007, 128).

Yet the situation clearly was different in the Shishged in the late 1990s, when Darhad shamanism was not so much being explicitly reinvented by anyone but was instead imposing itself on everyone in the rude manner of an uninvited guest. In this context it is of limited analytical value to speak of shamanism as a way of dealing with the uncertainties of postsocialist transition, for the incomplete shamans and the restless spirits were felt to increase, rather than reduce, individual and collective calamities (a point also raised by Buyandelger in relation to her Buryat material).

For the same reason, the serious—and sometimes not so serious—shamanic cosmologies decribed to me in detail by various Darhad shamans and laymen cannot be interpreted in any analytically meaningful way as cornerstones of a social imaginary on which people drew to fill a void of meaning opened by the collapse of the socialist master trope (Lindquist 2005). To conceive of Darhad shamanism as a "strategy of empowerment" adapted by people in Ulaan-Uul to "make sense" of the uncertainties of postsocialist transition (Vaté 2009) would be to overlook the feeling of loss and ignorance, along with the sense of predestination and lack of individual agency, associated with it. Darhad shamanism, including the alleged lack of "genuine shamans," was indeed all about uncertainty. Yet, as I will show, this assemblage of discourses, practices, and things shamanic widened rather than curtailed, reproduced rather than reduced, the sense of latent cosmological breakdown associated with life after socialism.

It would not be ethnographically accurate, however, to speak of the shamanic spirits as the cause of people's sense of ever-increasing postsocialist uncertainties. Instead, to people in Ulaan-Uul, the half-shamans and the restless spirits simply *were* uncertainty as such; they were materializations, actualizations, instantiations, and condensations of the all-pervasive state of cosmological turmoil variously called "democracy," "transition," or "the age of the market." Thus understood, the sense that shamanism made of postsocialism, or vice versa, was not the result of people's inscribing cultural meanings onto a chaotic world as part of an existential quest to understand it. Rather, in northern Mongolia after socialism, an immanent state of transition was unmaking people's sense of themselves and their lives by causing the logic of shamanism to collapse into that of postsocialism.

Shamanism and Postsocialism

Darhad shamanism, and particularly in its variations "without shamans," is not an occult economy "of" postsocialist transition; it "is" a distinct ontological condition in its own right. As I hope will become clear in the chapters that follow, the Darhad shamanic predicament is thus a potential state of perpetual metamorphosis that may be assumed by any (impossible) form, whether drunken men, wild animals, sacred talismans, a decaying infrastructure, even certain kinds of mischievous joking. It is not a common cultural repertoire, or shared imaginary, which bestows meaning on every thing. Rather, Mongolian shamanism, like all post-plural forms, is an emergent assemblage of self-scaling practices, discourses, and materialities. This fascinating but also frightening constellation of things shamanic does not add up to a culture or ideology with one or more symbolic-functional roles. On the contrary, it is by virtue of its multiplicity, indeterminacy, and plasticity—its capacity for endless deferral, irresolvable paradox, and infinite self-extension—that shamanism is imbued with such a potent efficacy in northern Mongolia after socialism.

What follows is an ethnography, and a theory, of postsocialist shamanic agency in all its guises, manifesting itself as a bewildering multitude of impossible forms ranging from the wild animals of the taiga to the ghastly remains of socialist high modernity, and to an isolated village community's witchcraft-like exchanges of playful "lies." Yet in saying that this book amounts to a study of shamanic agency, I do not mean to suggest that it is simply a traditional ethnographic study of a certain people ("the Darhads") and their well-known traditional faith ("shamanism"). Nor is it a conventional anthropological investigation in which agency is taken to be a matter of human intentionality and individual volition alone. On the contrary, in this book shamanic agency is located above all in those persons who are *not* considered "real shamans," whose sources and vehicles of agency are located to only a limited extent in their own or other human minds and bodies. In what follows, shamanic agency is also—perhaps even predominantly— found in a bewildering wealth of nonhuman agents, such as vague presences and ephemeral atmospheres (a cool sensation in a hot room, a conspicuous silence between words); wild animals and plants (a mountain goat that appears in the shape of an old lady, a berry that glows in the dark); and particular things (a lone tree on a windswept grassland, a gift of meat from the hunt, a defunct electrical generator).

For the same reason, I do not consider shamanism to be limited to those practices that some might want to call "religious," nor do I see it as a way of clothing the undeniably harsh political and economic realities of neoliberal governmentality and global capitalism in the soothing garb of culture. As I intend to show, for certain people in Ulaan-Uul, postsocialist transition is what shamanism *is* (as opposed to is *about*): the labile manner in which the world arranged itself in the late 1990s. In northern Mongolia after socialism, shamanism potentially embraced every possible and impossible actualization of this "transition," which is precisely why my endless encounters with playful "lies," mischievous jokes, and subtle ironies did not just resemble shamanic maledictions; they were shamanic acts in their own right. Likewise, the *agsan* persons causing havoc in Ulaan-Uul in the late 1990s did not just resemble shamans; they were possessed by spirit(s) in transition in their own right.

1 Shamanic States

Once, the vice governor of Ulaan-Uul was beaten up after spending a drunken evening with a local strongman (*ataman*). The surprising thing about the incident—more so than the vice governor's partaking in late night vodka sessions—was that, despite having been badly hurt, he did not take any punitive measures against his aggressor. "It was my own mistake," he explained from his sickbed the following day. "I was drinking with the *ataman*," he sighed, "and then we started discussing local politics. The next moment he turned *agsan*. And as you know, I am no fighter. I am just an accountant. So now I look like this," he said meekly, pointing to his swollen face.

I had first heard mention of the *atamans* during my first week in Ulaan-Uul, when the wife in my host family took my friend from Ulaanbaatar aside to warn him about certain persons we ought to avoid. It was, she stressed, his duty as my friend to relay this vital information to me before his imminent departure. As I later learned, she then named and described four men who, as she put it, were the most difficult and dangerous in town. Collectively she referred to them as "our *atamans*," as if this designation provided all the explanation needed to understand their peculiar yet prominent role in the community.

Atamans, or "strongmen," were omnipresent in Mongolia during the 1990s.[1] They could be found not only in desolate villages like Ulaan-Uul but also in working-class neighborhoods in the cities, as well as in a whole range

---

1. The word *ataman* may have entered the Mongolian language as Cossack colonial militias expanded eastward into Siberia (Forsyth 1992). Its contemporary Russian meaning (military leader, strongman) may in turn be identical to that of the old Turkic word *kasak*, which means "free warrior" (Gordon 1983, 63; Kornblatt 1992, 8).

of institutional contexts. (There were even cases of *atamans* threatening university lecturers into giving better grades.) Essentially the term refers to a person—typically, but not necessarily, a young man—who is willing and able to transgress the ordinary threshold of violence, and is thus imbued with the capacity to preside over (*bar'j baidag*) a band of followers, typically (but not always) consisting of gangs (*büleg*) of unemployed and restless men or, in more urban contexts, criminal networks of ex-convicts.

The problem with *atamans* in Ulaan-Uul was significantly worsened by the fact that people were hesitant about instigating punitive action against the perpetrators of *agsan* violence. For one thing, they might know them, or know someone who did. And then there was always the risk of retaliation. Furthermore, since official law enforcement was largely defunct in Ulaan Uul at this time, it was assumed that violent people would face criminal charges only for very serious offenses. Indeed, the two Halh police officers who, in keeping with standard policy, were stationed in the district for a three-year hitch made it clear to me that they had given up enforcing the letter of the law. While one spent most of his time at home—especially, as he emphasized, when there was trouble in the streets—the other was increasingly drinking and brawling on equal terms with the local youths. Of the two officers, the latter had more authority even though he was considered a bad cop: "he likes guns and vodka too much," one young man told me, but "at least he knows how to fight."

Through accounts of interwoven phenomena as diverse as *ataman* violence and the breakdown of local government, and from national election campaigns to the altars in shamans' homes, this chapter paints a disturbing picture of a community, and a state, where the invisible forces of spirits and the market were perceived to have gained the upper hand during three turbulent weeks in the spring of 1999. Engaging with recent ethnographies of the (post)socialist state by Nikolai Ssorin-Chaikov (2003) and Alexei Yurchak (2006), as well as, more implicitly, writings about the "magical," "imaginary," or "phantasmatic" nature of the postcolonial state (such as Hansen and Stepputat 2001; Navaro-Yashin 2002; and Taussig 1992, 1997), I show that the state remains omnipresent in northern Mongolia after socialism, despite—or perhaps because of—its purported collapse. Yet to say that the postsocialist state is everywhere is not to say that it is there all the time. That is, just because something is omnipresent, it is not necessarily omnipotent. Indeed, I detected a widespread perception that the Mongolian state was not quite in the places where it used to be. For the same reason, people were often struggling to find the state before, as it were, it found them.

As we shall see, while what little that remained of the socialist welfare state gradually disappeared, there was a widespread sense in Ulaan-Uul that a multitude of invisible shamanic energies had been unleashed, which were now slowly but irreversibly working their way through every crack in the firmament of the village and the community. Yet despite the atmosphere of postsocialist crisis and neoliberal gloom, I could not help noticing that many institutions which since 1990 had hovered on the verge of collapse (such as the school and the district administration) had managed to stay afloat. Eventually I realized it might be more accurate to say that, rather than having collapsed after socialism, the Mongolian state had found a new modus operandi in a time of transition. Perhaps the many problems people were facing in Ulaan-Uul in the 1990s resulted not only from a perception of too little state but also from the obverse perception of too much state. Perhaps the postsocialist chaos had not come about just because the shamanic spirits were on the loose after decades of state socialist repression; perhaps the new state that had emerged was itself shamanic.

To substantiate these observations, I begin the chapter by discussing people's responses to a temporary electric power cut that took place in Ulaan-Uul in the spring of 1999. It was taken to be a sign of an incurably weakened postsocialist state and, more implicitly, as a portent of an imminent "age of darkness" (*haranhui üye*). At the same time, the case introduces various elements of what I subsequently describe as the shamanic state.

The Underneath of the Infrastructure

In the first weeks of March 1999, cases of *agsan* and *ataman* violence reached a new peak in the village community of Ulaan-Uul. This coincided with a number of scandals involving the perceived deterioration of the state. People were worried about two disruptions in particular: first, the shutdown of the locally run diesel generator owing to lack of funds to buy fuel; and second, the collective decision by schoolteachers to go out on strike until their salaries were paid, or "at least," they announced, "the money owed to us since autumn."

It took me a while to understand that the lack of electricity had broader-ranging effects than simply the dimming of lights. "What is the big deal?" I asked my hosts in response to their complaints. "Electricity is available here only from eight to eleven PM anyway, and you guys are used to doing everything by candlelight at your summer place." The wife strongly took issue with my offhand attitude. Apart from the immediate negative impact on the pocketbooks of the people working at the power station ("These people have hardly any animals, you know?"), for her the darkened light bulbs pointed to a more profound source of malaise, namely, the demise of the state in the powerful, enduring form she had known all her life. Indeed for this family, the pitch-dark streets were perceived as an omen of more terrible things to come.

To understand how and why they were led to think this way, it is useful to remember that infrastructure has always been one of the cornerstones of state socialist modernity, and this was especially true in the remote and unforgiving population centers scattered across northern Eurasia. Thus, argues Caroline Humphrey (2005), the fantasy as well as the reality of infrastructure acquired an overdetermined quality in the Soviet Union in conjunction with the grand collectivization programs of the mid-twentieth century. Here, at the peak of Soviet modernism, and especially in the model settlements established across Siberia's taiga and tundra, *infrastruktura* was seen as the precondition for socialist modernity; without this productive basis, there could be no material (and therefore no ideological) progress. Since rural Mongolia was subject to a very similar mix of Stalinist economics in the postwar period (Bawden 1986, 303–15), there is every reason to assume that the same hypermodernist imaginary dominated there as well, at least until 1990.[2] As Ole Bruun writes about a district in central Mongolia, "state construction...rose dramatically, thoroughly modernizing the countryside in the spirit of socialism....A large number of new buildings turned the sum center into a miniature metropolis" (2005, 20).

In socialist rural Mongolia as much as in the remote corners of Soviet Siberia, investment in infrastructure was thus not rational in any narrow economic sense; instead, building "miniature metropolises" was understood as investing in a new being, a new humanity, a new cosmos.[3] Even more than in the Soviet Union, electric light was an absolute cornerstone in Mongolian socialist discourses of modernity. David Sneath writes:

> In Mongolia the electric light became a central symbol of modernism, and indeed the particular project of Leninist state socialism. Elderly herders told me that when electricity was first introduced to their rural district centers in the 1930s and 40s they had called it Ilyichiin Gerel— "Lenin's Light"—the electrification policies were attributed to him personally.... This new form of light was ideally suited as a vehicle for

2. As Büchli notes, the USSR was "the most complete realisation of European modernity" the world had yet seen (2000, 2; see also Scott 1998). It is this state socialist "hypermodernity" (my term) that I am interested in here.

3. As Ssorin-Chaikov points out about state subsidies in Siberia during socialism: "They were allocated not to make collective farms viable economic entities but to develop state infrastructure. This infrastructure, in turn, did not produce any goods but merely built more state infrastructure" (2003, 129). His observation seems to square well with the Mongolian communists' ideas about growth: "Public capital [was] looked upon mainly as the process of forming the necessary 'material and technical basis' for achieving the ultimate aim, the building of communism" (Bawden 1986, 394).

the particular imaginative construct of modernity and progress (*högjil, devshil*) as it was powerfully produced by the new revolutionary state of Mongolia.…[B]y the early twentieth century there was a powerful association between light and higher understanding—as the English term "enlightenment" denotes. These associations suffused the language. The term *gegeersen,* for example, meant (and means) enlightened and the verb *gegeeruuleh* to educate or enlighten. The title of a Hutagt—the reincarnate senior lama of the Buddhist church—was *Gegeen,* a word that means daylight, brightness, splendour and brilliance. (2009, 74–76)

In an unintended fulfillment of Marx's revolutionary formula, the collapse of infrastructure accentuated by the power cut was felt as a full-blown cosmological crisis in Ulaan-Uul. To my host family, it was as if "everything solid was melting into air." Nowhere was this more apparent than in the spirit-like manner in which the loss of light from the bulbs was magically extended to encompass the concurrent upsurge in violence in the community. It was not just that the darkened village streets made people more vulnerable to attacks from *agsan* persons, although this was indeed a major source of concern. Rather it was as if a horde of unknown forces and energies had suddenly been unleashed from beneath the infrastructure, where it had previously been held at bay by the ideological and material form assumed by the socialist state at its northern Mongolian margins.

Thus in Ulaan-Uul in the late 1990s, the shamanic spirits were not being imagined solely in "traditional" shamanic terms, as the souls of dead ancestors or the spiritual masters of wild animals. Other shamanic imaginings took an ostensibly more "modern" form, as the spirits were associated with concepts of technology, science, and the state. As a Darhad shaman once told Otgony Pürev, "natural electrical currents such as spirits…are strongest in the dark of the night" (cited in Humphrey 2007, 163). Consider, as a contemporary example of this "modernity of shamanism" (to paraphrase Geschiere 1997), the words of a truck driver as he was angrily fixing a flat tire late one night at the edge of Ulaan Taiga: "Spring is approaching, Morten, so beware. Every year, the masters [*ezed*] wake up with the thaw. They begin to move as the first flowers break through the earth's icy crust. If you pick one, poisonous gases [*hort hii*] will slip out from below." Surprised by the shamanic beauty of the image, I urged him to elaborate. "Well," he retorted, "if you were to ask a shaman, he would say that the spirit comes from the trees themselves. But it doesn't. It is an electric current [*tog*]—a natural element [*bodis*]."

Interestingly, no such spirit problems were associated with the socialist period. Indeed, with a few notable exceptions (to which I return in the next chapter), the spirits had left people alone back then, at least according to what people remember (or say they remember). Why is that so? An answer may be reached by taking a look at people's memories of and narratives about life during the collective farm (*negdel*) period and comparing these with their concerns about life in the postsocialist transition.

Collectivized Bodies and Repressed Souls

People in Ulaan-Uul talked about "the socialist age" (*socializmyn üye*) all the time, but they seldom went into details about what their lives had actually been like back then. All I got were resigned conversation stoppers like this: "Just as people are now getting used to democracy, we learned to live with [*dasah*] the collectivization of our animals back then. What else is there to say?" Acting out of increasing frustration, I set up some interviews and explicitly tried to ask selected people, "In your view, what about life during socialism was good, and what was bad?" Here is how an old woman, my hosts' next-door neighbor, responded, unable to hide her lack of interest—if not disbelief—in my question:

WOMAN: Life was acceptable back then [*dund zereg*].

ME: Acceptable in what way?

WOMAN: Well, they took our animals, didn't they, and made them into collective livestock [*zasgiin mal*]. They added them to the new *negdel*. A household was allowed to keep only a certain number of animals. We managed to keep three good cows and three horses. They took the rest. They also left us with two camels but came back and took them in the spring.

ME: What about the situation was good back then, and what was bad?

WOMAN: Well, we did have a home, didn't we? But hardly any animals. We were just living. Life was mediocre [*taaruu*]. Everyone worked for the state, getting a salary. That was it.

This woman, who was "around ten" when most of the livestock of her family was collectivized, was not alone in describing life during the *negdel* period (1956–1990) as predictable, if not flat and boring. Many others, however, had much fonder memories of this era of changelessness. A strong (*hüchtei*) state made sure that there was law and order ("The criminals were actually punished back then!" a retired teacher huffed) and above all, material plenty. So, while not necessarily remembered as an exiting time, the *negdel* period was praised as one in which no one had to worry about basic things: everyone was fed, clothed, and kept warm. As the grumpy ex-teacher went on to explain while his wife served salty black tea, having deeply apologized for the lack of milk ("We are still waiting for our daughter to send new supplies of white food from the countryside"):

> After the livestock were collectivized in 1961, goods became plentiful, and life was nice and easy. The herders received a state salary. There was free electricity and even hot water. Everything was available. Now everything is about the market. There is no state control [*töriin medel*] and no state property [*töriin höröngö*]. Because we are living in a very remote place, things have become very expensive. Before, Russia was helping us to build our own factories and produce all varieties of goods, so everything was cheap and plentiful. A naked guy could have bought everything he needed in the *negdel* shop and still had money left over! House upon house, storeroom upon storeroom, was stacked with wares. Things were like that in the 1970s and 1980s. Then, after democracy came in the early 1990s, everything became scarce.

This passage is instructive in several ways. First of all, it provides a good illustration of the nostalgia with which a great many people spoke of the socialist period—and particularly the *negdel*—in the late 1990s. This, of course, is hardly the whole story about socialism in the Shishged context, as the available accounts from the period attest. (Recall the many complaints about the 1920s mentioned in the introduction to this book.)[4] Nevertheless, a clear majority of the people I spoke to in Ulaan-Uul—and by no means only former state cadres—associated socialism with prosperity, stability, and security.[5]

Indeed, there is little doubt that for a majority of people in northern Mongolia, many of the indicators commonly used to measure the material quality of life, including access to medical services and formal education, were at a consistently higher level during the *negdel* years than at any other time in Mongolian history, including the present (Morris 2001; Rossabi 2005). This, of course, is not to deny that collective or individual life trajectories from decade to decade of socialism—or even from year to year—assumed countless

---

4. Debunking another postsocialist myth—that the *negdels* were not afflicted by drunkenness and alcoholism—Bawden reported fifty years ago that one "problem which continually exercises the Mongols is that of addiction to alcohol. This is considered as a serious social evil.... [I]n a sample year, 1959, over three-quarters of 'offences against public order' were said to be due to drunkenness, as were nearly half the cases of assault" (Bawden 1986, 394).

5. For a small but outspoken minority, however, "socialism" carried only negative associations. Interestingly, such anticommunist voices were not restricted to relatives of former lamas or shamans purged in the 1930s; in fact, some such descendants were among the staunchest defenders of the socialist project, perhaps because they, owing to a particularly sinister yet effective policy, had been enrolled in the party apparatus to inspire them to turn against their "counterrevolutionary" parents (Humphrey 1994b; Pedersen 2006b).

Figure 4. Village shop

variations, just as it is obvious that for long periods, the shops were not exactly bursting with wares, especially in a remote place like Ulaan-Uul. Perhaps a naked guy really could have dressed himself fully in the village shop and still had cash to spare, but he might well have had to make do with *bakal* (leather boots) a size or two too big and, if he was lucky, a quickly forgotten promise that next time he would be first in line for a pair of jeans.

According to Ole Bruun's apt summary of the last decades of socialism, "life was good, but there was too much hard work" (Bruun 2006, 22). As the wife in my host family recalled, though only after her husband had first praised the *negdel* years for several minutes,

Actually, life was pretty hard back then, especially when the children were small in the mid-1980s. We were living more than ten kilometers outside the Center because of your [points at husband] job for the Youth Communist League. It was quite a walk to the school every day. Still, it wasn't so much the walking. I actually enjoy walking a lot. It was more the fact that I had to get up so darned early every morning and always had to stay up so late. I hardly slept! Before leaving, I first had to milk the cows, then boil the milk and prepare tea, only to get the children out of bed, clothe them, and feed them. When I returned from work in the Center, it was already after sunset, and I had to the same things in reverse. Often I was alone with the children and Mother because you [smiling to the husband] had left to check a *ferm*. On these days I also had to round up the cows and the sheep every evening and sometimes also search for the horses. (I seldom found them.) Yes, those were quite hard times, also because a lot of people tried to hide things from us because of your job in the *negdel*.

Perhaps it is from "everyday" recollections such as these that one gets the best impression of what life was like in northern Mongolia for much of the second half of the twentieth century. That is not necessarily because they are more accurate than other kinds of recollections (Rethmann 2000; Ries 2002), but because they convey just how fundamental the *negdels* were, not only to the way people evaluated their lives at the time, but also to their imagining how they might live in the future, and how they would remember having lived when looking back on the past. The most lasting impression one gets from this description and many others like it is of an almost overpowering sense of normality, a predictability of life of such massive proportions that it almost seems to border on the oppressive, even, or especially, for someone like me, raised in a Scandinavian welfare state. It was not that the hardship or the quality of people's lives did not fluctuate over time. Far from it. (For instance, on several occasions in the 1970s, northern Mongolia was hit by such snowy winters—*zud*—that thousands of animals couldn't find forage and died.) And of course individual lives took the usual twists and turns, such as falling in and out of love. But the overarching narrative and even sociological frame of events, whether public or private, official or nonofficial, was always already in place.

In short, no matter whether people expressed nostalgia for the socialist period or the opposite, or something in between, everyone associated it with a deep sense of sameness, predictability, and inevitability. Like it or not, life in rural Mongolia back then unfolded according to a certain preordained form—that of the *negdel* and associated institutions—a form so powerful that it became the very precondition for a concept of the everyday to emerge, both as a way of framing people's lives and as a template for imagining past and future versions of them. So while countless small issues were questioned and ridiculed during the socialist period, and sometimes even criticized (at least during its first and last decades), one thing was, as it were, too big to fail: the state socialist order itself. Small wonder, then, that the speed and ease with which this system collapsed left people in a state of near-paralysis. "People who lived through socialism," Manduhai Buyandelger writes, "had not expected that the transition from socialism to a market economy would actually mean the collapse of the state....The disappearance of a strong state was shocking" (2007, 129).

All this calls to mind Alexei Yurchak's highly suggestive work on "the last Soviet generation" (1997, 2006). He argues that for people in their twenties and thirties who came of age in Leningrad and other Russian cities during "late socialism," the USSR was "experienced as eternal." Yet crucially, despite this "profound feeling of the Soviet system's permanence and immutability, and [the] complete unexpectedness of its collapse" (2006, 1), people did not necessarily *believe* in the system. On the contrary:

> The perception of the social world's immutability was based on the personal experiences of the Soviet citizen that nearly all mechanisms of representation in the official sphere were centrally controlled. Under these conditions, the official reality was uncontested not because its representation was taken for granted as truthful, or because people were afraid to contest it, but, first and foremost, because it was apparent that no other public representation of reality within the official sphere could occur. (1997, 166–67)

Might this help us understand why the spirits mostly left people alone during the era of socialism, whereas today they seem to be everywhere and nowhere at the same time, like the "poisonous gases" released by certain innocent-looking plants as they break through the ice in spring? As one hunter explained, asked if he also thought that the spirits tend to be more active in the summer season: "Oh yes, did you not know that? In the winter there are no *lus savdag* [land spirits] around. When it begins to freeze, they become unable to move and leave us alone. They get stuck to the ground, temporarily frozen. Then, as spring approaches, they slowly start growing powerful again. And by late September, just before it begins to freeze, spirits are everywhere in the land and in the water."

Perhaps, like other nonofficial phenomena in socialist rural Mongolia, such as the so-called black economy that was thriving especially during the last decades of socialist rule (Wheeler 2004; Pedersen 2007b), the spirits during the time of socialism were unable to move within the "frozen" (immutable and changeless) framework of everyday *negdel* life, having been relegated to various "deterritorialized worlds," which, while existing in a reality parallel to the official communist order, "drew heavily on that system's possibilities" (Yurchak 2006, 132). On this reading, it was not that people didn't believe in spirits in the socialist period but rather that, like illicit goods, these and other black (*har*) and nameless entities were not admitted into what Yurchak calls the hegemony of representation at that time. Instead these entities figured only in the unofficial contexts of people's lives, and even in these parallel worlds they manifested themselves as vague presences, too ephemeral to speak of let alone see. It is telling, I think, that occult themes often were brought up after my hosts had gone to bed and could be heard whispering about the events of the day—not because they were any longer afraid that someone might hear what they were saying, but because certain phenomena could be spoken of only in this way (and, more mundanely, because they did not want to wake the children).

Of course, sudden and unpredictable changes must also have been perceived as having occurred in people's lives during the socialist period, and some of these circumstances and events must have been seen as having been caused by forces that were not fully visible, let alone fully understandable, to ordinary people. And apart from the common experiences of arbitrariness and paradox arising from the more absurd implications of socialist planning—for instance, the near-chronic scarcity of goods in the shops—some of these changes, like their opaque and possibly occult causes, must have been attributed to the party's suppression of religious practices, especially the purges of lamas and shamans in the 1930s.

So, surely, hordes of uncontrollable spirits were already on the loose back during the socialist years, especially after their shamanic (and Buddhist) masters had been killed or arrested or forced to practice "in secret"? Yes and no. Yes in that "actually, there were also cases of *agsan* violence and *ataman* extortion back then," as some people admitted to me, albeit only if pressed, and only if I happened to know them well. But also no because, according to the all-pervasive retrospective fantasy surrounding the socialist past, some very powerful if not omnipotent thing was imbued with the capacity to contain all forces of spiritual instability and physical violence (in the sense of rendering them invisible, not causing them to disappear). And that all-powerful thing was the state (*tör*).

Back in the socialist period, as everyone was eager to tell me when the always looming presence of the Mongolian state (*Mongol tör*) came up in conversations and interviews, the state was strong (*hüchtei*)—so strong, it appears in hindsight, that it was able to suppress (again in the sense of pushing into the background but not destroying) not only the shamans but also the spirits. But this did not make the spirits (or shamans) less potentially present as latent forms lurking in the shadows of *negdel* life. On the contrary, the more people tried—and today continue trying—to ignore the spirits by not talking about them, or refraining from constructing specific concepts of and names for them, let alone believe in them, the more omni-present (but not, it must also be noted here, omnipotent) they became.

In short, with the advent of transition, people in northern Mongolia ex-perienced an almost total collapse of the boundaries between official and nonofficial realms, and between ordinary (known) and extraordinary (un-known) causes. This generated a sensation of being overrun by a plethora of spirits and forces which had hitherto been tucked away in multiple parallel dimensions. Because these entities had been rendered as structurally invis-ible as the repressed lamas and shamans, they could not be talked about, and perhaps even thought about, even if everyone knew that they still lurked behind the scenes. Only in 1990, with the "spring of democracy" (to borrow one of the flowery phrases of transitology discourse), these forces were liber-ated from the "winter of communism" (another transitology cliché) as they leaked, gas-like, from underneath the crumbling infrastructure and other former emblems of socialist hypermodernity now subject to structural ad-justment, shock therapy, and the unpredictable and yet inescapable laws of the market.

The End of Progress

Having demonstrated why it makes sense in many ways to speak of "the modernity of shamanism" in northern Mongolia in the late 1990s, I now turn to the second "welfare crisis" that took place in Ulaan-Uul during the chaotic spring months of 1999, a crisis in which the disintegration of the postsocial-ist state was even more explicitly associated with the rise of the spirits: the events surrounding the schoolteachers' strike.

The teachers' strike had been under way for several weeks when the elec-tricity was cut off, which only added to the general sense of chaos. One day, as I was crossing the frozen river from the opposite shore, I ran into the director of the school outside the faded white wooden school building with moun-tains of logs stacked outside. He eagerly invited me for a "meeting" in his office. Lukewarm Chinese beer was produced from the steel safe beneath his desk, as he confessed that he was no longer able to resist the bottle. "Everyone hates me," he sobbed, "but I can't do anything about those unpaid wages. Only the regional government can." Indeed, another week or so into the strike, an official delegation from Mörön happened to pass through Ulaan-Uul on its way to a seminar, and soon an extra injection of funds enabled the teachers to be paid and the school reopened. By this point, however, an irreversible metamorphosis already seemed to have taken place in the director's—and more generally the school's—standing in the eyes of the community.

Figure 5. Female teachers on winter picnic

Even the normally stable domestic structure of my host family started to fall apart during these weeks of accelerated transition. The husband, who belonged to the enviable group of village men with a steady income and a relatively low alcohol intake, was suddenly observed downplaying his Halh ethnicity and participating wholeheartedly in the two most common activities of the unemployed: drinking vodka and playing the card game *durak* (Russ. "fool"). In another breach of convention, his wife, instead of scorning her husband, as any self-respecting Darhad wife should have done in this situation, teamed up with her striking colleagues from the school in a weeklong spree of drinking, smoking, and partying. As hard as the teenage daughter fought to maintain some semblance of normality by trying to keep the household neat and tidy, my host family eventually assumed the same disorderly (*zambaraagüi*) appaerance as the "bad families" (*muu ail*), from which the most notorious *atamans* reputedly came.

But the changes in the household went deeper than that. Whereas the wife would usually stress her ignorance about such "difficult" topics as shamanism and the spirits—themes, she would assert, that did not interest her very much—she now started to take an active interest in occult matters. She would quiz me about my visits to "the real shamans up north" and began to solicit help from local occult practitioners, including a renowned diviner from next door and a less respected shamaness from an impoverished *ail* at the edge of village, whose shamanic powers, for reasons that never became fully clear, were considered weak, even in her own eyes.

This was new territory for her, both as an area of interest and as a moral issue. Nowhere was this more clearly illustrated than in the striking transformation that took place in her view of her elder brother's son, a notoriously *agsan*-prone young man in his early twenties who had moved in with my host family after his parents decided to put some distance between him and the law in his hometown, a large industrial city in central Mongolia. Whereas the youth's constant binging and fighting had previously been attributed to unemployment and a troubled ("lazy") personality, he was now being referred to as a potential shaman. Indeed, the wife confessed in one of her gossipy tea sessions with the elderly widow from next door, her nephew had expressed several signs of the shamanic capacity (*udha*), which, it now suddenly transpired, ran in her mother's family line (*udam*). But a "however" was quickly added. Because the wife in my host family had been adopted as a child by the sister of her biological mother, who was herself an adoptee, there was "of course" no possibility that she could have the *udha* herself. In any case, the possibility that her nephew might turn out to be a potential shaman was explored no further, since the young man vehemently refused to travel with his aunt and grandmother 100 kilometers north to Tsagaan Nuur to see a shaman for additional divinations. (A failed attempt had been made during a previous visit to the same shaman when the nephew was a teenager and "for a long time had been acting strangely.") Instead, after a particularly wild drinking binge, he was unceremoniously shipped off in the weekly mail van to the regional capital, Mörön, in the direction of his hometown, semiconscious and with a severe hangover. In a final gesture of guilt, his aunt slipped a wad of money into his pocket. (Apparently the nephew did not make it all the way back home but decided to try his luck in Mörön instead.)

Meanwhile, my host's world underwent a no less dramatic transformation. A former leader in the Communist Youth League in the Happy Living *negdel* and a lifelong member of the Mongolian People's Revolutionary Party (MPRP), for which he served as party sectary for a number of years in the 1990s, he had also briefly been leader of the village *bag*. ("No one else seemed to want to do it," he told me.) This well-liked Halh migrant to the Darhad homeland had secured himself a sought-after job prior to my first arriving in the region, namely, that of national park warden.[6]

---

6. I came across several former Communist Party members of Halh background who, having been dispatched to northern Mongolia after graduating from universities in Ulaanbaatar and even abroad, ended up marrying local women and settling down. In fact, during the socialist

Established in 1992 with support from the U.S. government and foreign NGOs, the Lake Hövsgöl National Park and the neighboring Hordil Sar'dag Mountains, which is classified as a protected area, mark the Shishged's western boundary with the Lake Hövsgöl region. While the area is not very well suited for herding, it has for centuries been a popular hunting spot. Indeed, one of the primary reasons for establishing the national park in the first place was to protect endangered animals such as the argali sheep, the mountain goat, and the brown bear, whose numbers had been declining rapidly since the end of state control over hunting.[7]

This, of course, did not stop hunters (or, in more official parlance, poachers) from entering the area, which explains one reason for the national park's desirability as a place of employment.[8] Although many wardens (including my host) took their status as law enforcement officers very seriously, the job also gave ample opportunity to make money on the side. I'm not referring to outright bribery (although this also took place, at least according to hunters who complained about how much they to pay) but rather to the possibilities for making additional income though so-called informal economic transactions, which, so to speak, arose naturally from the job of warden. While my host to the best of my knowledge was never involved in the former (indeed he was relentless in his criticism of those who were), his position presented unique opportunities for making *tanil* (acquaintances), with whom, as he happily demonstrated, one could engage in more or less formalized exchange relations. His patrols involved visiting practically every household on his route, from which he would carefully select a "target" and then spend the night as a guest of honor. Invariably, upon my host's return to his family waiting eagerly in the village, his saddlebags were bursting with cheese, butter, and other so-called white food (*tsagaan idee*). He was also the bearer of a no less prized commodity: "news" (*medee*) and gossip from the countryside.[9]

---

period it was official doctrine that "closer national integration [could be] measured by the degree of inter-ethnic marriage" (Bulag 1998, 33).

7. Hunting was strictly regulated in the Shishged *negdels* (Badamhatan 1986, 28–34), and while unauthorized hunting was not unknown during socialism, it has skyrocketed since 1990. As a result, wardens like my host—and many hunters as well—reported a dramatic drop in the population of several species of animals, in some cases (such as argali sheep and mountain goats) to the point of extinction.

8. Unlike, say, schoolteachers, wardens were paid not by local or regional governments but by the relevant ministry in Ulaanbaatar. In addition to the status associated with being close to state power, this meant that the salary of these few lucky people came from a source less sensitive to local budgetary fluctuations.

9. When going to the countryside, villagers would often carry a selection of goods to exchange for surplus products from the pastoral economy. Thus my host brought candles, sugar,

This time, however, something had changed. While it had long been true for many people employed by the government that "'work' [was] no longer a career or a calling but...a strategic value" (Humphrey 1998, 460), others still seemed to take great pride in the fact that they were working for the state. My host very much belonged to the latter category; in fact, given his background as a Halh migrant, a prominent member of the MPRP, and a local *bag* leader, he was in many ways the archetypal state official. Perhaps this is why, although most of his time on the job was spent with his many *tanil*, he would never have admitted to a clash between his own interests and those of the state. In fact, it probably never would have occurred to him. Paraphrasing Michael Herzfeld (1985), we might say that a warden's job was indeed a genuine calling for my host, since being good at being a warden (embodying the state) was more meaningful to him than being a good warden (representing the state).

Only with the most recent deterioration of welfare services in the spring of 1999 did it seem to dawn on my host that perhaps there was no state at all—in the sense of a unified, enduring, and strict but benevolent paternal, authoritarian sovereign body. It certainly is striking that I never again heard him praise his job in the overeager manner so characteristic of former lower-ranking communist cadres, who have seen their status (and income) fall as a new contingent of very different (business) men take over. From this point on, his job in the park, having been presented until recently as a position of national importance of which he and the family had good reason to be proud, was dismissed as just another means of survival in "the age of the market."

What seems to have taken place during those spring weeks was nothing less than the irreversible end of "progress" and "modernity" in the form of an (imagined) linear progression of time toward ever higher stages of societal development. Faced with the shadowy underside of self and community, both husband and wife in my host family had been halted, if not reversed, in the linear march toward enlightenment (in the dual socialist-Buddhist sense) on which they had previously been embarked, and which they, more than most former cadres in Ulaan-Uul, and perhaps postsocialist Mongolia as a whole, had until that moment personified. They had once been unrelenting in their Bolshevik "expectation of modernity" (Ferguson 1999). But now it was as if the unmistakable manifestation of the shamanic *udha* in their own household, in combination with the overwhelming reality of poaching, clientelism, and bribery, succeeded in shattering their rock-solid

---

cigarettes, candy, and soap with him on his trips, which he then exchanged—through barter or for money—for butter, dried curd, meat, and hides.

belief in progress. As a result, they came to realize what most others around them had known for a while. Now for them, too, the "age of darkness" had commenced.

In many ways this dark and negative vision was more in tune with the realities of "transition" than the enlightened and optimistic vision they had previously entertained. After all, the slow but relentless disappearance of the old socialist welfare state in the Mongolian countryside throughout the 1990s has been well documented (Bruun 2005; Bruun and Narangoa 2006; Bruun and Odgaard 1996), and there is no reason to think that the situation in the Shishged was any better. In fact, because of its remoteness, this region probably suffered more than most. As I noted in the introduction, it is no coincidence that Ulaan-Uul, with some justification, had a reputation as a deprived, alcoholic, and lawless place, for the available data indeed give the same picture.

Against this backdrop, the stubbornly law-abiding and defiantly optimistic attitude of my hosts in the years before the crisis stands out as an enigma. In what looks like an inversion of Slavoj Žižek's concept of cynical reason (1993), my hosts—and, it is fair to assume, other "good households" (*sain ail*) as well—had been surviving the transition period by adhering, in an over earnest (as opposed to a pretensive and cynical) way, to an imagined "normality" (Fehérváry 2002), built on generalized social trust and a deep-seated faith in the state. This decidedly anti-cynical imaginary, whose peculiar combination of statism and a no less strong emphasis on individuality may be traced back to Genghis himself (Humphrey 2008), provided a sort of chronotropic filter by which my hosts, throughout much of the 1990s, kept the forces of darkness at bay.[10]

Nikolai Ssorin-Chaikov, in his important historical ethnography of the state in subarctic Siberia, paints a similar picture. Far from representing an

---

10. Unlike the citizens of many postcolonial states, Mongolians do not as a rule conceive of the state as an alien entity imposed on them from the outside. On the contrary, people tend to have a highly intimate if not downright affectionate relationship with *Mongol tör*, as witnessed, for example, in the striking degree of awe and respect commanded by state emblems such as seals, stamps, and coins. Indeed anyone who is tempted to compare Mongolia with postcolonial contexts should keep in mind that even though Mongolia was a de facto part of the USSR and before that a colony under the Qing Empire, many Mongolians see themselves not, or at least not only, as postcolonial subjects but rather as colonizing, postimperial subjects. (The case of Inner Mongolia is, for a variety reasons, different; see for example Bulag 2002.) To be sure, few people believe that Genghis's empire is about to rise from the ashes of history, and one encounters much resentment of China's rise to power and worry about the dependency on multinational companies and development agencies. Still, the Mongolian political self-conception is more that of a former imperial master than a former imperial subject.

indigenous culture preserved by a long history of failed government interventions, he argues, the local Evenki people have appropriated these same failures to make "successful claims to statehood and [to] display a considerable mastery in using tools of state power" (2003, 12). Thus, instead of illustrating the weakness of the Russian (and before that the Soviet) state in a remote corner of Siberia, Ssorin-Chaikov's analysis shows how that state made itself "conspicuous by its absence" in social life (9).

This argument is clearly relevant to the Darhad case. As described earlier, for centuries if not thousands of years the Shishged has been positioned at the edge of Inner Asian polities that sought to rule the population and their land in accordance with the dominant imperial (and Buddhist ecclesiastical) policies of the day. While each of these polities produced very different impacts on local life, one thing they all had in common was a record of failed, or at least incomplete, political interventions. Throughout the 1970s and 1980s, for example, the Revolutionary Party repeatedly let it be known—in language reminiscent of its nineteenth-century Buddhist predecessors (see chapter 3)—that although a fair amount of progress had certainly taken place in *sums* and *negdels,* the real potential of the region, and the country as whole, had "once again" failed to materialize because of insufficient vigilance on the part of the comrades.[11] In that sense the premodern Buddhist estate and the hypermodernist socialist collective farm emerge as two instantiations of the same "poetic of unfinished reconstruction," to use the apt term coined by Ssorin-Chaikov (2003, 113).

The spring of 1999, however, saw the end of this myth of linear progression. It was as if an irreversible realignment had taken place between the general thrust of social life and certain "good" and "influential" persons' (mis)perceptions of it. Until the crisis broke, no matter how grave the escalating deficit in the Ulaan-Uul *sum* budget, and no matter how obvious the guilt of the latest official caught up to his neck in sleaze, my hosts had been living their lives—and expecting others to live theirs—as if these were freak incidents destined to disappear with the long-awaited return of "normality." With the twin crises of the electrical blackout and the school strike, however, attitudes and behaviors that had previously been deemed evil, corrupt, or indeed irrational and shamanic, suddenly became understandable, if not downright commendable.

---

11. As Bawden observed about the situation in Mongolia in the mid-1980s, "with painful regularity, year after year, [the Mongolian press] exposes the chronic faults of apathy, fecklessness, carelessness with machinery, neglect of collectivized livestock, dishonesty in the management of public funds and property, and, above all, it deplores the lack of enough people of a proper standard of competence and reliability (1986, 393).

As similar shifts in perception no doubt took place in other leading Ulaan-Uul households, the community as a whole may be seen to have undergone a carnivalistic rite of inversion, were it not for the fact that while one "good husband" after another fell victim to the same symptoms of *agsan* usually associated with the "bad husbands," no one from the latter group took on the respectable appearance of the former in mocking imitation. Rather, as if having been part of a collective rite of passage, for a period of several weeks that spring the entire village found itself in a spirit-like condition of pure and perpetual transformation—or chaotic and permanent transition—as its otherwise more or less stable adult subjects dissolved into a multitude of conflicting wills, desires, and strategies.

Within this limbo, where the dynamics of village politics, religion, and economy were suddenly put on hold, every member of my host family (myself included), and perhaps those of other "good" households too, was turned into a potential victim of the shamanic predicament. Clinging to a ground that could not even be imagined as solid anymore, we were all subjected to spirit-like forces which had spiraled out of control. Far beyond the relatively limited nuisance of the teachers' refusal to teach, what was at stake during these weeks was nothing less than the very form of community as it had hitherto been imagined. Everyone seemed to have become momentarily a potential shaman, and the new world(s) that they—that we—could see from this occult perspective was altogether different from before.

From the Multinaturalist Taiga to the Postsocialist State

What, then, emerged on the other side of these critical, indeed transgressive weeks? Bearing in mind that unwanted and unplanned rituals have irreversible effects (Houseman and Severi 1998), I propose that what became irrefutably clear in the aftermath of the spring crises was the essentially shamanic nature of the postsocialist state. If up to this point people like my host family had imagined the Mongolian state as a singular and stable thing—a unified, stratified, and predictable sovereign body made up of components and relations of a certain predictability if not, in their own limited terms, equity—then from this point on, the state started to assume the form of a labile and ephemeral spirit-like presence rendered visible in fleeting, conflictual encounters arising from confusing, unpredictable, and unintended events.

Much like the shamanic spirits, then, the postsocialist state in northern Mongolia in the late 1990s was "an apparition—now you see it, now you don't—an intangible nonentity that appear[s] constantly to change hands" (Navaro-Yashin, 2002, 175). But how do we best theorize the occult aura that hovered around things political during my time in Ulaan-Uul? Wherein lies, to adopt Michael Taussig's apt phrase (1997), the magic of the postsocialist Mongolian state?

In recent years a number of political anthropologists have posited the postcolonial, and indeed the postsocialist, state as a fundamentally fragmentary, spectral, and phantasmic entity, which citizens only imagine to exist in a reified, unified, and transcendental form (Hansen and Stepputat 2001; Mueggler 2001; Navaro-Yashin 2003; Taussig 1992, 1997). As Erik Mueggler writes in his perceptive ethnography of perceptions of the state in southwestern China, states are "loosely coordinated systems of institutions, policies, symbols, and processes. Their capacities to affect events, produce meanings, or work themselves into the bodies of their subjects depend on how they are imagined collectively as unitary entities" (2001, 4).

While my argument is wedded to the general theoretical thrust of these studies, it departs from them in terms of the consequences of the state's purported "fall" from a single transcendental thing to an immanent multiplicity. From Mueggler's and others' arguments it thus seems to follow that if people were to stop imagining the state as that single transcendental thing and instead begin to see it for what it "really is"—an immanent multitude of heterogeneous agents and effects—then it would lose its distinctive magic. But why should states not remain godlike, in terms of both the elevated respect they elicit and the occult potency they exude, even if such sovereign bodies are no longer perceived as singular and transcendent? Why, that is to say, is the irreducibly multiple and radically immanent not imbued with a distinctive political magic in its own right?

I begin my exploration of the radically immanent shamanic state by drawing an apparently unlikely analogy between the postsocialist imaginings that I encountered in northern Mongolia and the so-called perspectivist cosmologies discussed by Eduardo Viveiros de Castro and other anthropologists working on Amerindian animism (Descola 1996; Fausto 2007; Taylor 1993). In his 1998 paper "Cosmological Deixis and Amerindian Perspectivism," Viveiros de Castro explores the wider anthropological and philosophical ramifications of the fact that jaguars and other wild animals are considered by some Amerindians to see the world as humans do. *What* they see, however, differs from what humans see. Hence the intriguing idea, found in much of the Amazon, that

> in normal conditions, humans see humans as humans, animals as animals and spirits (if they see them) as spirits; however animals (predators) and spirits see humans as animals (as prey) to the same extent that animals (as prey) see humans as spirits or as animals (predators). By the same token,

animals and spirits see themselves as humans: they perceive themselves as
(or become) anthropomorphic beings when they are in their own houses
or villages and they experience their own habits and characteristics in the
form of culture—they see their food as human food (jaguars see blood as
manioc beer, vultures see the maggots in the rotting meat as grilled fish,
etc.), they see their bodily attributes (fur, feathers, claws, beaks, etc.) as
body decorations or cultural instruments, they see their social system as
organized in the same way as human institutions are (with chiefs, shamans, ceremonies, exogamous moieties, etc.). (1998a, 470)

This is what Viveiros de Castro calls "ontological perspectivism" or, more
provocatively, "multinaturalism"—the notion that it is not different human
worldviews that are relative to one another but the world that is relative to
itself, given that the cosmos is composed of multiple perspectives residing
in different kinds of plastic bodies.[12] So if conventional cultural relativism
"supposes a diversity of subjective and partial representations, each striving
to grasp an external and unified nature," the alternative, *natural relativism*,
"poses the opposite: a representational or phenomenological unity which is
purely pronominal or deictic, indifferently applied to a radically objective
diversity" (1998a, 478). So whereas naturalism and cultural relativism are
based on "the unity of nature and the plurality of cultures," multinaturalism
and natural relativism, conversely, hinge on "spiritual unity and corporeal
diversity" (1998a, 470).

What happens if we extend the analytical scope of perspectivism beyond
the scale of the Amazonian hunter facing the jaguar to ask what shape Northern Mongolian social life takes from the point of view of different postsocialist political bodies? While perhaps alien to Viveiros de Castro's project, this is
not as farfetched as it may seem. For if perspectivism can be defined roughly
as the "process of discrete switching of points of view between forms of
agency populating the cosmos" (2007), it is pertinent to ask: What might the
postsocialist Mongolian state look like from a shamanic perspective? In what
follows my aim is to do with the Mongolian state what Viveiros de Castro
and Marilyn Strathern have accomplished for Amerindian cosmology and
Melanesian kinship respectively, that is, to ask: What does it take to see—and
to be seen—with different bodies?

12. Although the entities (hunters, jaguars, and so forth) undergoing perspectival metamorphosis in Amerindian animism are sometimes referred to in a sort of shorthand as "bodies," it is
important to stress that these entities are not "Western" bodies in the sense of fixed physiological
forms, but are continually changing assemblages of "affects, dispositions or capacities which render every different species unique" (Viveiros de Castro 1998a, 478).

The postsocialist state, I submit, is imbued with indexical or "deictic" properties, in the sense that its different "attributes are immanent in the viewpoint, and move with it" (Viveiros de Castro 1998a, 477).[13] Thus in Ulaan-Uul in the late 1990s—especially in the aftermath of the chaotic spring crisis of 1999—statehood was identified in whatever person or thing that enabled people to *become* the point of view of some political body, for, as is the case with all indexical or deictic attributes, the Mongolian state was now perceived to exist in a multiple cosmos, where each point of view was embedded in a distinct body, or more precisely a partly connected and yet partly detached assemblage of corporeal affects. For people in Ulaan-Uul, the question was thus not so much how "to see like a state" (Scott 1998) but rather how to *be seen* like a state. Like the Amerindian hunter, who *is* (as opposed to *has*) the point of view of a wild animal soul in the multinaturalist taiga, every citizen is (as opposed to has) the point of view of a certain attribute of the state in the chaotic age of permanent postsocialist transition. At no point was this more apparent than in the decoration of a Tsagaan Nuur–based shaman's home in conjunction with Mongolia's national elections of 2000. Here, as we shall see, I witnessed the first of three instances of "shamanic politics" in the postsocialist context.

Shamanic Politics I

Although I had not been present in the Shishged for the national elections in the early summer of 2000, their effects were still visible on my return to Ulaan-Uul that August. In practically every household, people had been appropriating the generously disseminated election material to decorate their homes. As a devoted member of the Mongolian People's Revolutionary Party, my host had a clear reason for this choice. Gaudy posters showing local party hopefuls mingling with famous pop stars from Ulaanbaatar were displayed in the honorary position above the altar, rubbing shoulders with the permanent lineup of Lenin, the revolutionary hero Sukhbator, and the president at the time, Bagabandi, of the MPRP. Most

---

13. In linguistics, "deixis" refers to those language situations in which the meaning of a term relies absolutely on the context in which it is uttered. Personal pronouns such as "I" and "you" are thus generally considered deictic indexes, as are, sometimes, other proforms, such as "here" and "there." Viveiros de Castro's novel claim is that in certain Amazonian contexts, concepts that are not commonly thought of as deictic in the West, such as "person" and "human," are radically indexical as well. He writes, "Amerindian souls, be they human or animal, are ... indexical categories, cosmological deictics whose analysis calls not so much for an animist psychology or substantialist ontology as for a theory of the sign or a perspectival pragmatics" (1998a, 476).

Figure 6. Home decorated with election posters

households, however, seemed to evaluate the election material according to more aesthetic criteria. "Because they look so nice," was the laconic reply I received when asking why someone's home was adorned with portraits of smiling politicians.[14]

In the case of Nadmid Udgan, a renowned Darhad shamaness (since deceased) who was living in the Tsagaan Nuur district, this seemingly frivolous use of politics as ornamentation reached a level that merits special attention. Although her home was always decorated, I was taken aback upon entering it this time. The spirit talisman (*ongon*) in the corner was as imposing and flamboyantly designed as ever, but its occult radiance was now matched by a montage-like tableau of election posters, flyers, and newspaper clippings, which left practically no surface uncovered. Even the ceiling was plastered with them. Just above the altar, amid an impressive collection of ceremonial

14. This is not to say that people did not feel the need to judge the same politicians in light of the "content" of their policies; indeed, that was done throughout the election year, and with great fervor and wit.

silk scarves (*hadag*), was a portrait of a local Revolutionary Party candidate with the sacred Delger Khan Mountain towering behind him.

"They are all about the election," Nadmid Udgan explained unnecessarily, before launching into a long monologue making it abundantly clear that here was someone who knew more than a little about national—and international—politics. There is nothing unusual about Darhad shamans being interested in politics. As the Darhad shamaness Baljir told the Mongolian ethnographer Otgony Pürev in 1994: "The...Ongon is a powerful and clever thing, which gives all kinds of information from all over the world....As an old woman, I am often tired of [it]. Last year it told me that a war would take place in Europe. (It did so in Russia and Yugoslavia)" (2004, 138). "Indeed," Pürev notes with no little admiration, Baljir "foretold the emergence of Mongolian democracy in the 1990s as long ago as 1978" (2004, 130).

Several anthropologists have explored the prominent role of political imagery in Mongolian shamanism (Buyandelger 2007, in press; Humphrey 1994a, 1996). But that is not my concern here. More than the ability of shamanism to represent or symbolize the state, I am interested in the isomorphism of form between things shamanic and the statist phenomenon in postsocialist Mongolia. Rather than presenting details about Nadmid Udgan's shamanic views on, say, the deployment of NATO forces in Kosovo in 1999 (which she, along with many other Darhads, was vehemently against), I want to draw attention to the unique shape assumed by the political in her eyes. For that, I propose, is precisely what the election poster display was: a visualization of what politics looks like from a shamanic point of view.

To substantiate this point, it is useful to consider one of Maurice Merleau-Ponty's more interesting ideas, namely, the deeply perspectivist notion that the ability to see something from a certain point of view involves seeing (or imagining seeing) that same thing from all other potential points of view (1962; see also Kelly 2005; Holbraad and Willerslev 2007; and Willerslev 2009). According to this "animist" theory of perception,

> to see is to enter a universe of beings that display themselves....Thus every object is the mirror of all others. When I look at the lamp on my table, I attribute to it not only the qualities visible from where I am, but also those which the chimney, the walls, the table can "see"; the back of my lamp is nothing other than the face which it "shows" to the chimney. I can therefore see an object insofar as objects form a system or a world and insofar as each of them treats the objects around it like spectators of its hidden aspects and a guarantee of its permanence. (cited in Kelly 2005, 76)

I suggest that the concept of national politics made visible in the shaman's election tableau was similarly animist or perspectivist in nature. The difference was only that, instead of lamps and other everyday objects, as in Merleau-Ponty's (characteristically) mundane example, the "universe of beings" that displayed themselves in the Darhad shaman's house were "spectators" of an altogether more esoteric (some might say occult) object, the shamanic Mongolian state, put on display in conjunction with the elections.

Like the shamanic spirits, the shamanic state is not normally visible to the human eye—not because statehood (and, for that matter, spirit-hood) is invisible or transcendental as such, but because its different modes of existence, its multiple metamorphoses, are not under normal circumstances *simultaneously* visible. In the shaman's home, however, it was as if the diverse assemblage of faces through which the Mongolian state—like the spirits—manifested itself had temporarily been gathered into a montage-like totality of heterodox perspectives. For what did the poster display constitute other than a sort of political talisman, an iconographic instantiation of the multitude of changing bodies through which the postsocialist state compels people to be seen as citizens?

Needless to say, it is hard to imagine anyone, whether shaman or layman, decorating his or her home like this during the socialist period, not only because there were no democratic elections then, but also because it would undoubtedly have been deemed improper if not illegal to depict the state in this manner. In fact, shamans in Mongolia have traditionally considered the state beyond the reach of their (nearly limitless) powers (Pürev 2004, 149–64). Thus, explains Pürev, Darhad shamans

> have always taught respect for state emblems, pictures of its head and officials, bank notes and coins with their symbols and such like. Some shamans...who were able to find and fetch lost items with their own magic gifts, said, 'It is possible to bring back anything, which was lost by someone....But no shaman can fetch a bank note or a coin, because of the state emblem on it.'...So, a shaman, who has fallen into an Ongon's trance, though capable of bringing anything of a weight of five to eight kilograms within a distance of up to ten kilometers, cannot pick up even a small brick of tea if it has a state or national emblem on it. (2004, 153–54)

How do we reconcile this veneration of state iconography—which, as noted earlier, is typical of Mongolian perceptions of the state more generally—with the shamanic election images? On the one hand, Nadmid Udgan clearly considered her poster display a show of respect. The shaman was not depicting the postsocialist democratic state in all its bewildering multitude of individual candidates because she disapproved of it; she did so precisely because she found the images of politicians appealing and powerful. On the other hand, if Pürev's account of the situation before 1990 is representative, then a significant change has evidently taken place in terms of shamanic perceptions of the Mongolian state. Whereas the state used to be conceived of singularly, and was in this respect conflated with the Eternal Blue Sky (Tenger), the postsocialist state has taken on a more multiple appearance, akin to the so-called ninety-nine skies (*tenger*) (see chapter 4). This suggests that Nadmid Udgan's concept of the political in the 1990s underwent a transformation not unlike that which my hosts experienced in the same period: from believing in the unity and stability of the postsocialist state (despite mounting evidence to the contrary), she too began to see it as fluid and multiple.

If the story of the shaman's election poster display offers an apt illustration of the deictic nature of the postsocialist Mongolian state, then that is because the state, in an unusually literal manner, was here composed of a multiplicity of perspectives (portraits), each of which, so to speak, took on a life of its own by being looked at by the shaman's many visitors, and thus by those visitors imagining being looked at by all the politicians depicted in the posters. Far from representing a superficial appropriation of "the political" for decorative purposes, the shaman's poster tableau in that sense amounted to a genuinely shamanic act. By displaying, in all of their irreducible heterogeneity, portraits of each and every candidate for election, she was effectively creating an *invocation* of the postsocialist state in its radically immanent incarnation as a multitude of different faces, agents, and strategies. Thus Nadmid Udgan and her visitors were made to see themselves through the state's many eyes. Not only were the viewers of her poster display being seen from multiple points of view at the same time (reminding them of their splintered selves in the age of transition), but also they were made to see the state as a multitude of spectral political faces, thus turning them, willingly or not, into citizens of a chaotic ("democratic") state.

This suggests that the shamanic state that emerged in northern Mongolia after socialism was not simply a multitude of actors and their different strategies unmasked behind the fetishized garb of a decaying monolithic socialist state. Instead it was a deeply shamanic state composed of multiple and endlessly shifting points of view, implying that people needed to resort to occult means in order to be seen by it. Far from being less "magical" (in the sense of being endowed with occult capacity to mold people's perceptions of political realities) than its hypermodernist predecessor, this new, non-modern state was magical in a different way. For instead of seducing people into imagining it, as well as themselves as its citizens, as unified, stable, and singular beings, the shamanic state compelled its subjects to see both itself and themselves as irreducibly heterogeneous. The postsocialist Mongolian state was multiple through and through, dispersed across a multitude of political faces, each containing a world of its own.

Shamanic Politics II

It took a while for me to understand that Ulaan-Uul's *atamans* were not perceived as mere brutes. I wondered why my friend the vice governor, who had been beaten up by one of them, never accused his assailant of any wrong-doing. Indeed, it seemed to be commonly accepted that "as an accountant," the vice governor ought to have known better than to get into a drunken argument with an *ataman*. As I would eventually learn, the brawl had been over a much-contested loan made by the district administration to a distant relative of the governor. While the vice governor had apparently not gained personally from this dubious transaction, he was widely condemned for hav-ing approved it in the first place, a criticism he seemed to accept as valid. In beating up my friend, then, the *ataman* had displayed not only an obvious physical advantage but also a more abstract moral superiority in the eyes of the community. By taking on the role of a postsocialist "social bandit" (Hobsbawm 1959), he had evidently succeeded in policing the murky realm of rural politics, and in so doing revealed that the vice governor was not just a lousy fighter but an incompetent accountant.

All this suggests that the *ataman* is a leader (*darga*) of sorts. But what kind of leader is he, and what does this tell us about the political efficacy of shamanism in northern Mongolia in the late 1990s? Unlike other leaders, formal or informal, Ulaan-Uul's *atamans* had no one above them. This set them apart from more familiar mafia types in the postsocialist world, who are often organized, or thought to be organized, into gangs of thieves and other secret networks transcending the mob (Humphrey 2002; Ries 2002; Volkov 2002). As an ex-*ataman* from Ulaanbaatar explained to me: "There can be only one *ataman* in each district. No one can be above the *ataman*, not even Genghis Khan," he said, laughing. "Everyone obeys his words, and his words only. They don't pay any attention to the law. Whatever the *ataman* says, people will do."

Indeed, there was no explicit hierarchy among Ulaan-Uul's *atamans*, ei-ther in their own eyes or the eyes of others, though of course people engaged in all sorts of speculation about who would be victorious in the likely case of a lethal showdown. Perhaps this is why they seemed to put so much effort into avoiding one another, as if doing otherwise would break some implicit rule dictating that no two *atamans* should recognize that they are in fact very much alike.

Atamans, then, are political singularities: they exist only in the form of One, for the prominence of each one of them cannot be divided, nor can it be subsumed under any higher level of sovereignty or administration or by any greater cosmological scale. And yet Ulaan-Uul's *atamans* were not—at least not in any simple sense—in opposition to the Mongolian state. Instead they were imbued with a unique prominence that was, I suggest, deeply shamanic in nature. Let me explain by recounting a revealing incident that took place during the lunar New Year celebrations (Tsagaan Sar).

Across Mongolia, Tsagaan Sar is known as a time when junior generations (in particular children) must show respect and thus submission to their parents and to elders more generally, who in turn respond by bestowing blessings and gifts. It is a weeklong (and in rural contexts often longer) festive period during which everyone gets together with above relatives but also friends to eat, drink, and sing traditional songs. Given the conservative air of the occasion, one might assume that the *atamans* would be entirely marginal in the Tsagaan Sar context. Yet on more than one occasion I witnessed them playing a prominent role in Ulaan-Uul's lunar New Year celebrations. Once an *ataman* turned up at one of the many Tsagaan Sar gatherings at my hosts' home. Entering the house in a characteristically crude (*büdüüleg*) manner, his gown unbuttoned, its belt hanging loose around his waist, and totally ignoring the male elders seated in the *hoimor* (the honored northern section), the *ataman* parked himself in front of the altar, where he was served food and drink. He then underwent a remarkable transformation. Instead of becoming *agsan,* as many people (including myself) might have feared, based on previous experiences with him and his followers, he proved to be a skilled manipulator of *yos* (custom). But instead of tapping into the conventions of traditional male oratory and fortune-bestowing gestures, as the elderly men were doing, the *ataman* proceeded to subvert the Tsagaan Sar tradition from within by, for example, substituting words in well-known proverbs and sayings.

This performance was highly appreciated. People laughed at the *ataman*'s daring word games, but they also displayed a deference altogether different from the sheer angst I had witnessed on other occasions. My impressions were confirmed that same evening after the departure of the *ataman* and the other visitors. Puzzled by the event, I asked my hosts to explain what had just taken place: Why had the *ataman* acted as he did? "Oh," exclaimed the wife with an awe normally reserved for respected teachers, senior lamas, and high ranking officials. "That *ataman* is so clever. At my school, he was the best in class. Later he went to prison. Yes, he drinks and fights all the time, but his head works very well. He knows all the songs and sayings. He is so well spoken."

So if the *ataman* incident recounted at the beginning of this chapter revealed to me that the strongman tactics of *atamans* are by no means always seen as inherently unwelcome, this second incident exposed a peculiar switching mechanism by which *atamans* are at times able to shut off the warrior-like source of their authority. As the wife in my host family explained, again unable to hide her fascination, "it is not enough to be a first-class fighter if ones lacks the ability to speak nice words," meaning words that not only sound correct and beautiful but also are uttered at exactly the right moment, often to humorous effect. A proper *ataman,* then, is both clever and wise. In addition to his violent capabilities, he needs good timing, a poetic streak, and a well-developed gift of gab. *Atamans* dominate with their words as much as with their fists.

All this suggests that the personhood of the *ataman* is qualitatively different from the amorphous personhood of the subject of *agsan,* who is not considered to be the author of his own acts. Indeed, a large and very heterogeneous assortment of persons in Ulaan-Uul were imbued with the potential for inflicting physical violence on others, but only some of them—most wrestlers, some but not all police officers and military men, and, to a greater degree than anyone else, the *atamans*—were considered to be in control of this potent capacity. If *agsan* persons were thus looked down on because of their inability to speak once the spirit(s) of intoxication took over, *atamans* were admired for becoming even better speakers when drunk. This was indeed a recurring theme in conversations with middle-aged Darhad men, who would stress that they were "skilled drinkers," and thus differed from the hordes of disorderly *zaluuchuud* (youth) who could be heard roaming *agsan* around the village streets. Moreover, while only a few men would admit to having been the victims of *agsan,* many would describe themselves with ill-disguised pride as former *atamans* who, after having established families and "ceased being young," had now stopped fighting.

It seems that a concept of singular and purposeful will lies at the heart of the difference between *agsan* persons and *ataman* persons. To be sure, *atamans* are also subject to sudden outbursts of violence, but even such *agsan*-like manifestations tend to be seen as purposeful and decisive, even when no moral justification such as in the case of the vice governor is available for this conduct. More than the fact of inhabiting the moral high ground of the conventional social bandit, what seems to constitute the *ataman*'s authority is, first of all, the perception that there is a clear intent behind his violence, or threat of violence, along with the perception that he is able to manifest this willfulness as strongly and transparently as possible, even when he is violently drunk.

In sum, the *ataman* emerges as a distinct "political type" (Sahlins 1963). On the one hand, he is an informal leader of sorts, for his power is essentially political in nature, and he inspires a sense of awe (and perhaps of identification), as do other informal leaders in postsocialist rural Mongolia. On the other hand, the *ataman* is also a kind of shamanic persona, for his capacity to enter into states where others cannot go—and, even more important, to be in control of what he is doing while he is in them—in many ways resembles the shaman's. Like the shaman, who is in charge of when she enters and leaves the world of the spirits, the *ataman* has the capacity to turn his magnificent potential for violence on and off. In that sense the shaman and the *ataman* share a characteristic dual composition. Shamans and *atamans* both contain within themselves an irreducible duality or indeed composite self, which is also the ultimate basis of their authority, since both are imbued with the magical ability to bridge it.

Two distinct kinds of persons have now emerged from the "violent chaos" of postsocialist transition (Nazpary 2002), which at first glance was characteristic of life in northern Mongolia in the late 1990s. First, there are the shamans, who, unlike their "fake" peers, have the capacity to convert the manifestation of shamanic spirits (in the form of *agsan* incidents, for example) into religious status. Second, there are the *atamans,* who, unlike the drunken brutes who act as their followers, are imbued with the capacity to harness the forces of the market and democracy into political capital. As a political singularity, the *ataman* embodies the unpredictable faces of the postsocialist state in much the same way that the shaman, as an occult specialist, personifies the invisible paths of the spirits. And that, surely, is shamanic politics in my second sense of the word.

Shamanic Politics III

So far I have discussed the nature of the shamanic state at the scale of local village communities in the Shishged. In my third and final exploration of shamanic politics, I consider the ramifications of shamanism on the Mongolian political imagination as a whole.

Perhaps the only truly black aspect of Darhad shamanism involves the deliberate invocation of the spirits with the aim of harming someone who is considered an adversary. Indeed, cursing (*haraal*) is one realm in which shamanism and politics were already imbricated during the socialist period. Consider the following tale, which was part of a talk about "the old days" (*deer üye*) between an old herder and his adolescent grandson:

HERDER: When your great grandfather shamanized, he would hover in the
           air above the ground. In the Holy War [the Great Purges], he was
           accused of being counterrevolutionary, so they caught him and tried
           to send him away

GRANDSON: In 1937?

HERDER: Yes. They wanted to kill all the best shamans. But after three days, our
           father managed to [escape and] return. He then donned his gown and
           shamanized until dawn, tying cotton from the door to here and there,
           and then cutting it with scissors. When I asked him why he did this, he
           didn't reply. Many years later I was told that he had been cutting the
           hel am [malicious slander]. If you cut things like that, you can fend off
           powerful spells [*hüchtei tarni*] from far away.

GRANDSON: He was undoing the *hel am* [*hel amgüi bolson*]?

HERDER: Yes, you could say that! Two of the party cadres who [first] caught
           him came back for him. But on their way here, they both turned
           into goats. After this, they did not even try to catch such magician-
           shamans [*id shidtei böö*] anymore.

Keeping in mind this pointed shamanic message to the communist per-petrators of the 1930s purges ("Don't mess with us Darhad shamans unless you want to end up a goat"), we now turn to a more recent example of such "assault sorcery" (Whitehead and Wright 2004), which was played out on a popular Mongolian Internet chat site in the summer of 2003. For some time its users had been engaged in a heated debate about Lamjav Gündalai, a well-known but controversial business tycoon and populist politician associated with the Democratic Union, who had been elected to Mongolia's national parliament (*Ih Hural*) several times from electoral districts strategically situated in his hometown of Mörön in the heart of Hövsgöl province. This debate came to a head when, in response to another scornful critique of Gündalai's politics and business activities, an avatar calling himself "The Darhad Sha-man" posted this warning: "DO NOT SOIL THE REPUTATION OF OUR DARHAD BOY! HAVE YOU NOT HEARD ABOUT DARHAD SHAMANS? BE AWARE OF YOUR LIMITATIONS [*HIREE MEDEEREI*], OR ELSE…" In order to understand how an elected member of the Mongolian parliament could evoke such passionate feelings, let alone what Darhad shamans have to do with this, we need briefly to consider the tense political situation that sparked this Internet debate in the first place.

Figure 7. Cutting *hel am* (malicious gossip)

Like every election in Mongolia since the suspension of the one-party communist system in 1990, the national elections of 2000 were generally deemed fair by the independent international observers who monitored them. At stake for the electorate, however, was not so much the finer details of democracy but rather what was seen as the blatant incompetence and rampant corruption of the incumbent government, a shaky coalition of Democratic Union members. It therefore came as little surprise to anyone (apart from some foreign observers) that the Mongolian People's Revolutionary Party was returned to power in a landslide victory, securing eighty out of eighty-four seats in the parliament. The four seats taken by the liberal-conservative opposition were won in prosperous central Ulaanbaatar, and interestingly, in the thirty-fifth electoral district, encompassing, along with four other Hövsgöl districts and part of Mörön, the Shishged districts of Tsagaan Nuur, Renchinlhümbe, and Ulaan-Uul.

The same pattern could be seen in the elections for local and regional government. In fact, within the remote (and not at all prosperous) electoral district to which Ulaan-Uul belongs, those parties that are not formerly communist have done well in every election since 1900, even when the MPRP has been dominant elsewhere in rural Mongolia. Why is that? According to a Darhad hunter and blacksmith who, in the early 1990s, was actively involved in the new opposition to the former communist rulers, "shamanism and democracy are as closely connected as Buddhism and socialism are." In light of this man's troubled personal history, which is explored in detail in the next chapter, it is perhaps not so strange that his sympathies for the People's Revolutionary Party (and for Buddhism) are limited. But the question remains whether, in some limited way, he was correct: Is there a sense in which shamanism takes sides in Mongolian politics?

The eccentric figure of Gündalai fits this picture. Born in Hövsgöl province's Hatgal district to a Darhad father and a Buryat mother, he made a fortune importing goods from (East) Germany, where he had studied during the socialist period. Partly because of his background and partly because of the nature of his businesses (in the late 1990s he ran an "executive" nightclub in Ulaanbaatar known as Attila, which featured, according to the rumor mill, bare-breasted Nubian waitresses serving alcohol from his own breweries), many people considered Gündalai the quintessential "new Mongol" (*shine Mongol*) tycoon, a man of dubious morality whose tacky tastes and ultraliberal politics distinguish him from most members of the old elite (see also Rossabi 2005). Yet, although more or less everyone in Ulaanbaatar seemed to despise Gündalai around the turn of the millennium, he enjoyed widespread support in his Hövsgöl constituency. According to his website (2003), this popularity reflects his "unparalleled success" in attracting both foreign (German) investment and aid money to the Mörön area. While there is evidently an element of truth to this claim, one should not underestimate the combined effects of Gündalai's wealth and his skills as a campaigner. As one middle-aged Darhad man from Mörön reflected:

> Our MPRP candidate, Togtohnyam, was a woman who is also from Hatgal. But she was not elected. For one thing, Gündalai had a better slogan [*tör hiigüi bol bi hiine:* "What the government can't accomplish, I can"] than Togtohnjam's [*töröö hyamralaas gargaya, tümnee yaduurlaas gargaya:* "The government is not working, we will make it better"]. For another thing, he had more funds. Unlike Togtohnyam, he had a helicopter so he could visit every corner of the constituency, even the Reindeer People [Duha] in the taiga! Ever since the election, every time the old nomads see a helicopter, they exclaim, "Look, Gündalai is returning with money, just as he promised us!"

Already an enfant terrible, Gündalai reached new heights of infamy in the summer of 2003, when he was arrested at the Ulaanbaatar airport as he was about to board a plane to Seoul. It was, the authorities explained, illegal for Gündalai to leave the country as he was under criminal investigation for his scandalous release of certain top-secret government documents to the vibrant Mongolian press. Yet, retorted Gündalai, it was precisely the shocking content of these documents (which a retired general had supposedly shared with him) that had forced him to make his controversial accusation that Tsendiin Nyamdorj, minister of justice and internal affairs from 2000 to 2004, had "contacted a foreign intelligence agent."

The fact that a violent scuffle broke out between the police and Gündalai's private bodyguard at the stairway to the plane, and later again at opposition headquarters, only heightened tensions further, as did the subsequent rumor that Gündalai and his wife had been beaten up by paramilitary forces associated with Nyamdorj's ministry. Nonetheless, the affair eventually came to a relatively peaceful conclusion. Following protest demonstrations in Ulaanbaatar organized by the Democratic Party and numerous petitions from human rights watchdogs, Gündalai's arrest was deemed illegal by the Mongolian High Court of Justice because he was still protected by parliamentary immunity, and he was later returned to parliament in the 2004 elections (which led to an unstable status quo between the two political blocs) and later served as minister of health. He still remains a divisive figure in Mongolian public life.

I have provided a fairly detailed account of this controversial politician for two reasons. First, his story highlights a number of characteristics of the postsocialist Mongolian political imagination. Not only did the Gündalai affair test the official and popular tolerance for critique of the government. If the taxi drivers I spoke to that same summer in Ulaanbaatar are to be believed, he was seen as having gone too far in his self-appointed role as public watchdog. But also the way in which he orchestrated his reelection in 2000 is typical of postauthoritarian democracies at the margins of dying empires. That is, in the poverty-stricken rural peripheries of the postcolonial and the postsocialist world (the margins of the margin, as it were; compare with Das and Poole 2004; Tsing 1993), politics is a competition between big men, each of whom is the master of a neo-patrimonial chiefdom, like an upscale (and wised-up) *ataman* running his own fiefdom in a backyard or village near you.

Second, we are now in a better position to understand the logic behind that Internet warning, which, as it happens, was posted at the very height of the Gündalai affair. Clearly it was no coincidence that the author of this chilling message had chosen to call his or her avatar "the Darhad Shaman," or indeed that the term "shaman" was part of this user's email address. Nor, presumably, was it any accident that, whereas up until this point Gündalai's defense had amounted to polite arguments authored by intellectuals from Ulaanbaatar's burgeoning civil society organizations, this intervention was characterized by its rejection of the "civil" norms of "debating culture." In all its blunt subjectivity, and the decidedly nonliberal manner in which it refused to tone down its aggressiveness, the message was democratic in content but not in form. It was as if its harsh words acquired their authority by rejecting two otherwise dominant styles of postsocialist Mongolian political discourse, the "traditional Mongolian" (*yos*) and the "modern Western" (liberal democratic) rhetorics, by opting instead for a "truly Darhad" form: the curse. For that was exactly what it was—a good old shamanic malediction cast through the new medium of the Internet.

Other political actors in Mongolia in the late 1990s reverted to even stronger shamanic methods. According to several Darhad shamans I spoke to in Tsagaan Nuur, this is one crucial difference between local clients and those from afar. Said Nadmid Udgan, the shamaness: "Whereas people from here mostly come to find their lost horses and so on, some outsiders come, or send their representatives, to have someone destroyed all the way down to the root! [*ündes ugsaagaar n' ustgah*]." And that, she continued, now whispering, was what "certain powerful businessmen and politicians from Ulaanbaatar may demand from us shamans—to have family X with Y number of people wiped out! [*ustgaad tsaash haruulah*]." "Of course," she immediately went on to stress, she would never perform such assault sorcery herself, even if it meant that the client would return to the city and "ask one of the black shamans who have moved there" to perform the dark deed, now extended to Nadmid Udgan herself as one of the victims.

Nevertheless, "unlike certain shamans in Ulaanbaatar" who, according to this shamaness, like to boast about their ability to "shamanize from the dark side" (*haryn talaar böölöh*), the shamans I met in the Shishged all referred to themselves as "white shamans," who above all defended the well-being of their communities. As Nadmid Udgan would emphasize, she and other white shamans would revert to "heavy" (*hünd*) forms of assault cursing (*muu üil zasal*) only under exceptional circumstances, in which someone's life (including the shaman's own) was at stake. While there is every reason to believe what she told me, the terrifying examples detailed to me by this woman and her fellow Darhad shamans also attest that in postsocialist Mongolia as much as in the Amazon interior, the "link between the body-politic and individual bodies…reveals the way in which techniques of dark shamanism [are] entwined with the exercise of political power" (Whitehead and Wright 2004, 8). And that, I submit, is shamanic politics in the ultimate sense.

Too Many States

In a final ironic twist to my argument about the nature and the efficacy of the shamanic state, I contend that what characterized political life in northern Mongolia during the late 1990s was not only the much-lamented demise of a strong and predictable modernist state, familiar from so many other postsocialist contexts, but also the obverse perception of too much state, or more precisely too many states—a largely implicit, deeply contradictory, but hard to ignore sense that the faces of the Mongolian state were too many, too fleeting, and too unpredictable, so that people in Ulaan-Uul did not feel equipped to recognize them, let alone appropriate and potentially benefit from them. As with the shamanic spirits running wild because of the shortage of shamans to tame them (more on which in the chapters to come), ordinary people like my hosts found themselves lacking the appropriate political bodies through which the capricious perspectives of the postsocialist state could be made visible. Still more positionings were imagined as potential perspectives through which an omnipresent—but not omnipotent—shamanic state could be made to come into being by assuming one of its many faces; yet as an inevitable result of this inflation in what might possibly count as a site of the Mongolian state, it was even more difficult to figure out what kind of person one needed to be—what kind of body one needed to have—in order to be seen by it.

As an illustration of this postsocialist paradox—that there were any number of "subject positions" (or, in a sort of perspectivist reversal of Foucault's phrase, position-subjects) in northern Mongolia after socialism, yet at the same time, many people did not feel capable of embodying any of them—it is useful to consider what happened to my host family, and in particular to my host, in the months and years after the spring crisis of 1999. For what happened was that—ever so slowly but no less irreversibly—my host's position in the community embarked on a downward spiral, so that, by the time I got back in contact with the family several years later, it was abundantly clear that they were no longer considered to be among the most prominent *ails* in the Center (although they were still deemed "a very good household"). Had the Revolutionary Party's partial return to power in 2000 occurred just a few years earlier, it would have catapulted my host back into power as well as opened new opportunities for jobs and favors. Instead, he and the rest of the *ail* seemed to have become detached from the most influential networks of acquaintances. More than ever, it was as if the world had moved on while my host had stood still, for while he and his brother-in-law, the discredited vice governor, were still seeking to be elected or appointed to low-paid, minor, and temporary offices (*bag* leader, party secretary, chairman of the local district board, and so forth), and often succeeding, other smart (*uhaantai*) people around them could now be found pursuing very different—and from the perspective of my host, alien and/or disreputable—work options in new fields such as small-scale, illicit mining (a big gold deposit was discovered in the taiga some 100 km west of Ulaan-Uul in 2008, and since then thousands of illicit minors—or "ninjas" as they are called because of their plastic helmets—have flocked into the Shishged, with radical economic, social, and environmental consequences), the tourist sector, and various forms of trade. While these sectors were not directly controlled by the Mongolian government, let alone heavily taxed or in any other sense regulated by it, they were often run by different big men (*tomchuud*)—retired colonels or civil servants, former wrestlers, and ex-*atamans* who had, in not always transparent ways, come into money. These men in turn were dependent on maintaining good connections (*holboo*) with various officials at the district, regional, and national levels in order to secure the flow of new permissions and the necessary passing of inspections, or to ensure that these would not be required in the first place.

Somehow my host had missed being admitted into this emerging "post-post socialist" socioeconomic network of officials, patrons, and their clients; in fact, he probably neither would nor could have been included. This had now placed him in the same position most people around him had long been in, a position that, so to speak, had no state subject, in the sense that in the body my host was stuck in, and from the vantage point he was endowed with, it was virtually impossible to be seen by anybody who mattered in the emerging age of the market. It is in this sense that the challenge faced by people like my host during the late 1990s (especially after the spring crisis of 1999) was not so much the lack of a state but rather a lack of vehicles for bringing it into view. He and countless others like him found themselves without the bodies through which the faces of the postsocialist state could be made manifest and harnessed.

It is against this backdrop that we must understand the continued popularity of politicians like Gündalai in northern Mongolia and perhaps other rural postsocialist contexts as well. Like the *atamans* at the community level, Gündalai and other tycoons personify the inherently transgressive nature of transition in a way that more conventional politicians and leaders do not, and cannot, do. As political shamans specializing in "the informal politics of the occult" (Bubandt 2006, 414), these upscale *atamans* are imbued with a magical capacity to embody the multiple faces of the postsocialist state in such a way that their clients, their voters, and—not to be forgotten—their victims see themselves being seen, and sense themselves being touched, by a spirit-like sovereign that is simultaneously too small and too big, too distant and too close.

The Shamanism of Modernity

This chapter has demonstrated how, much like the Cameroonian concept of *djambe* explored by Peter Geschiere in *The Modernity of Witchcraft* (1997), the shamanic spirits in northern Mongolia during the spring of 1999 were woven into every aspect of social life, including such quintessentially modernist phenomena as a centralized energy supply, a state-run education system, and national elections. Yet, while the general object of my exploration has in this sense resonated with the literature on "occult economies" in the postcolonial world (Comaroff and Comaroff 1999), my conclusions differ from these writings in a subtle but crucial way. The difference may arise from diverging ethnographic realities on the ground, but it is also a necessary result of our fundamentally different theoretical stances. Contrary to what has been described about much of sub-Saharan Africa (the spirits as metaphors for market forces, thus serving as "symbolic-functionalist" instruments in a purported existential quest for "making sense of" the transition to capitalism and democracy), the association between shamanism and modernity that I encountered in northern Mongolia was not about overlapping content but about the isomorphism of (impossible) form. That is, the shape of the shamanic spirits, the capitalist market, and the liberal state were all equally labile, fluid, and inherently multiple. Thus, as we have seen, the unlit village alleys during the spring crisis of 1999 did not merely remind in a purely metaphoric manner my hosts of an imminent "age of darkness"; they were perceived as shamanic phenomena in their own right. Similarly, the dual personhood of the *atamans* did not merely resemble that of shamans; the *atamans* were shamans of a sort in their own right.

In this light it is perhaps more accurate to characterize the postsocialist reality I witnessed in Ulaan-Uul not as "the modernity of shamanism" (as I did earlier) but as "the shamanism of modernity." This is more than a play on words. The shamanism of modernity, I think, captures the key ethnographic fact that is also the theoretical premise of this book as a whole: that in northern Mongolia after socialism, it is not the state that encompasses the spirits, and thus defines their mode and their purpose of existence, but the spirits that encompass the state. Because of the inherent capacity of shamanic spirits to turn into anything or anybody—their latent potential to take up residence in all human and nonhuman bodies, in all animate beings and all inanimate things—it is they that logically and ontologically exhaust the state and not the other way around. Indeed, that is what shamans are so good at, whether genuine or not so genuine: making visible the spirit of transition in its ceaseless jumping from one body to the next.

As I have demonstrated in my three excursions into shamanic politics in Mongolia, the postsocialist state is deictic in the same way as the shamanic spirits themselves; that is, its "attributes are immanent in the viewpoint, and move with it" (Viveiros de Castro 1998a, 477). Thus in Ulaan-Uul, statehood is assigned to whatever person or thing is perceived to embody the point of view of the fleeting and labile Mongolian state. It is precisely for this reason that the issue is not one of "seeing like a state" (Scott 1998), let alone not seeing like a state, or not being seen by it (Mbembe 1992). The question is how to be seen by the state's many guises, for as an *ongon*-like sovereign, the state is multiple through and through, dispersed across a swarm of different faces, each of which is the deictic vantage point of a world of its own.

In this light, Nadmid Udgan's display of election posters emerges as even more emblematic of the general spirit of the time. For it becomes clear in hindsight that the characteristic design of her political talisman was in perfect accordance with Mongolia's political realities, and its predominant post-authoritarian political imaginary more generally. In the 1990s, and to some extent still today, the postsocialist state was perceived as a dispersed assemblage of political singularities, each pursuing its own hidden agenda through "corrupt" pathways of relatives, friends, and acquaintances, so that every prominent politician or tycoon was in effect the visible surface of an invisible netherworld composed of patrimonial networks and mafia-led "icebergs" of quasi-governance (Humphrey 1991; Verdery 1996).

This, then, is the magic of radically immanent things like shamanic spirits: they know no limits, for they can extend themselves, or be extended, into everything. As post-plural scalings that are automatically generated out of the relentless movement of social life, they take their form in the continuously changing image of the world itself. This is in contrast to modernist sovereign bodies such as the Mongolian socialist state, which, by virtue of their will to mold the world in their own image, must always leave a deterritorialized residue that is not influenced by their transcendental "magic." It is precisely in this sense that we may speak of the postsocialist state as omnipresent but not omnipotent: like all spirits, it is everywhere and nowhere at the same time. For by being composed mostly of what it is not yet but potentially could be, the state that has emerged in northern Mongolia after socialism has so many faces, so many bodies, that at any given moment, it is as if this swarm-like multitude of political affects is not quite there.

2 The Shamanic Predicament

"Some years," Gombodorj told me, "the bears go crazy. Usually there are plenty of berries in the taiga during late summer and early autumn, and the bears will stuff themselves before hibernating in October. But some years the berries are scarce, and the early autumn becomes a very dangerous time." At first, he explained,

the hungry bear will try to compensate by eating red ants. But when these enter the bear's stomach, they turn into worms—really big, hungry worms. When the bear tries to eat, it is not really eating. The worms are eating it from within, so it becomes hungrier, and it cannot sleep. At this point, the bear has become a roaming bear [*yavuulyn baavgai*], one that never sleeps, and is destined always to be on the move. It may attack anything: dogs, livestock, even people. Not so long ago, an entire household was killed: wife, husband, and two daughters. The bear crashed into their yurt and ate everyone. As people say, it must have been completely wormed-up [*horhoitson*]. By early November, all the wormed-up bears will have perished. Desperate to get rid of the worms, which are wriggling out of every opening in their bodies, they throw themselves into holes in the frozen rivers and freeze to death.[1]

But it is not just the bears that occasionally cause havoc in people's lives. In another narrative, which was a favorite theme of gossip in the late 1990s, the

---

1. Other hunters confirmed to me that many bears do get worms from eating berries and other foods in the taiga, although none of them mentioned that ants turn into worms or claimed that such intestinal worms might drive the bears crazy.

same man who told me this story was himself the key topic. In this tale the hunter himself becomes the unwilling victim of forces manifested through him but beyond his control. In this capacity the man is emblematic of the central subject of this book: he is a shaman, but not quite. This was a general problem in the Ulaan-Uul community. As I noted briefly in the previous chapter, one elderly woman living on the outskirts of the Ulaan-Uul district center was sometimes referred to as an *udgan* (female shaman), but she was not considered at all powerful (*hüchtei*), even in her own eyes. ("I don't have a shamanic gown," she apologized to me the first time I visited her.). Nor did she perform possession séances. And she was widely referred to as "only a diviner—and not even a very good one"—as opposed to being a "genuine shaman." Thus people found themselves in a tricky situation: there were far too many potential shamans around, and far too few shamanic teachers who could make these "half" shamans "whole." The disturbing presence of the former indicated a generational rupture in the shamanic institution, for the continuity between senior and junior shamans had been severed after half a century of state socialist purges.

This chapter traces the multifarious effects of this politically orchestrated shamanic rupture by exploring the predicament of one incomplete or potential shaman in whose life I became especially closely involved: Gombodorj (as I shall henceforth call him). A renowned bear hunter, blacksmith, and self-acclaimed expert in shamanic knowledge, he in many ways represents the archetypal half-shaman. Like the "wormed-up bears" that roam ceaselessly from place to place, Gombodorj personified an unpredictable occult undercurrent perceived to run beneath the surface of everything, which was constantly threatening to burst out into the open—a proliferating multiplicity of labile forces set free by the disintegration of the Mongolian state and the Buddhist church, and rendered more uncontainable by the present lack of shamans resulting from past state socialist policies. While the tragicomic tale of Gombodorj and his shamanic forebears unfolds, I introduce a number of quasi-shamanic practices that will be explored further in subsequent chapters, notably those of hunting, cursing, and joking.

There are two interrelated messages I wish to convey through my tale of Gombodorj and his fellow potential shamans, all of which concern the overarching question of the nature of shamanic agency in northern Mongolia after socialism. The first, largely empirical point concerns the ethnographic observation that in the Shishged, if not elsewhere in Mongolia, shamanism is understood to be a predicament, if not a destiny—as opposed to a religious repertoire or cultural resource that people choose, or choose not, to appropriate strategically. As we shall see, in the late 1990s a half-shaman—or for that matter a whole one—was not something that persons had themselves decided to be; instead it was what the spirits and such people's life circumstances more generally had determined they *must* be. This flies in the face of most literature about the so-called revival of religion in postsocialist contexts, which often presents faith, be it Christian, Muslim, or shamanic, as a voluntary act on the part of its adherents, whether a strategic choice by autonomous individuals or a common response to a social and/or existential void of meaning generated by the collapse of socialism (Lindquist 2005; Pelkmans 2009).

The second point is in many ways a theoretical corollary to the first one. It involves the dramatic existential, social, and indeed political effects caused by the failure of shamanic predestination in this corner of Mongolia in the late 1990s. In relating my ethnographic account of Gombodorj and his shamanic forebears to anthropological literature on the personhood of various occult specialists—whether Melanesian great men (Godelier 1986; Strathern 1991), Siberian hunters (Willerslev 2004, 2007), or above all other kinds of Mongolian shamanic subjects (Buyandelger 2008; Hamayon 1994; Hangartner in press; Humphrey 1996)—I trace and theorize a distinct form of human (and nonhuman) agency: the shamanic capacity to be different as such, that is, to differentiate not only from others but from oneself as well.

This, then, is another reason why it makes only limited sense to speak of the return of Darhad shamanism in the 1990s as a response to a quest for meaning in the wake of a loss of religious traditions accumulated over half a century of oppression. Some of the most vociferous party cadres active in the Shishged were themselves Darhads—which may explain why I seldom heard people blaming the disappearance of shamans (and lamas) on outsiders. On an even more basic level, the shamanism without shamans that flourished in Ulaan-Uul during those years almost by definition did not lend itself to existential quests for the individual or collective "sense-making" that has been described in so many postsocialist and postcolonial settings. On the contrary, as we are about to see, the presence and the actions of the potential shamans essentially served to destabilize if not destroy whatever sense people had left of themselves and others.

Gombodorj, a Not-So-Genuine Shaman

A youthful-looking man in his late thirties when I first met him in 1998, Gombodorj was living with his wife and four children in a small wooden barn situated a couple of kilometers outside the Ulaan-Uul district center,

Figure 8. Blacksmith's forge

across the Guna River.[2] Like other Darhad hunters, he spent much of the main hunting season from September to March away from his family, traversing the taiga in search of various species of game, armed with a selection of guns and bullets, some of which he fashioned himself, for Gombodorj is also well known as a skilled blacksmith. The forge, which was located next to the family's home, was filled with equipment that Gombodorj, in true *bricoleur* fashion, had constructed largely out of materials available in his immediate surroundings. The bellows were made from birchwood and hides from the musk deer, and tools had been molded from metal scrap left behind by the Red Army.

Gombodorj is indeed of shamanic ancestry, and although he is not a shaman in his own eyes or in those of others, it became increasingly clear as I got to know him (as well as some his friends and foes) that he would like to be

2. This residence pattern is characteristic of other occult specialists in the Darhad context. Pegg describes Baljir Udgan's home as "tucked away behind a barren, rocky slope close to the river Harmai" (2001, 122).

one. Hidden away beneath the forge he kept a "secret" (*nuuts*) collection of notes, newspaper clippings, and crumpled pages torn from Mongolian, Hungarian, and Soviet ethnographic books. "All of these," he would whisper in my ear, "are about shamanism," adding in a confiding tone, "People like you study the relationship between humans, whereas people like me study the relationship between humans and wild animals, and between humans and souls."

Gombodorj seldom missed the chance to emphasize that, unlike the herding of domestic animals, hunting is an inherently dangerous activity. For the same reason, he would add in a worried, paternal voice, "experienced hunters" like himself are troubled by the loss of shamanic knowledge (*böögiin medleg*) in the community which took place during the socialist period. Indeed, Gombodorj lamented, both the technical skills and the knowledge about animals and spirits needed to be a good hunter have "become a secret." And without such knowledge, hunting can be very dangerous. He explained:

> Some animals are good for humans, others are bad. Animals do not have souls [*süns*]. But then again, some wild animals do. Some game is okay. But other game gets hit [*tsohiulah*] by the souls of dead shamans. The *süns* enters the hunter after he kills it. Because of this, he will become ill, maybe even die. A good hunter knows this from his premonition [*ööriin sovin*]. If he does not know whether there is a *süns* or not, he is a bad hunter. It is dangerous for him, and for his wife and children. Hunting is hard. Every hunt is a unique event [*sodon*]. The hunter must recognize signs [*temdeg*] of the spirits, which can be either big or small, but always new and different. Many young men have died from hunting because they did not know about these things.

Still, even if one knows how to distinguish between animals that possess a soul and those that do not, hunting is an activity that requires the utmost care. For the spirits will behave toward you in either a benevolent or a harmful way, depending on whether your interactions with them—or rather your interactions with the wild animals over which they are "masters" (*ezed*)—are sufficiently respectful. The following story, according to Gombodorj, offers a lesson about the importance of taking good care of the prey and its masters:

> Recently a hunter shot four mountain goats dead, only to die soon afterwards himself. He went with his son to hunt at the spring of the Tengis River. There they saw four mountain goats. The man killed all four of them, but then he started to feel bad. He died just like that, despite being a young man. Before he died, he managed to tell his son: "I cannot go

on anymore. You must return to the village. Do not kill anything on the way. Go and get our people and bury me here." So the son returned and brought people back with him, and they buried him. That is what the masters are like. If they see that hunters are doing something bad, they respond by releasing harmful intentions. If, on the other hand, humans look properly after [*iveej harah*] their prey, then the masters will protect [them] in return.

Such male narratives about encounters with the souls of dead shamans and other spiritual entities while hunting were not restricted to Gombodorj; many other hunters told me similar stories. What made his case special was the elaborate and explicit manner in which his own personhood was associated with these occult entities, according to both himself and others. In that sense the case of Gombodorj points to a crucial distinction in Shishged social life between those shamanic persons who are in control of their occult capacities and those who are not. Indeed, as we shall see, the problem with Gombodorj is that he is an amorphous person, unable to control what forms his body and his mind take.

"He is wormlike"

I once spent an eventful week with Gombodorj and his family. It was late spring, and, as happens every year at this time, the thaw had created an almost insurmountable barrier of melting snow and glacier-like ice between the family's home on the western side of the Guna River and the village center on the eastern side. The sense of isolation was intensified by the location of their home on a sloping hill at the edge of the taiga. Over the next several days, Gombodorj would climb frequently onto the roof of his forge, ostensibly to survey the vast expanse of taiga stretching away from the back of his house. To my surprise I discovered that, rather than looking for signs of wild animals through the binoculars held to his well-trained eyes (as vigilant hunters do, he had explained), Gombodorj seemed to be more interested in registering from his elevated vantage point the unfolding of life in the village. Only after some time did I realize that, far from representing a frivolous waste of time, as I initially could not help thinking, this peculiar activity in fact served a purpose. By engaging in what may be described as the gathering of visual gossip, Gombodorj was in a sense trying to compensate for his exclusion from the endless flow of village gossip and rumor-mongering. The irony, as we shall see, was that much of the most malicious slander circulating in the Ulaan-Uul community that spring centered on him.

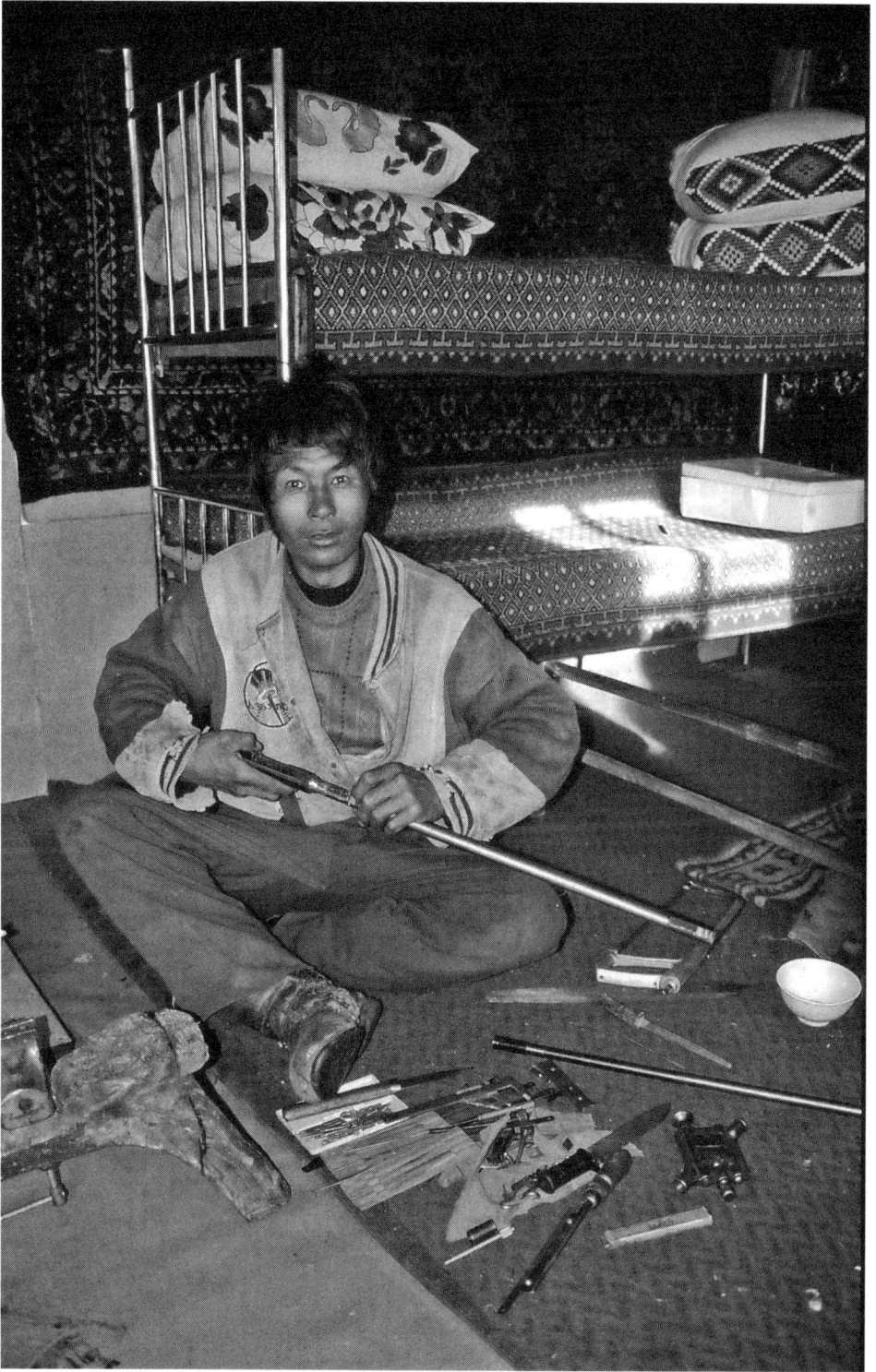

Figure 9. Preparing for a hunt

With few exceptions, Gombodorj was not a welcome guest in people's homes. My hosts, while recognizing Gombodorj's skills as a huntsman and smith, dismissed him as a "liar" (*hudalch*), and always suggested other people—"good people"—whom I should visit instead to learn about hunting and shamanism. In fact, the opportunity was seldom missed to discuss his flaws with relatives and friends. Gombodorj, it was widely agreed, "is not normal in the head." Besides, someone would add, "his mood changes all the time." An elderly widow from a respected household was the first to link this psychological profile directly to the shamanic themes of sorcery and witchcraft. "My son, stay away from him," she urged me. "He is a bad person. His father was a thief, and his grandfather a black shaman [*har böö*]. Both he and one of his sons harbor dark intentions [*har sanaatai*]. Be afraid! They could cause you harm."

Most people seemed to share this feeling, although the subtext of sorcery and witchcraft was not always present. Some people made it quite clear that they simply did not like Gombodorj very much, although occasionally someone would whisper to me that a close relative of Gombodorj's was one of Ulaanbaatar's most infamous Darhad shamans. "She used to live in the Shishged, in Tsagaan Nuur," the same gossip would continue, but without ever mentioning the *udgan*'s name for fear of attracting her or her spirits' attention. "There she cast many spells [*tarni*] and was the instigator of many conflicts between people and even between entire households. Eventually, it is said, the village turned against her, so she had to flee to the capital."

At one point a bitter falling-out took place between Gombodorj and my host family. He had been escorting me home after another late-night conversation in the forge, and now insisted that we wake up my hosts. Already intoxicated, Gombodorj demanded more vodka, well aware that my host family usually kept a secret stock. When Gombodorj's request was ignored, he became very angry. The husband tried to calm him down but was violently pushed away. Gombodorj then launched into a long monologue, the full meaning of which I did not catch, but the words *haraal* (curse) and *hel am* (malicious slander) figured prominently. My host became strangely subdued, and everyone else in the room looked confused and frightened, for gossip and cursing are not taken lightly in Mongolia, especially when they involve people of shamanic ancestry (see Højer 2004). Finally, Gombodorj ran out into the cold winter night, still screaming and crying in his state of *agsan*.

The following morning my hosts tried to downplay the incident. Yet they could not hide their distress: *hel am* and possibly *haraal* had been hurled at them, and they feared that misfortune (*horlol*) might strike (*tsohih*) members of the household (especially the teenage children as they are always most prone and vulnerable to such attacks), whether as a result of Gombodorj's intentions or because in the course of the previous evening's argument he had unleashed shamanic forces and spirits of which he was unaware.[3] Still, to my knowledge, my host family did not instigate any formal shamanic response to Gombodorj's *hel am* (for example, by seeking help from one of the shamans in Tsagaan Nuur). But not surprisingly, they began to talk about him in an even more negative manner than before, referring to him as "primitive" (*balar*), "mad" (*galzuu*), and "nuts" (*teneg*).

Another thing that made Gombodorj "strange" (*hachin*) was the peculiar way in which he carried himself. In fact he was widely known in Ulaan-Uul as "the monkey," presumably because of his wild gesticulations, sudden jumps, and above all his constant and seemingly involuntary display of facial tics. Indeed, it was as if Gombodorj had never learned or internalized the otherwise age- and gender-specific bodily comportment dictated by Mongolian custom (*yos*), as epitomized in the calm and dignified manner in which all men, and older men in particular, are supposed to carry themselves (Lacaze 1996). One of the strangest and most irritating things about Gombodorj, I was repeatedly told, was that he was "a person who moves about a lot" (*ih hödölgööntei hün*). As my hosts once remarked with a sneer, "that Gombodorj, he is wormlike! [*öt shig*]."

Interestingly, a comparable notion existed among Daur Mongols before the revolution, when, writes, Caroline Humphrey, some "people remained in the state of being potential shamans all their lives. They were known as *butur* (something like an insect hidden in the silk-worm cocoon and waiting to emerge)" (1996, 185). We can view in a similar light a notion among Nepal's Tamang, who, according to David Holmberg, distinguish between two types of shamanic specialists: *bombo* and *sangtung*. Essentially, *sangtungs* are incomplete *bombos,* for *sangtungs* have not undergone any proper shamanic teaching and initiation, nor do they wear a shamanic costume (1989, 142–47). Consequently, *bombos* tend to "look down on" *sangtungs,* because *sangtungs* "are said to shake 'hard' under the effects of *lente* [shamanic spirits] and to be out of control" (1989, 147).

Does the perceived "wormness" of Gombodorj reflect a similar conception within a postsocialist context that he is an incomplete shaman whose occult potential has never been fully realized? Over the sections that follow,

---

3. In Mongolia, to speak—or even think—about someone in a too negative (or, for that matter, too positive) way is widely seen as imbued with occult efficacy, even if such *hel am* is done unintentionally (Højer 2004). In fact, malicious gossip, whether in its "black" (*hel am*) or "white" (*tsagaan hel am*) variety, is sometimes perceived as carrying the greatest risk of all, perhaps because of its inherently open and collective nature—it is, as it were, a public and authorless spell.

I explore this possibility through a discussion of social practices imbued with transformative potential, such as joking, blacksmithing, and hunting. As we are about to see, Gombodorj's association with these practices points to a key distinction between people who are in control of their occult powers and those who are not.

The Overspill of Form

Gombodorj was himself acutely aware of his stigmatization in Ulaan-Uul, and he had several ways (some might call them excuses) of accounting for it. According to one explanation, as a young man he frequently became *agsan* and eventually earned a reputation as a local *ataman*. Then, as he grew older and established a family, the vodka started to make him ill, and he was forced to leave the village to escape the drinking. But often he simply said that since he has no friends, he might as well live on his own. "People don't like it when I am joking," he once told me. "It is only you who appreciate my sense of humor." Indeed, as the next anecdote illustrates, there was a lot of truth in his observation.

Once, after having crossed the river to Gombodorj's home, I found it to be full of visitors—a rather unusual occurrence. As part of the customary greeting, I inquired after his elder brother. Suddenly looking horrified, Gombodorj replied: "But haven't you heard? He passed away yesterday!" As it happened, I had seen his brother that day in the village shop, so I did not fall for Gombodorj's cunning trap. But I was still taken aback by what in a Mongolian cultural context can only be called the obscenity of his joke. Death is a highly taboo subject throughout Mongolia, and to imply that someone has died, even jokingly, is considered a bad omen (*muu yor*). Small wonder, then, that the other visitors were not at all comfortable with the joke. They all looked away, their faces expressing anger, embarrassment, and above all fear. Only members of Gombodorj's own household joined him in his loud fits of laughter, although his wife's giggles sounded decidedly forced. (It was, after all, *her* relatives who were visiting.)

This incident was only one of many. In fact, Gombodorj is notorious for his social gaffes and improprieties. Sexual allusions figure prominently in his obscene joking, often in creative combination with food. Fish, meat, and vegetables are used to mimic sexual organs, giving rise to cheap laughs at the expense of blushing nomad maidens and not a few wives. More generally, he has a propensity to mix things (or words) that ought not to be mixed in Mongolian context, such as so-called upper things (like hats) with so-called lower things (such as boots).

Is there any connection between Gombodorj's transgressive humor and the fact that as a blacksmith and hunter, he has access to extraordinary areas of knowledge? As Mary Douglas once suggested, the joker is a "minor mystic. Though only a mundane and border-line type, he is one of these people who pass beyond the bounds of reason and society and give glimpses of a truth which escapes through the mesh of structured concepts" (1968, 373). I believe it is instructive to think of Gombodorj as a living trickster. More than anything else, it is his often misplaced jokes and social gaffes that render him "a person without custom" (*yosgüi hün*). Far from confining his humorous transgressions to certain contexts, as people ordinarily do, Gombodorj might transgress "beyond the bounds of reason and society" at any given time. A compulsive destroyer of conventions who is never content with taking things at face value, Gombodorj is like "the trickster who is both inside the play and outside the play: he is the cheat, who is playing with the rules of the game" (Oosten 2001, 25).

This, I suggest, is precisely the role that Gombodorj had come to play in the Ulaan-Uul community, quite unwillingly, and with often disastrous consequences for himself and others. His jokes and improprieties were quasi-occult modalities through which existing norms of sociality, language, and the very cosmos itself were broken and reinvented. As we are about to see, a similar breach of convention with respect to the prevalent forms of matter itself occurred at Gombodorj's forge, the place where he brings his molten metals to ever higher temperatures and molds them for hitherto unseen purposes and into hitherto unseen shapes.

Most visits to Gombodorj were restricted to his forge and involved men only. Gombodorj's wife never entered the forge, nor did his two daughters. His two teenage sons, however, regularly took part in his activities, both at the forge and in the taiga. Clearly they (and the younger son in particular) were their father's apprentices in several respects, en route to becoming blacksmiths, hunters, and, perhaps, potential shamans themselves.

The magical power of Buryat blacksmiths, Liubov Abaeva writes (1992, 106), is based on their "direct relationship with the elements of nature," which enables them to transform matter into something "qualitatively new." Picking up this idea, I suggest that a homology can be posited between Gombodorj's amorphous personhood and the labile nature of the molten metal he forges. Both the Buryat material and my own experiences with Darhad blacksmiths thus suggest that the "qualitative deformation or transformation" involved in forging activities amounts to an "overspill of form" (Deleuze and Guattari 1999, 410), and that such acts of *sui generis* world creation are closely bound up with concepts of life and death.

This notion—that blacksmithing is an occult practice in its own right—is clearly brought out in one Darhad origin legend, in which a Darhad black-smith enters into a magic contest with a non-Darhad blacksmith. The Dar-had smith produces a bronze pot that surpasses the pot produced by his counterpart in strength and beauty, earning him and his clan (*ovog*) the right to settle in what is today the Shishged.[4] Indeed his victory is the ultimate one, for soon after being defeated, the other smith dies. Just as in the case of two *atamans* fighting, then, the contest between blacksmiths takes the form of an encounter between unique entities whose rules are dictated by an aesthetic of warriorhood whereby the winner literally takes all (including the loser's life). The tale also suggests that the violent agency of forging activities is un-derstood to derive from the transgressive nature of the blacksmithing process itself. The smith, through his "direct relationship with nature," has the capac-ity to extinguish the flame and thus the very flow of life. This point is further illustrated in the Buryat idea that a blacksmith may kill someone by heating a piece of iron, tying it into a knot, and saying, "Die, dry out!" (Galdanova 1997, 90).

I have not come across such explicit allusions to blacksmith sorcery in the Shishged, or for that matter elsewhere in Mongolia. Nonetheless, what took place at Gombodorj's forge amounted, I argue, to a cosmological destabiliza-tion of the same caliber—a fundamental overspill of form brought about by his ability to expose the potential of metal to spill into new forms, not unlike the way certain larvae have a potential to spill into insects, or indeed the way in which certain persons contain a hidden potential to "spill into shamans" while still not quite getting there.

The Half People

Like the blacksmith's forge, the *taiga* constitutes a site of latent metamor-phosis, where the forms of humans, animals, and spirits are constantly at risk of spilling over and blending into one another. One of the most strik-ing examples of this conception is found in the lore of the "half people" or *badagshin*—semimythological creatures living somewhere in depths of the taiga, who appear to man as "vertically halves" (in the shape of a person with one arm and one leg, a deer with two legs, and so forth). While there is some disagreement about precisely what kinds of spiritual beings *badagshin* are, all people describe them as a small life-form (*jijig am'tan*), which may be

---

4. Interestingly, some Darhads used to "explain the name [Darhad, which among other things means "smith"] by saying that their ancestors were two smiths" (Sandschejew 1930, 9).

encountered while hunting, alongside all the other nonhuman persons inhabiting the taiga.[5] As an old hunter explained,

> *Badagshin* are people of the wilderness (*heer*). Their minds are like humans, but their bodies are half (*tal*). They are small as dwarfs, only the size of an elbow (*neg tohoi*). Sometimes, when the hunters rest in the taiga, *badagshin* take the food that has been thrown away. *Badagshin* are covered in yellow hair, especially during winter, when a thick growth from their noses covers their faces. Tears are always running from their eyes. If one tries hard, one can spot the *badagshin* in the moonlight, roaming around as they always are like small children, stark naked. However, despite their small size, they are extremely strong. Their pull is harder than a horse being tied to a nail in the ground. No one can resist. Once, a *badagshin* caught a wild reindeer and curled its antlers up. No human can do that. For sure, they are masters.[6]

In this and other stories about half people, one recognizes several themes from the eleborate hunting lore of Siberia's indigenous peoples (Bogoraz 1909; Ingold 1986; Hamayon 1990; Willerslev 2004, 2007). Both cases can be described as animist or indeed perspectivist (Viveiros de Castro 1998), for, in Mongolia as much as Siberia, a safe and successful hunt hinges on the hunter's soul's ability to move between bodies by taking on the perspective of the different beings inhabiting these (Broz 2007; Kristensen 2007; Pedersen 2001, 2007; Willerslev 2004, 2007).

But there are also noteworthy differences between the two cases. According to Rane Willerslev, the Yukaghir hunter seeks to attain "a 'double perspective' whereby he can assume the animal's point of view but still remain a human" (2004, 648). Thus, Willerslev convincingly argues, Siberian animism is all about mimesis, even if the hunter never tries to "become an animal and adopt its point of view in any absolute sense"—indeed, "that should be avoided at all costs" (2004, 638). Compare this idea with the following tale about half people, told to me by a chain-smoking truck driver from Ulaan-Uul:

> Once, at the fifteenth moon, Dashnyam and I went hunting at a place called Bosgot Ulaan Maraa. We were resting in the moonlight when a male deer came to drink from the salty bog. Only as the deer turned, I realized that all of it was half (*bugyn öröösön tal*). It had one antler and half the legs (*tal höltei*). Terrified, I woke my mate up, and asked, "What *is* this strange thing?"

5. The etymology of *badagshin* is uncertain (it does not seem to be of Mongolian origin).
6. A similar version of this story was told to me by Duha hunters in the mid 1990s (see Pedersen 2009).

"It is something from the South," he said, "We must leave here immediately."
So, we left without shooting it. After we had galloped for some time, we asked
each other, "What did you see?" "I saw a half deer," I said. To my surprise, my
mate said, "I saw an old one-legged woman with a stick." A few weeks later,
he died. Two persons saw two different things. I saw a half of male deer, he
saw a half woman. There are thus two ways of seeing such things; a good way
of seeing them and a bad way of seeing them (*tiim yum hünd haragdval muu
talaar haragddag, esvel sain talaar haragddag hoyor uchirtai*).

In Willerslev's terms, what happened to Dashnyam was a fatal case of total
mimesis. The fact that he saw *badagshin,* not in their "normal" shape of a
half animal (as the truck driver did himself), but in the even more uncanny
guise of a half human, suggests that his poor friend had unwillingly assumed
an animal perspective (in his sleep, perhaps?) in what eventually turned out
to be an irreversible and therefore deadly metamorphosis. Yet, how are we
to understand that, according to the truck driver, "there are two ways of seeing *badagshin,*" both of which merely allow for these beings to appear "half"
(*tal*)? In Darhad shamanism, the hunter does not hover halfway between two
perspectives at the same time (as in the Yukaghir case); rather, he fully inhab-
its two perspectives that are each only half. In every narrative I heard about
badagshin, they never had two parts (one human and another animal) joined
into one hybrid form as in some Indo-European fable animals (centaurs,
mermaids, and so forth). Instead, I was left with the clear and yet paradoxical idea that *badagshin* are only half—that is, wholly half—for all there is of
them is half the torso and half the limbs of some body (a deer with two legs,
say, or an old woman with one leg).

What this allows us to surmise, then, is that *badagshin* are not so much
half-people—or half-animals—in the sense of occupying a mimetic space
betwixt and between humans and animals. Rather, *badagshin* are irreducibly
dual beings, who are composed by two contrasting halves "without it being
the case that the[se] halves represent one another" (Deleuze cited in Badiou
2000, 36). Seen in this light, and recalling my characterization of Gombodorj
as a living trickster, is there a sense to which *badagshin* and people like him
are mirrors, or reversibles, of one another, where the trickster role played by
half shamans in the village is analogous to that of half people in the forest?

Gombodorj's Curse

To explore the ramifications of this possibility—that half shamans are sort
of spectral spirits—I now recount the tragicomic tale of how Gombodorj's

own life and that of many of his relatives was predestined by a curse cast several generations ago. The tale, which consists of several parts, begins with an incident for which Gombodorj is infamous in Ulaan-Uul. I paraphrase his account, since he did not allow me to record it.

During the late summer of 1997, Gombodorj's household was staying at a place called Baga Bilüü. One night some neighbors came to visit, and they all started drinking and talking about something unusual that had just taken place. A few hours earlier, an old man had killed two bears, which had been spotted near some children out berry picking, who had run back to their camp to report it. The hunt itself had been easy enough, but it was a strange occurrence, because bears usually stay in the depths of Ulaan Taiga. At midnight, after countless discussions of the event amid much drunkenness, the visitors stumbled out of Gombodorj's *ger*. Inside, Gombodorj was on his way to bed when he suddenly felt a cold sensation in his left shoulder. Mysteriously compelled to look up, he saw a smoke-like thing (*utaa shig yum*) hovering around the *ger*'s smoke hole, a common entrance point for shamanic spirits. Gombodorj instantly began to pull the burning logs from the stove and threw them in all directions. Led by another mind (*öör uhaan udirdsan*) and unable to control his own actions, Gombodorj burned down his home. The fire woke his wife and children, who escaped from the *ger,* leaving the head of the household alone in the burning inferno. The next morning people came from all directions to inspect the site. What they beheld was very strange. Out of each pair of boots, one was burned and the other intact; of two wooden buckets, only one had suffered damage. The spirit talisman (*ongon*) was intact. Clearly it had not been a normal fire. Then, a few days later, the old man who had killed the bears fell ill and died, and soon afterwards, so did his wife. There was general agreement that this was because the land spirits (*lus savdag*) had been offended by the killing of the bears.

This explanation did not quite satisfy Gombodorj, however, for how did this account for the strange thing that had happened to him? No, he maintained, the entire spectacle must be understood in light of an ancient dispute between two male shamans (*zaarin*), one of whom was his great-grandfather. What took place at Baga Bilüü was a continuation of this original fight, now taken up between the shamanic spirit souls (*ongon süns*) of the two shamans. The old man had been unfortunate enough to kill a bear that was in fact a metamorphosis (*huvilgaan*) of a deceased shaman. Gombodorj had been led to set fire to the *ger* by his own great-grandfather's soul. This had been a good thing, for had the ancestral spirit not intervened at this point, he and the rest of his household might easily have perished. "My great-grandfather's soul saved us," Gombodorj concluded. "It led me to set fire to our home to scare off the other shaman's soul."

Who, then, was Gombodorj's great-grandfather? Like many shamans-to-be, the great-grandfather had been "a very difficult person" (*ih hetsüü hün*) when he was young. He drank excessively and was continually involved in violent, *agsan*-induced fights. Occasionally he would wander for days or even weeks in the taiga, completely oblivious to his surroundings. A devoted ecclesiastical serf (*shabi*) on the Buddhist estate of the Darhad Ih Shav', the young man's father (that is, Gombodorj's great-great-grandfather) first went to Urga to seek advice from the Jebtsundamba Khutuktu himself, who decreed that what the youngster needed was more responsibility and so appointed him *zaisan* ("a kind of governor") of the ecclesiastical estate. This, however, only made the young man's condition worse, so the father reluctantly sought advice from an experienced *zaarin*. Soon the young man became his student and was eventually consecrated as a shaman himself.

Over the years, Gombodorj's great-grandfather sired seven daughters. After each birth he threw a big party, inviting people from near and far, treating them to rare roebuck meat (for, like his great-grandson, he was a gifted hunter). On every occasion, the shaman teacher (*böö bagsh*) was invited as a guest of honor. When, finally, his wife gave him a son, the great-grandfather threw the biggest party of all, where he served an extremely rare delicacy, meat from the mountain goat. But this time the old *zaarin* was not invited. "There is no reason to invite that geezer," the great-grandfather exclaimed with a haughty sneer. "I am now far stronger than he is." The shaman teacher naturally heard about the party and his former student's disrespectful words, and of course the news made him furious. He turned up at the party to demand an explanation, and a terrible argument broke out between the two. As the old *zaarin* departed, he said: "Perhaps I shall die from you cursing me, but you will not remain unhurt. For the next three generations, you and your descendants will suffer from diseases, debt, and humiliation!" Less than a month later, the *zaarin* died.

The old shaman was right. The curse has since manifested itself in the lives of the great-grandfather's descendants, albeit in different ways and to different degrees. Disease and premature death have haunted some households, like that of Gombodorj's younger brother, who has lost several children. Other descendants have experienced severe problems with money. Gombodorj's own father, who was "a very talented man" (*ih chadvartai hün*), suffered in this way. As part of his occupation in the *negdel*, he had developed a new technique for producing oil or soap from bones, and even appeared on television to talk about his invention. The communist authorities, however, were not impressed. Undeterred, he continued improving it, but was soon ordered to stop. "You need permission," he was told. This taught him a lesson for life: never work for the system, only for yourself and your family. If you carve a nice bucket, sell it at the highest price you can get. Don't make the mistake of adding it to a common pool of buckets, most of which will be badly made, and for which you will receive only a fixed price.

The authorities loathed Gombodorj's father, but his talent could not be ignored. Eventually he was made vice deputy for unprocessed products (*tüühii ediin erhlegch*) at the local branch of the state trading office (*beltgeliin angi*) in Ulaan-Uul. He worked for the socialist state for many years and received numerous decorations. This all changed one day, however, when some Soviet soldiers cheated him, and a lot of government money was lost. Desperate to redeem these losses, he devised a way to manipulate the centrally planned economy. Together with a trusted friend, a driver at the collective farm, he brought "his" surplus of hunting pelts from Ulaan-Uul to a neighboring district and sold them to his local counterpart there. He was taking advantage of the difference in the ability of two units in the planned economy to meet their annual production quotas for furs. Over the next several years, the two partners successfully expanded their *bizness* (as Gombodorj called it) to an increasing number of *negdels* and for a growing range of products. They made a lot of money, and his father was able to pay back his debt, which he had managed to keep secret.

But then they were discovered. For their "appalling example of speculation," capital punishment was an option, but the two men ended up serving eight years in prison. Meanwhile, their families suffered humiliation and discrimination. People would shout at Gombodorj's mother in the village streets, and despite doing well in school, Gombodorj and his brothers were not allowed to go on to higher education. Instead, Gombodorj became the pupil of a famous craftsman, a man who happened to be a childhood friend of his beloved father. As for the latter, he ended his days bearing the stigma of a convicted thief and counterrevolutionary, the memory people still have of him. In Gombodorj's own eyes, however, his father's only mistake was to be ahead of his time. "My father," Gombodorj proudly concluded, "was Mongolia's first capitalist."

At this point I could recount the colorful story of Gombodorj's grandfather, a man renowned for indulging in the riskiest forms of gambling, trading, and flirting, most famously with Duha reindeer herders living in the depths of the taiga. Of all the great-grandfather's descendants, however, it is Gombodorj who has been most intimately connected with the curse, so let us take a closer look at his life story. To Gombodorj, the old curse manifested itself in strange fires and mysterious encounters with bears, that is to say, as a sort of continual replay of the original dispute between the two shamans.

It all started when he was fourteen, on an autumn night, when it happened that Gombodorj was the oldest male present in the household. A bear suddenly crashed through the *ger*, but the young lad resolutely jumped out of bed, got hold of his father's rifle, and put two bullets through the bear's heart. He had saved his family. (This, by the way, is a true story, which everyone knows.) Many years later a newly wed Gombodorj, upon his return from a successful hunt, encountered a bear on a forest path close to his house. Immediately he knew that his home had been destroyed, and so it was. But his family was unhurt. That morning they had been taken to the village because his wife was in labor. And that same night, as his first son was born, a mysterious fire broke out at the clinic. No one ever discovered its cause, nor could anyone explain why the flames did not create more damage. But for Gombodorj it made perfect sense: his great-grandfather had been fighting his old teacher again.

A Genealogy of Difference

As the story of Gombodorj and his forebears makes clear, being subject to the shamanic predicament is no guarantee of happiness and prosperity. Quite to the contrary, shamanism in Mongolian societies is often perceived as "a psychological burden which contains its own force of perpetuation" (Humphrey 1996, 211–12; see also Balzer 2008). Indeed it is telling that Gombodorj told me the story I just related the first time we met and hardly ever mentioned it again. Presumably he not only found it painful and shameful to talk about the strange events at Baga Bilüü but also did not really understand what had happened, let alone why.

Certainly the tale of Gombodorj and his forefathers is not unique. Darhad—and more generally Mongolian—lore is awash with origin stories about shamanic spirits which share the same plot (Humphrey 1996, 198). Once upon a time, a dramatic event took place (usually involving one or more people with magical abilities), which led to the creation of a new shamanic spirit (*ongon*). Since then, the lives of later generations have been influenced by this primordial shamanic event, especially descendants of persons who were involved in the original creation of the new *ongon*, who may have inherited the *udha* and become shamans themselves (Badamhatan 1986, 185–87). As Sandschejew pointed out more than eighty years ago, "only Darhad persons with shamanist ancestry can become shamans. These people have not only the right but also the duty of becoming shamans" (1930, 56).

Indeed, the tale conveys the unmistakable message that Gombodorj himself ought to be a shaman, for he is presented as one of those "unusually gifted" but also "very difficult" persons who, like his great-grandfather, have been "called by the spirits to be their new representative on earth" (Even

1991, 194). Whether Gombodorj has any choice in this regard is beside the point. Gombodorj is, to use a cliché, the chosen one, and not only does the soul of his great-grandfather remind him and everyone else who wants to listen about this by "leading" him into doing strange things, but also this spirit's interventions convey the message that Gombodorj's firstborn son is meant to take over from *his* father one day, as witnessed by the fact that it intervened when the son was born.

Now, across Mongolia, a person's abilities, whether considered extraordinary or not, are widely understood to have been inherited from his ancestors. But crucially, unlike, for instance, clan affiliation (*ovog*), shamanic ability (*udha*) is not necessarily passed down in the predictable (unilateral) way associated with the patrilines (*yas ündes*), which used to provide a hegemonic model for social and political relations in Mongolian contexts, and to some extend still do (Vreeland 1962; Humphrey and Sneath 1999). As Humphrey writes about the Daur Mongolian case, "the connection between shamans was in principle not a patrilineal affair.... The link could zigzag from women to men and vice versa" (1996, 36). In much the same way, in the Shishged as well as elsewhere in Mongolia, shamanic ability may be passed down through both male and female ancestors; but not all siblings or even all generations are destined to become shamans, as the *udha* sometimes skips a generation or two before manifesting itself anew.

Still, in those contexts in which clans have played a key role, much emphasis has been placed on keeping the *udha* within the patriline. According to Roberte Hamayon, women were sometimes prevented from becoming shamans among western Buryats (1984); indeed, as she herself puts it, "given the connection between shamanic and patrician institutions, the bilinear transmission of the shamanic essence...constitute[s] a source of potential conflict" (1984, 310). Given that clans used to play a key role in Darhad social life, it should come as no surprise that the tale about Gombodorj's forebears conveys a similar patricentric message, even if most people today (including him) do not claim any clan affiliation. For one thing, we are told that Gombodorj's great-grandfather needed a male—as opposed to a female—shaman in order to be nurtured into a shaman himself. More to the point, the story communicates how important it was to the great-grandfather to have male offspring (the bigger party, the rarer meat). Only with the birth of his first son did he dare challenge his teacher by not inviting him to the party. The great-grandfather's surpassing of his teacher's strength, then, coincided with his securing the continuation of his patriline.

One lesson of this tale is therefore that shamanic neophytes become stronger than their teachers only at the moment when they produce a male heir to the *udha,* for at this moment these junior shamans become senior themselves. At the same time, the moral of the tale is also that seniority does not automatically make one shaman superior to another; in fact, concepts of occult prowess are closely bound up with concepts of youth across Inner Asia (Hamayon 1994, 85; Humphrey 1996, 37–39). This is not to say that senior shamans are unimportant. They are crucial for the nurturing of junior ones in the role of shaman teachers; but they must eventually give way to a new generation, or be prepared to pay the price.

But the story of the great-grandfather challenges not only patriarchal conceptions of seniority and respect but also the equally hegemonic position of the Buddhist church at the time. Thus the first part of the tale conveys a clear message about the limitations on ecclesiastical power in the Shishged during the tumultuous years leading up to the revolution. Even intervention by Mongolia's holy emperor, the Bogd Khan himself, proved futile in the face of the violent manifestation of *udha* in a troubled Darhad adolescent; for not even the *agsan*-prone great-grandfather's appointment to the high office of *zaisan* turned out to be a viable remedy for the so-called shamanic illness (*böögiin övchin*).[7]

The tale about Gombodorj's father contains a no less subversive message, only this time in opposition to the socialist state, not the Buddhist church. Gombodorj's father, we are told, used his occult skills to turn himself into a "capitalist ahead of his time." Like the skills of the blacksmith, this creativity resided in his capacity for revealing the invisible potential in things, in this specific case the latent potential of animal pelts (and wooden buckets) to be assigned individual values as opposed to what Martin Holbraad calls the "arthritic" nature of prices in state socialist contexts (2003). Thus understood, the father's invention was to fuse together two separate economic logics, namely, those of the supply-driven centrally planned economy and the demand-driven capitalist market (Verdery 1996). By extending the market-like logic of Mongolia's illicit black economy into the heart of planned production, which organized the activities of the rural trading bodies in the socialist period, Gombodorj's father turned the centrally assigned production quotas into items of market exchange. In that sense, the father's crime was that he revealed a shady potential for capitalist profiteering hidden beneath the surface of the socialist economy.[8] Whereas, during the socialist period, this led to his conviction as a "speculator," today he might well be

---

7. The symptoms of "the shamanic illness" (jaundice, fever, sudden fits of violence, solitary roaming in the forest, and so on) have been well documented in the literature on Mongolian shamanism (Even 1991; Humphrey 1996).

8. During the last decades of socialism, there were transactions in many kinds of goods at semi-illicit "black markets" (*har zah*), which sprang up across Mongolia and typically were located on the outskirts of larger towns and cities (see Pedersen 2007b).

commended for his "entrepreneurship" by some foreign NGO promoting "small and medium-sized enterprises" in Mongolia.

Taken together, this chain of episodes from the lives of Gombodorj's great-grandfather and his descendants provides a rare insider's glimpse of a shamanic genealogy. The tale not only provides valuable insights into the nature of shamanic predestination but also reveals a homology between Gombodorj's social status and that of his forebears, despite the radical changes that have taken place in Mongolia over the past hundred years. Gombodorj's ancestors, we are told, were not ordinary men. They were fighters, shamans, gamblers, inventors, and entrepreneurs, and Gombodorj has inherited a propensity for the unique and extraordinary himself, as witnessed by his own array of special abilities. In fact, as the story about the fire at his *ger* demonstrates, Gombodorj is capable of momentarily becoming one of his forebears, or rather the other way around, for his great-grandfather's shamanic soul sometimes makes him do things against his own will.

What we have here, I suggest, are the contours of an inherently shamanic genealogy of difference—an ongoing, intergenerational return or "rebirth" of difference itself (Deleuze 1994). Following Humphrey (1996, 357–60; c.f. Strathern 1988), we can conceive of Gombodorj's social status in postsocialist Mongolia as a "substitution" (as opposed to a "replication") of his father's status during the socialist period, which itself is a substitution of his grandfather's position around the time of the Mongolian revolution, which again is a substitution of his great-grandfather's position in the Darhad Ih Shav'. In other words, an analogous marginal social position is repeated across succeeding generations of specialists, but it takes on heterogeneous forms. These substitutions occur not only in accordance with the individual life trajectory of the person concerned (whether or not he is subject to any shamanic calling), but also in accordance with the political-economic context against which his marginality is defined. (Today's businesspersons, for instance, are not burdened with the stigma that was once attached to "speculators," and it is inconceivable that Gombodorj would be considered one of them.) Indeed, as Gombodorj predicted, his sons are well on track toward becoming potential shamans themselves, continuing an unbroken family tradition for replicating difference as such.

Occult Specialists

Marginal and sometimes stigmatized people with occult abilities like Gombodorj and his forebears have a long history in Mongolia. The Shishged, and Mongolia more generally, have for centuries been home to a plethora

of different kinds of shamanic practitioners, who have been competing—
and fighting, often in competition with Buddhist lamas endorsed by local or
imperial rulers—for the attention of various human and nonhuman others.
To understand better how Gombodorj and his forebears do—and, equally
important, do not—fit into this general picture, it is useful to provide an
overview of the different kinds of occult specialists (as I call them) present in
Ulaan-Uul before, during, and after socialism.

Around the turn of the twentieth century, a wide range of occult specialists were practicing in Mongolia, in an often uneasy truce with lamas and
others in roles sanctioned by the Manchu colonial polity and the dominant
school of Gelugpa Buddhism (Heissig 1980, 1–6; Jagchid and Hyer 1979,
163–75). Of these, the shamans have been subject to the most scholarly attention, and with good reason: they were, after all, usually at the top of the
occult pecking order. Still, in more than a few cases one might as well have fo-
cused on blacksmiths, midwives, "bonesetters" (*bariach*), diviners (*meregch),*
astrologers (*zurhaich*), or even hunters. All these people were also imbued
with powerful abilities (*hüch chadal*), which marked them as qualitatively
different from ordinary people.

All these kinds of occult specialists—barring, as I was repeatedly told,
shamans—could be found in the Ulaan-Uul community in the late 1990s, as
they apparently also could throughout the socialist period. While age, gender,
and wealth were not ignored in people's estimation of these persons' skills,
none of these markers seemed to play any decisive role in determining a given
specialist's strength and general status in the community. What mattered above
all was how good the specialists were at putting their occult knowledge to use,
preferably in ways no one else could. Thus, when people in Ulaan-Uul were
asked to explain why a specialist had been able to "rise above" (*deshee garah*) his
or her peers, they would sometimes describe him or her as *sodon* (outstanding,
unique), as if this was sufficient to account for the possession of occult skill. Indeed, a Buryat saying goes, "'*Böö böögiin böölöh ondoo*'; literally, every shaman
shamanizes differently from every other" (Buyandelger 1999, 227).

Consider as a concrete example the half-dozen or so people who were spoken of as blacksmiths in the Ulaan-Uul community in the late 1990s. All of
them, if in varying degrees and with different levels of mastery, were imbued
with *hüch chadal,* in the sense that these specialists either had been gifted
from birth or endowed later in their lives with extraordinary capacities that
other people simply did not have (like the ability to "see"—*üzeh*—things), or
because they mastered common abilities (like the ability to hunt) in a way
that vastly surpassed the capacities of ordinary persons.

Apart from being different from the nonspecialists, Ulaan-Uul's smiths
were also perceived to differ from one another. For example, as has also been

reported from Buryatia (Abaeva 1992, 103–10; Galdanova 1997, 87–91), two of them had a reputation as good diviners. They did, however, use different techniques, one stone divination (*chuluu tatah*) and the other scapulomancy (*dal shataah*), divining with the shoulder blades of sheep; and there was much disagreement, not only about who was the better diviner but also about which technique was able to elicit the best answer to which kind of question. Two of Ulaan-Uul's smiths were also considered gifted hunters (*mergen hün*). Once again, the skills and wisdom of one specialist did not correspond at all to the skills and wisdom of the other. For example, according to one of them it was taboo to hunt deer in Tujid Taiga, whereas to the other, who was living close by, this presented no danger.

Ordinary people in Ulaan-Uul seemed to accept if not enjoy this heterogeneity among specialists. Both in their ways of speaking about specialists and in the reasons they presented for visiting them, my hosts made it clear to me that "different kinds of occult ability were related to different kinds of religious knowledge" (Humphrey 1996, 51). It is this division of occult labor, or occult knowledge, that interests me here, for it seemed to be even more extreme in the Shishged context than the already quite heterodox picture conveyed by anthropologists writing about other Mongolian shamanic contexts, be they contemporary or historical (Buyandelgeryin 2007; Humphrey 1996; Hamayon 1994).

Consider this tale, which was told to me by an old nomad couple who kept on interrupting each other, eager to correct or improve on what the other had just said:

> Back in the old days, there was a very powerful and skillful *zaarin* called Delden Mend. He had an old flint gun. Once he became very seriously ill, so he handed the gun to a friend and said: "Now I will shamanize, and you must shoot me. Then I will be okay." So, although Delden Mend was close to dying, he began shamanizing. "Now go and ahead and shoot me!" he grunted. As requested, the friend shot Delden Mend through the head, who then fell down flat. For a long time he was lying completely still, but suddenly he got up and resumed the shamanizing. Soon he became better. The only thing left was a scar at the back of his head where the bullet went through.
>
> But then one day things went wrong. Delden Mend was bewitched by someone [*neg hünii horlol bolson*]. For some time a *zaarin* called Borigka had been chasing after him. So far it had not come to a fight, for Delden Mend had successfully been hiding in the mountains. Each time Borigka came looking for him on one mountain, Delden Mend moved to another mountain. Eventually, Delden Mend had had enough. He prepared

[*tsagaalj,* lit. "purified"] a drill, and went to Borigka and used the drill to cut through the canvas of Borigka's *ger* with the intention of killing his adversary. But at that same moment Borigka's wife came close to the canvas and ended up having a hole drilled through her head. Aghast by this turn of events, Delden Mend revealed himself to Borigka and said: "The person I wished to kill has not perished. Instead, I have erred by killing a person who was innocent. My shamanic abilities must have turned bad for something like this to happen. Bring me to whatever place I need to be brought [*avaachdag gazraa avaach*]! Make me meet the destiny that I am supposed to meet [*hürgedeg gazraa hürge*]!

In its surprising shifts between valor and slyness, and between mischievousness and earnestness, this narrative captures the way in which many people in northern Mongolia speak of the great shamans (*aihtar böö*) of the past. More to the point, the tale of the conflict between Delden Mend and Borigka confirms that shamans, and possibly other occult specialists as well, are always conceived of in the singular. It thus seems that the only way to compare two Darhad shamans is by having them fight to the death, if not necessarily in a face-to-face collision, then at least by proxy (as in cursing). Somewhat as with goods exchanged in direct barter transactions outside standardized price systems (Humphrey 1985), there is no fixed, abstract scale through which the relative value of two occult specialists can be measured in advance. Like pears and apples brought together with the aim of facilitating a swap, only an unmediated encounter between their occult capacities will determine their respective value, for they do not automatically belong to the same world (Strathern 1992). As with Godelier's Melanesian "great men" (1986), we could thus say that specialists are "non-equivalent," for the *sodon*-ness of one is not commensurable with the *sodon*-ness of another. It follows that, more than simply being a means of establishing their respective places in the local shamanic pecking order—that is, their societal status—the fight between Delden Mend and Borigka, like the one between the two blacksmiths recounted earlier, was about different ontological statuses: about being alive or being dead.

Informal Leaders

If Ulaan-Uul's occult specialists stood out from other persons by constituting political singularities, how did they compare with other kinds of prominent persons, such as the husband in my host family? To engage with this question I need to present an overview of the different kinds of leaders, formal and informal, who have emerged in rural Mongolia after socialism. In Ulaan-Uul in the late 1990s, the more formal leaders holding top political and administrative jobs such as *sumyn darga* (district governor) and *zasgiin darga* (chief administrator) were still mostly recruited from among various professionals, such as doctors, economists, accountants, veterinarians, and so forth, many of whom had also held analogous positions during socialism. Still, three more informal kinds of leaders were also gaining—or regaining—distinct prominence.

First, there were the "eldest men" (*hamgiin ah*[*mad*]), who played a key role on various festive occasions, such as weddings and other calendar or life-cycle rituals within or between households, as well as certain community rituals organized by local leaders (such as the so-called *ovoo* mountain ritual, which is described in chapter 3). As implied by their designation, *hamgiin ah* must be somehow perceived to embody the very essence of an old man, much as the comparable category of elderly men known as *utaachi* did in presocialist Daur Mongolian society, where each *utaachi* was considered the epitome of experiences accessible to every (senior) male person, and for the same reason would "emerge from the ranks of men in general" (Humphrey 1996, 60). Unlike the Daur *utaachi* presiding over communal rituals (including mountain rituals) who were known as *bagchi*, however, the Darhad *hamgiin ah* I came across were not considered to have specific oratorical skills or ceremonial knowledge. In fact, apart from their advanced age, there seemed to be nothing unique about them: they were not particularly wealthy, nor were they known to have any special knowledge. They hardly seemed to do anything at all at the parties and rituals in which I took part, apart from always being present in their very midst, as if exuding an invisible magnetism compelling all the other persons present to gather around them. The one way in which *hamgiin ah* did stand out was by doing what all old men must do according to *yos*, namely, remaining as immobile as possible, for as with other social categories, the bodily comportment of elderly men is supposed to reflect their stage in life (Lacaze 2000).

Second, there were the leaders of Ulaan-Uul's six subdistricts, who were known as *bagiin darga*, a low-ranking, semi-elected politico-administrative office whose historical precedents can be traced all the way back to the Darhad Ih Shav' in the form of the so-called *otog* leaders (Badamhatan 1986, 80, 127; Sandschejew 1930, 28–33).[9] Among other things, these *bag* (subdistrict) leaders were responsible for the twice-annual livestock count, the collection

9. In the late 1990s the district governor formally appointed each *bag* leader but usually followed the proposal put forward by the elected *bag* council (*bagiin hural*) (Enhbat 1993, 8–10; Enhbat and Odgaard 1996).

of certain taxes, and the organization of (more or less voluntary) communal tasks such as the construction of fences and the extinguishing of forest fires. Invariably respected and relatively well-off herders and often former wrestling champions, all of Ulaan-Uul's *bag* leaders were archetypical "masters" (*ezen*, pl. *ezed*) in the traditional patriarchal sense, whose continuing importance in Mongolian contexts has been discussed by several anthropologists (Humphrey and Sneath 1999; Sneath 2000, 2007).[10] Thus all five rural *bagiin darga* in Ulaan-Uul were senior males, who not only were admired for their talents as herdsmen but also had large households and herds. Like my host (who himself used to lead the village *bag* in the early 1990s), they were known as hardworking, respectable, polite, and trustworthy figureheads from "good households." Like him, they might get drunk occasionally, but so did everyone else; or they might fight occasionally, but so did everyone else. This was all considered perfectly fine (after all, they were men), as long as they did not do "too much."

The third type of informal leader was "businesspersons," an increasingly influential group of men and women comprising shop owners, jeep and truck owners, and a variety of traders, who were all making quite a comfortable living from shifting various goods to and from the countryside (this was done almost exclusively by men), or from the Ulaan-Uul village to the regional capital (done by both men and women), where some of them (predominantly women) were also directly engaged in selling goods at their own stalls at the sprawling market in Mörön (Pedersen 2006a). All were rumored to be very wealthy, and I was often told (in what turned to be quite an accurate prediction of things to come) that "soon they will be running everything here." Invariably they were spoken of as smart and well connected. Indeed, many had held leadership positions during socialism and were now taking advantage of their *tanil* from back then, just as some of their most valuable assets (such as trucks) had been acquired in the murky privatization of the early 1990s.

In other words, if some people in Ulaan-Uul in the late 1990s turned into informal leaders because of their advanced age and dignity (the "eldest men"), others did so by being exemplary and trustworthy patrons in their respective communities (the *bag* leaders), while still others became informal leaders of sorts by being particularly wealthy (the businesspersons). I suggest that the prominence of all kinds of informal leaders (barring shamanically inclined and transgressive ones like the *atamans*) in that sense arises from their being

---

10. As Sneath points out, the *ezen* concept is "a central theme in the construction of asymmetrical social relations, and one which applied to a series of social scales—from the Imperial to the domestic" (2000, 43).

perceived as "hyper-similar" to other persons (that is, more similar to others than others are to others), as opposed to the occult specialists, who, as I explained earlier, stand out by being "hyper-different" from other persons (that is, more different from others than others are from others).[11]

So if the prominence of informal leaders in northern Mongolia can be said to inhere in a capacity to be hyper-similar (equivalent) to various categories of others, then the prominence of the occult specialists, conversely, can be seen to inhere in an ability to be hyper-different from (non-equivalent to) all persons, including not only, as we have seen, other specialists (including those with the same specialty as themselves) but also—as if they were striving to take the logic of hyper-difference to its limit—themselves. Nowhere was this excessive differentiation made more clear than in the case of Gombodorj and his shamanic forebears, who, as I argued in the previous section, were predestined to differ not only from others but also from one another. Indeed, if there was one thing that all of Ulaan-Uul's half-shamans had in common, it was this will or destiny to be different, an unparalleled capacity to differ from other men, including leaders, specialists, and—because of their wormlike bodies and trickster-like minds—themselves.

Against this backdrop, the Darhad case emerges as even more heterogeneous than what Hamayon (1984), with ill-disguised structuralist disappointment, has lamented as the "fragmentary" nature of much Mongolian shamanism (as opposed, she seems to imply, to much shamanism in general). For not only were there several kinds of occult specialists (shamans, diviners, hunters, and so forth) in Ulaan-Uul, as among the eastern Buryats, according to Hamayon (1990, 1994), but also there was considerable variation within each of these sociological categories, in that each specialist was understood and indeed praised for having his or her own *sodon* way of doing things, an observation that Humphrey convincingly made for the Mongolian case as a whole (1994a, 1996, 2008). Yet, as if this did not already present shamanic diversity enough, I want to add a theoretical twist to this insight based on my Darhad material, namely, that beyond the individualism of occult specialists identified by scholars like Humphrey and Buyandelger, the shamanic persona I met in northern Mongolia were also *internally differentiated,* in that each one was composed of many layers of agency, some human and others nonhuman.

---

11. While informal leaders stand out by being more similar to others than anyone else, they are not radically similar to the same others. If the "eldest men" are radically similar only to all other old Darhad men, the businesspersons are radically similar to all adult Mongolians, women and non-Darhads included. *Bag* leaders, for their part, are perfectly average men; in fact, if they have one outstanding characteristic, it is that they are so exceptionally good at being like other men.

A Lost Generation

To close my account of Gombodorj and his shamanic predicament, it is worthwhile to recall what took place when I returned to my hosts after having been told the tale of Gombodorj's forebears, during the very first week of my stay in the Ulaan-Uul community. "So, what did he tell you?" they rushed to inquire. As I hesitated, they came out with the answer themselves: "He probably told you about the *ger* fire. Well, he certainly was extremely drunk that night. But all that talk about *ongod* and *chötgör*...we're not so sure."

My hosts were not alone in their doubts. Several months later, after their falling-out with Gombodorj, they introduced me to a hunter who, it was emphasized, "used to be Gombodorj's friend." The man, who was tipsy, exclaimed that I was finally going to be told "the truth" (*ünen*). Gombodorj, he said, used to be his best friend and hunting partner. They always drank and fought together, and Gombodorj was certainly a man of multiple skills. "But," he continued, "I got frightened that night. I was there drinking with the other hunters when Gombodorj became violently drunk [*agsan tav'san*] and threw us all out. Next he threatened his wife and children, so they also had to run away. Soon everything was on fire. Then, the next morning, he said that an *ongon* had taken control of him and made him *agsan*."

This doubt, I was gradually to find out, was shared by many people in Ulaan-Uul. Because of his trickster-like character, it was simply impossible to know whether an ancestral shamanic spirit really had possessed Gombodorj that night or not. Nevertheless, the specific object of people's misgivings is interesting. They did not doubt the existence of the shamanic spirits (or at least they did not express such doubt). What they doubted was whether Gombodorj's actions in this instance had been caused by sources of agency beyond his control. As the wife in my host family complained, the problem with Gombodorj is that it is impossible to know where you stand with him, because he just "tells lies" all the time.

Gombodorj was far from being the only potential shaman in Ulaan-Uul. Indeed, as we saw in the previous chapter, the capacity to inflict physical (and psychological) harm was understood to reside in complex affective states involving exterior influences and forces (souls, spirits, and so forth) as much as in individuals' self-contained minds, which is undoubtedly why these conditions were also generally considered difficult to explain and, for the same reasons, difficult to do away with—so difficult that only occult intervention by skilled specialists could improve the situation.[12] I came across several cases

---

12. For more about uncontrollable rage in Mongolia, see Delaplace (2009). Note also, in the spirit of comparison, what a Sakha (Yakut) shaman once told Balzer: "I was very out of it when

of young as well as not so young men (but never women) who were deemed so "difficult" by their families that they were brought to shamans in Tsagaan Nuur and provided with Jew's harps (*hel huur*), always an important yardstick for measuring shamanic *udha* in the Darhad context (Diószegi 1963, 63–64). But for reasons that seldom were clear to me, these potential shamans never responded to the call of the spirits.[13]

What was clear, however, was that whatever the reasons for their lack of shamanic careers, these troubled men in their twenties, thirties, and sometimes forties were doomed to remain in a hyper-shamanic state of permanent transformation—or, as in the case of their country as a whole, transition—for the rest of their lives. As I was told, "they aren't shamans, but they are sort of shamans" *(Böö ch baihgüi. Harin böö uhaany yum baigaa.)*

All this suggests that northern Mongolia in the late 1990s was home to an entire generation of young men who were forever stuck in the process of becoming shamans. Marjorie Balzer makes a similar observation about indigenous groups in Siberia: "One of the many tragedies of the Soviet repression of shamans is that the shamans only with great difficulty found appropriate youth to whom to bequeath their secret knowledge and practice" (2006, 90). As the first decade after socialism came to a close, it looked increasingly difficult to redress this sociological time lag, or "social moratorium" (Vigh 2006), since by this time these troubled men "ought" to have become senior shamans imbued with the wisdom to nurture and teach the next generation of shamans, as opposed to hovering forever in the transitional state of being merely potential shamans, who were themselves still in need of shaman teachers to become complete shamans themselves. Like the millions of young men whose transition to adulthood has been put on permanent hold in postcolonial Africa, and the urban hustlers and drifters in Ulaanbaatar in the late 1990s (Pedersen and Højer 2008), northern Mongolia's half-shamans were like a lost generation whose subjectivity was one of many unintended casualties of large-scale political transformations. As occult Mongolian versions of Alexei Yurchak's "last Soviet generation" (2006), these half-shamans formed a quintessentially postsocialist cohort that, more than anyone else, was trapped between two societal orders.

It has proved difficult for me and other scholars to find a fully satisfactory answer to explain what went wrong. What happened to all the "genuine shamans" of the past? Where did they go? It is clear that, in comparison to

I drank, and through this, I suffered *éttéénii* [shamanic illness] without at first understanding what it was" (2006, 87).

13. One almost bluntly clear reason was presented in the case of the *ataman* nephew in my host family, who, as described in the previous chapter, simply rejected the possibility that he was a victim of the shamanic *udha*.

Figure 10. Man with *hel huur* (Jew's harp)

the virtual annihilation of Buddhism in the Shishged, Darhad shamanism fared somewhat better under socialism. Of course, like the other occult specialists who were active in those years, the shamans were forced to practice outside official contexts to avoid political repercussions from the authorities, which could range from public denunciation and the loss of social rights (such as access to high school or university for one's children) to, in the more extreme instances, imprisonment or even, in the 1930s, execution. Still, it was repeatedly confirmed to me, shamanic ceremonies were performed "in secret" throughout the period, just as shamans were consulted for divinatory and other purposes that did not require full-blown rituals in which the shaman is possessed by shamanic spirits.

The paradox of the missing Darhad shamans is underscored by the fact that the Mongolian ethnographer S. Badamhatan and the Hungarian ethnographer László Diószegi, who both visited the Shishged around the middle of the twentieth century, met a large number (more than sixty) of what they referred to as "former shamans," at least some of whom were no doubt active at the time.[14] Yet about a generation later, by the mid-1980s, there seems to have been only a few shamans left in the region, despite the fact that by then the most serious political repression was over. What happened? The Swiss anthropologist Judith Hangartner, who has conducted fieldwork in the Renchinlhümbe district, writes:

> When asked about the practice of their ancestors during socialism,
> present-day Darhad shamans usually answer that their parents halted
> their practice due to the persecution. Some informants said that they
> did not know at all that their father/mother was a shaman, hiding their
> practice even from their children. During some of the conversations,
> shamans revealed that their parents had stopped, restarted in a case of
> unexplainable sickness or livestock loss, abandoned shamanizing again
> and restarted on the demand of their spirits....Considering the memories
> of descendents of shamans and senior people it seems that local officials
> put some pressure on shamans to restrict their practices to the private
> realm but that this pressure fluctuated, causing shamans to renounce
> their practice or to resume shamanizing in periods of dwindling pres-
> sure....It furthermore appears that the number of practising shamans was
> decreasing towards the end of the socialist period. (Hangartner, in press)

---

14. As Hangartner points out, while "Badamhatan and Diószegi presented shamans and their practices as an historical phenomenon which was alive until the 'the turn of the century[,]'...[they] could not refrain from disclosing in footnotes that they actually encountered numerous practicing shamans" (Hangartner, in press).

These observations about the shaman situation in Renchinlhümbe during socialism correspond to what some people told me about Ulaan-Uul (compare also Buyandelger 2008 for the Buryat case). Others, however, insisted that there were "no shamans" (or lamas) back then at all, and this sometimes led to arguments in the middle of interviews ("What do you mean, there was a living shaman just next door?"). But the most common responses to my question "What happened to the shamans?" were vague, guarded, and contradictory, as in this exchange from an interview with an elderly lady:

ME: So there were no shamans here during the socialist period?

LADY: None whatever. Lamas, *zaarin, udgan*—they were all caught.

ME: Might there perhaps have been a couple of them? Other people have told me this....

LADY: Well, I guess there were a few around. Some moved up there [pointing to the taiga] and came back [in the early 1990s]. Some returned after being imprisoned for ten years, but they were lamas. About two of them, I think.

ME: One man told me that there were always shamans around here in Ulaan-Uul during socialism. There were one or two, he claimed, shamanizing in secret....

LADY: Yes, there were. There were also a few lamas. But none of them were really that good.

It is safe to conclude that shamans could be found practicing unofficially in the Shishged throughout the socialist period, even if this took place under quite difficult, restricted, and sometimes dangerous conditions, and even if it seems that there were only a few shamans left during the late decades of socialism. But for reasons that were never made clear to me—or, it seems, to other researchers either (perhaps because it would have been too painful to do so, or perhaps because these reasons were not entirely clear to people themselves)—the Darhad shamans virtually died out in the 1980s and early 1990s. What is abundantly clear, however, is that this shaman deficit had major ramifications on social life in the late 1990s.

Destined to Differ

It is important to emphasize that not all occult specialists in Ulaan-Uul were stigmatized like Gombodorj and the other potential shamans; in fact many were quite popular in the community. While other people often spoke of them by reference to their specific occult skill ("Which Bayraa? Ah, Bayraa the diviner"), their special liaison with the spirits did not permeate everything they did as in Gombodorj's case. For instance, when playing the Russian card game *durak* with their acquaintances, they did so as *tanil,* not as persons with occult capacities. Exposure of the latter was confined to those situations in which they acted as specialists toward ordinary people as clients.

Precisely because a clear-cut distinction was perceived to exist between the ordinary and the extraordinary states of mind of such "good guys" (*sain nöhör*), their neighbors were not constantly on guard against them. The problem with Gombodorj and other potential shamans was that there was only a thin wall—or none at all—between their ordinary and extraordinary states of mind. This, above all, was what made them so dangerous to be around. They might curse you, as Gombodorj possibly did to my hosts, or beat you up, as he allegedly did to everyone present on that frightful day at Baga Bilüü; or they might do something downright mad, as when Gombodorj burned down his *ger* in a fury of *agsan,* or as he does every time he indulges in his obscene abominations and mischievous "lies."

Nevertheless, some people (all of them, incidentally, male adolescents) privately confided to me that "perhaps Gombodorj is going to become a shaman one day." As yet, however, he was not quite a shaman. He was a recognized blacksmith and a recognized hunter, but he was also something more—or perhaps less—than that, namely, an inherently labile and amorphous being unable to attain any stable and singular form. In a sense, he was permanently trapped in the "very difficult phase" in which his great-grandfather had found himself caught until he became apprenticed to the old shaman. Unable to be the real shaman he was longing to be, Gombodorj was forever stuck in the process of becoming one. This marked him as a fundamentally incomplete, ambivalent, and dangerous person, who, for a combination of private and political reasons, had never learned to control his *udha,* as he ought to if he was to be a whole shaman and not just a half one.

* * *

The aim of this chapter has been to say something emblematic about the nature of shamanic agency in northern Mongolia in the late 1990s by focusing my ethnographic narrative on a single Darhad person and his eventful life. What I have presented, however, was not Gombodorj's "life story." It would certainly not have been a very complete or convincing example of a key informant's life story in the venerated tradition of autobiographical anthropology had this really been my intention.

We may, I suggest, think of the present chapter as something quite different from, and perhaps more experimental than, a conventional ethnographic biography, namely, an attempt to write the history of a certain affect or constellation of affects: the shamanic assemblage of human and nonhuman forces drawn, like clouds around the eye of a storm, to the bodies of Gombodorj and his forebears. It is, I submit, this assemblage of affects, and the cascade of intended and unintended effects sparked by the friction of this assemblage as it continually rubs against its surroundings, which defines an agency that may be called shamanic, and which, as I have argued, allows for the perpetual repetition of difference itself in Shishged social life.

Rather than telling the story of a specific individual's life in this chapter (as if the center of ethnographic narratives should always be individual human beings, chronicled through the linear and in my view therefore sometimes stale temporality of biography), I have aimed to trace the trajectory of a particular swarm of agency through its multifarious manifestations in Ulaan-Uul in the late 1990s, when transition was an all-pervasive fact of life, and the closest one came to shamans were potential ones. The fact that this assemblage of shamanic affects had a tendency to make itself visible in the bodies and minds of certain troubled and troublesome individuals should not lead us to commit the voluntaristic fallacy of assuming that they were its authors; certainly, as this chapter has shown, this was hardly how these persons or others in their milieu saw it. Instead, as we have seen, Gombodorj and the other half-shamans, were, so to speak, destined to differ. It was their predicament to be so different that they had hardly any self.

3 Layered Lands, Layered Minds

"There is a kind of uranium [*uran*] around here," a prominent hunter from Ulaan-Uul told me.

Nature [*baigal'*] contains it, and the flowers and wild animals receive it and pass it on to humans. For example, a mountain goat may have the *uran* and rest where the blueberries are growing. The blueberries receive the *uran,* and their taste and color become extremely nice. So people eat them and receive the harmful things. Their eyes become light blue and their eyesight turns bad. I think if we could avoid this influence from nature [*baigaliin nölöö*], Darhads would live for two hundred years. We are different because nature is different here. We receive many things from it—too many different things—and this makes our minds powerful and strange. What are these things? They are the many different things of nature [*yanz büriin baigaliin yum*], which influence people's minds. This is why we have shamans and the ability to curse. Some people will not admit this, but they really should, for it is part of them. Generally, people who have left here have had success; their heads work very well. During their time here, they received enough energy [*energ*] for the rest of their life. But those of us who stayed behind don't have good lives: we have received too much energy. So why don't we leave? We can't. Something is pulling us.

Perhaps not surprisingly, many Darhads who have migrated away from the Shishged entertain similar ideas. As a retired teacher living in the regional capital of Mörön said: "I am a Darhad, but I also did right in leaving my homeland. People in the Shishged are smart enough, but they can't see things through to the end" (*etsest n' hürgehgüi orhidog*). Shishged Darhads, he seemed to imply, are not "straight" (*shuluuhan*) in their minds, like Halh people are. Halh people, however, have the ability to make Darhads clearer in the head, to make them more single-minded. Said one middle-aged businessman from the (ethnically mixed) Arbulag district: "Here, Darhads are always doing well. We are the best in school, we are highly skilful, and we are hardworking. This is because we live in proximity to the Halh. In the Shishged, people do only what they feel like, which is sometimes a lot but usually very little. Here in Arbulag, the Halh leaders know to praise Darhads so they will work all the time."

Darhad persons, the central message seems to be, are out of balance, because something in their homeland is making their minds (*uhaan*) hazy and unclear. They cannot see properly. They are unable to carry things through to the end. Crucially, this "influence from nature" is strongly associated with the taiga. Thus the sources of "uranium" are all associated with the life forms of the taiga (blueberries and mountain goats), not the life forms of the steppe, such as the grasses on which the nomads' livestock feeds. Indeed, nature (*baigal'*) in the hunter's account figures as a plural and transformative concept, calling to mind the overspill of Gombodorj's and other half-shamans' minds and bodies. There are "many different things" in the taiga, we are told—"too many different things." Diversity, not unity, seems to be what the hunter's story is about, along with inherently unstable and therefore dangerous forms of power (*hüch*).

This chapter proceeds from the ethnographic fact and theoretical premise that Darhad concepts of the person cannot be understood without a careful exploration of the way people think through the landscape. Thus, many aspects of Shishged social life revolve around a spatial contrast between the taiga and the steppe, and an existential contrast between what many people take to be the two basic components of Darhad persons—the "yellow side" (*shar tal*) and the "black side" (*har tal*). The black side comprises everything that is violent, uncontrolled, harmful, morally ambiguous—and therefore shamanic. The yellow side, conversely, contains all that is peaceful, balanced, benevolent, morally unambiguous—and therefore Buddhist. Thus people often refer to shamanism as the "black religion" (*haryn shashin*) and to (Gelugpa) Buddhism as the "yellow religion" (*sharyn shashin*).

Someone might wish to think of these two "sides" as ethnic identities, for they spring from an imaginary shared by Darhads and non-Darhads as to what distinguishes the former as a "people" (*yastan*). I consider the concept of (ethnic) identity, however, to be analytically constraining if not misleading in the present context, if indeed not more generally. Not only does the term "ethnic identity" easily give rise to the dubious impression that Darhads subscribe to only one subjectivity in their relations with non-Darhads, but also it conceals the fact that Darhads see themselves as very much internally differentiated. For although both "sides" are understood to reside within each and every Darhad person, they provide a conceptual aesthetics by which Darhads distinguish among themselves. Thus every Darhad person is simultaneously black and yellow inside, but not on the outside, where certain persons (such as potential shamans like Gombodorj) stand out from others by being particularly black, while other persons (for instance, certain male elders) are prominent in a yellow way. Among Darhads, then, social agency to a large extent is derived from the way these two sides are drawn from the land, things, and people by different kinds of persons, specialist or otherwise, recognized as having the capacity to do so.

This has important ramifications for our understanding of shamanism without shamans in northern Mongolia after socialism. As we shall see, Darhads are not quite shamans in two senses. On the one hand, each individual Darhad is not quite a shaman in that he or she contains a black potential (though it is by no means always manifested as often and as violently as in incomplete shamans like Gombodorj). On the other hand, and on a different scale, Darhads as a collectivity are also not quite shamans in that half of their substance is composed of shamanic matter (the "black side"), while the other half is Buddhist (the "yellow side"). Thus Darhad personhood is fractal or self-scaling (Strathern 2004; Wagner 1991), and this must be the premise for any account of the politics of identity—if it makes sense to use this term at all—in northern Mongolia.

In what follows I lay out the complex historical process by which the "outer topography" of the Shishged landscape has become replicated in the "inner topography" of Darhad persons, as the often unintended result of different kind of "colonial" policies implemented first by the Qing or Manchu imperial polity, then by the prerevolutionary Mongolian Buddhist church, and finally by the socialist state. But I begin by describing the prevailing Darhad stereotype entertained by most people in Mongolia—a stereotype that, as we shall see, is strikingly similar to Darhads' conception of potential shamans such as Gombodorj.

The Darhad Stereotype

Darhads have a dubious reputation in Mongolia. We can identify several reasons for this. First, most people in Mongolia are aware that the Darhad homeland (*nutag*) is located in a cold, remote, forested northwestern corner of the country. Many people (wrongly) believe that all Darhads make their living from breeding reindeer, hunting, and fishing, as Duha people do. Indeed, people in Ulaanbaatar and elsewhere told me, with almost monotonous regularity, that "Darhads are not real Mongols [*jinhene Mongol bish*], for real Mongols are pastoralists." Undoubtedly this common picture is the result of a rather one-sided representation of Darhad "tradition and custom" (*yos zanshil*) in Mongolian public culture. In what is essentially a continuation of state socialist cultural politics (Bulag 1998; Marsh 2006), a steady flow of films, TV shows, newspaper articles, and cultural performances highlight the most "archaic" aspects of Darhad life, notably its shamanic faith (see also Lacaze 2000, 24–25; and Hangartner, in press). Little attention is paid to the significant role of Buddhism in Shishged history. On the contrary, Darhads are often presented as being *the* shamanic *yastan* in Mongolia, despite the fact that the revival of shamanism seems to have been more prominent among Mongolia's Buryat minority (Buyandelger 1999, 2007; Swancutt 2006, 2007).

Indeed for many non-Darhads, to visit the Shishged is to be propelled into a wild and untamed land full of unknown dangers, which nonetheless exudes a strangely compelling attraction, a sensation perhaps not unlike that which motivated the so-called itinerant lamas (*badarchid*) who spread Buddhism in the hinterlands of Mongolia (Pozdneyev 1971, 343–44). Tellingly, an English-speaking friend from Ulaanbaatar always refers to the Shishged as "The Dark Valley." Because outsiders like him do not know what to watch out for, they end up being suspicious of everything. Revealing anything about yourself is dangerous, as such information may be used to feed the jokes (*hoshin shog*) and maledictions (*haraal*) to which Darhads are supposedly prone. Thus visitors try to avoid giving any personal details to the local people (such as the names and ages of their family members) and make an effort instead to stick to the highly formalized decorum and customs (*yos*) that surround a visit to a nomadic household. During longer visits, they try to talk only about the most impersonal topics, such as the weather. Similarly, any suspicious-looking spot in the landscape is considered a potential source of harm. (As one woman warned: "Don't pick up anything from the ground here.") Examples range from lone trees on the steppe, to the impenetrable scrub growing around river pools, to the ritual cairns (*ovoo*) on mountain passes. Perhaps that pool is home to demons (*chötgörtei gazar*); perhaps the tree is a shamanic cult site (*böö mod*); and perhaps the *ovoo* harbors a land spirit (*lus savdag*). One cannot know, especially not an outsider visiting an infamous shamanic stronghold.

It is against this backdrop that we can understand the emergence of a distinct ethnic stereotype. When asked to characterize Darhads, non-Darhads tend to single out three traits: (1) all Darhads, owing to the harshness of life in their remote northern taiga, are wild, crude, and poor; (2) all Darhads are inherently shamanic and therefore have the ability to cast curses; and (3) all Darhads are inveterate jokers with uncertain and cunning intentions. This joking ability, while not necessarily a good thing, is imbued with a unique kind of efficacy. A seasoned market vendor from the regional capital of Mörön remarked:

> Darhads are a merry lot, and their company is good fun. But they are also dangerous, for they have the best shamans; one is at constant risk of being cursed up there. They are great jokers. If you stay overnight with one family, then the next morning you can be sure they will say something funny about you. Humor is their unique form of knowing things [*gants sain medleg uhaan bol shog*]. They have cunning minds. This is why they always win in business deals.

But there is a downside to these abilities, for they make it hard for people to trust those who possess them. As I was told by various people in Mörön, Darhads are not as *shuluuhan* (straight, direct) as other people are, especially the Halh, Mongolia's dominant majority, who are considered *ilen dalangüi* (earnest), *töv sanaatai* (balanced), and *töviig bar'dag* (also meaning balanced).[1] In fact the Halh have become the reference point against which the purity of all other Mongol peoples is measured. "The Halh," as Uradyn Bulag aptly puts it, have become "the indigenous Mongols, while Mongols elsewhere are semi-Mongols" (1998, 77).[2]

The inner state of Halh people, in other words, corresponds to their perceived position at the heart of Mongolia. Conversely, since Darhads do not occupy the center of the nation, their minds are not in balance either. Indeed they are seen as essentially "unbalanced" (*töviig bar'daggüi*, lit. "not holding the center"), and far from being *shuluuhan*, they are "always speaking in a roundabout way" (*dandaa toiruulj yar'dag*). Like Marilyn Strathern's Melanesian "dividuals" (1988), we could say that Darhad "minds" (*uhaan*) do not add up to a single intention, unlike the "minds" of Halh persons, whose "straightness" implies that their intentions can be condensed into a single,

---

1. As Sneath (2000, 144) notes, *töv*, whose most common meaning is "center" or "middle," also means "orthodox" and "righteous."

2. In the mid-1990s more than 80 percent of Mongolia's population was registered as Halh (Bulag 1998, 70–81). Officials estimated that 10 percent of Ulaan-Uul's inhabitants were Halh (no official figures were available). So, as Bulag writes, if, supposedly, the Halh originally constituted one *halh* (flank, shield) of the Mongolian heartland, they are now considered to be positioned at its very *gol* (core, center) (1998, 70–76).

unified will. Indeed the stem *shuluu-* forms the verb *shuluutgah* (or *shuluu-dah*), which, among other things, means "to concentrate on one aim" or "to decide completely" (Hangin 1986).

From the non-Darhad point of view, then, the Darhads' outward marginality in the Mongolian nation-state corresponds to an inward state of multiplicity: each and every Darhad person comprises a multitude within. These observations are underscored by the fact that Darhads were accused—but also secretly admired—by Halh traders in Mörön of having "layered minds" (*davhar uhaan*). Interestingly, the term *davhar,* in addition to meaning "double," "layered," or "stratified," also denotes processes of multiplication and hollowing-out (as in *biye davhar boloh,* meaning for a body to become impregnated). We seem to be faced with a concept of multiple layering, or infinite hollowness, which calls to mind the familiar Russian *matryoshka* dolls: every time you peel back a surface, another *davhar* will appear, so eventually you are faced with a "homunculus within homunculus problem," an infinite regress in which the "ultimate center can never be reached" (Gell 1998, 147). Indeed, images of multiple layers, infinite folds, and hollow surfaces pop up everywhere in Darhad social life, especially in shamanic contexts, suggesting that the concept of *davhar* is vital for understanding shamanic agency in northern Mongolia after socialism.

For many Halh, then, Darhads are not just marginal and multiple in geographic, economic, and political terms. They are also marginal and multiple in social and psychological terms. And, as we saw in chapter 2, there is in fact more than a glimmer of truth to this ethnic stereotype, at least when applied to a stigmatized person like Gombodorj, who seems as cunning to his fellow Darhads as they seem to other Mongolians. In that sense, we may think of him and other half-shamans as "hyper-Darhads"—as spectral, or more precisely fractal, figures whose individual stigmatization in Ulaan-Uul is homologous to the collective stigmatization of Darhads in general in postsocialist Mongolia. In this respect the previous chapter provided us not just with a genealogy of Gombodorj's marginality in his community but also with a genealogy (in the Foucaultian sense) of the Darhads' marginality in Mongolia as a whole.

The Black Side

Like many other marginalized people around the world, then, Darhads work hard to ensure that "the outsiders' stereotype [is] not wholly false" (Stewart 1997, 21). Even in the eyes of many people in Ulaan-Uul themselves, they are wilder, poorer, cruder, funnier, and (above all) more shamanic than the people living farther south. A couple of anecdotes illustrate this impression. Once, having for the first time been invited to a wedding in Ulaan-Uul, I asked my hosts what to expect. "Not much," the wife retorted. "Darhads are crude and harsh, and besides, we are too poor to hold weeklong weddings like the Halh." On another occasion an intoxicated young man tried to pick a fight with me. While attempting to fend him off, I asked, "But why are you attacking me?" To which he snapped: "You are a foreigner. I am a real Darhad. Therefore I must beat you up!" Above all, I was constantly reminded, jokingly and more seriously, about the special relationship between Darhad tradition (*Darhad yos*) and the shamanic religion (*böögiin shashin*). In the words of an Urianhai nomad from the westernmost reaches of the Shishged (a renowned shamanic stronghold): "I have seen much in my life, though not the entire world. But according to what I have seen, the most shamanic of all places is this. I warn you: be afraid! This is a very dangerously shamanic place [*ih ayultai böötei oron*]. You must be careful and vigilant when traveling here. The shamans want to eat your soul!"

This notion of the Darhad black side undoubtedly originates in the legendary conflict between shamans and lamas in Mongolia generally, and in the Shishged in particular (see, for example, Heissig 1980). The "yellow religion," Gombodorj liked to say—with the usual wild look in his eyes—"is weak." For whereas "the shamans drink vodka straight, the lamas mix it with water." The problem with lamas is that they "read too many books." Shamans, by contrast, are "strong" because, unlike the lamas, "they use their own bodies" (*ööriin biyeer*) to gain occult knowledge. More generally, there is a rich treasury of legends, shamanic maledictions, and ritual invocations, which play on the purported strife between shamanism and Buddhism. The following curse, for example, was cast by a renowned shamaness known as Sunchig Udgan:

Burhan burhan gedeg chin'	What is called Buddha, Buddha
Budag Shanhai hoyor	Is just some paint from Shanghai
Lam lam gedeg chin'	What are called lamas, lamas
Dönhör tolgoitoi mangasuud	Are just bigheaded monsters
Erüügee avch nuruugaa maaj	Take your chinbone and scratch your back
Elgee avch semjee oroo	Take your liver and cover it in its own fat
Darhind oruulj	Get into that fallen tree trunk
Butand buluul	And get buried in the bush
Amaa hürsen gazar mahaa urj idej	Eat as much of your flesh as you can gape over
Am'sgaa hürsen gazar tsusaa sorj uu	Suck as much of your blood as you can breathe in

This eerie curse contains a number of motifs typical of the doggedly anti-Buddhist rhetoric of some Darhad shamans. For one thing, the arrogant description of Buddha statues as mere "paint from Shanghai" underscores the shamans' claim to local authenticity, just as the insulting allusion to the lamas as "bigheaded monsters" plays on the widespread and to a large extent accurate notion that, unlike the shamans, the lamas draw their powers from reading books. More generally, the curse contains ideas, like scratching one's back with one's chinbone, that defy the naturalized social order, which for centuries dominated in Mongolia through a successful alliance between the Buddhist church and the heads of princedoms and households (Humphrey 1996; Sneath 2000, 2007). In fact, every single stanza challenges social and ontological conventions that are still taken for granted. Ordinary people, let alone lamas, are not supposed to eat their own flesh or be sacrilegiously "buried in the bush."

Indeed, the conflict between shamans and lamas is often expressed through the medium of the landscape. In a famous narrative, a female shaman is transformed into a rainbow that hovers over a valley where a caravan of lamas visiting the Ih Shav' is passing through. The lamas are terrified: the rainbow-shaman is defiling them, for what they see is the gigantic underside of a menstruating woman. Only when a high-ranking lama is summoned to cast a spell does the monstrous sight go away (Dulam 1992, 76; see also Humphrey 1996, 131–32). Consider also the following tale, presented here in the version originally collected by the Hungarian ethnographer László Diószegi in the late 1950s (I have been told the same story several times, but never with quite the same amount of detail and vividness):

> The Darkhat *xüree* (i.e. the Darkhat monastery) was established some 200 years ago. It was then near the Ivdiyn-gol. But the lamas fell ill, one after the other. A simple Khalkha lama lived in the monastery, and he said once that a *shulmas* (evil spirit) was strolling above the *xüree* and that the diseases were due to him. As long as the *shulmas* did not disappear—so he went on—the monastery would remain impure. But nobody heeded the warning of the simple lama. However, not long thereafter, a *xamb lam* (i.e. a Buddhist "bishop") also said that a *shulmas* was in the habit of descending through the eastern valley and it was she who has no peace, and that we should have troubles as long as she was continuing to stalk us. Being unable to destroy the female shaman, they decided to transfer the monastery to another place. Since shamanism was flourishing in the region where this *xüree* had been erected, they removed it to the east, beyond the present "sumun" of Rinchinlhumbe. Before having transferred the monastery they succeeded in destroying the female shaman nevertheless. When she descended in the eastern gorge, the lama managed to capture her, and she was put in a sac [*sic*]. The female shaman began leaping

in the sac. Opening it they found no female but a *chitkür* (devil): he had a round figure. They threw him into the stove. He began to skip there. So they took him out and interred him. Upon this, the lama calmed down and said they had destroyed all *chitkürs*. It was then that they moved to the second place. But this transfer of the monastery does not seem to have improved things since the shamans continued to make trouble in the new place as well. The *xüree* was then removed once more, to a place north of Rinchinlhumbe where it remained until 1937 when the government had it pulled down.

(Diószegi 1961, 202; parenthetical explanations are original, bracketed interpolations are my own)

The Yellow Side

Turning now to the concept of the yellow side, we find that things look very different. No warnings about disturbing "influences of nature" figure here, for on the yellow side, Shishged nature is particularly untainted. Indeed, life is calm, peaceful, and beautiful. Darhads figure as a chosen people, whose path through history has earned them the right (*erh darh*) to feel superior to, or at least purer and more unique than, other Mongol groups. Undoubtedly this discourse of positive alterity, as one might call it, is grounded in the Darhad people's historical status as Buddhist disciples of the Jebtsundamba Khutuktu, and in the complex semantics of their ethnonym, which, among other things, allows for an interpretation in which the term "Darhad" denotes an honorific title bestowed by Genghis Khan himself.[3]

It is written in the Secret History that Genghis Khan's forefathers crossed the river Tengis and also how Genghis himself traveled around a river called Irmegen Gün. And indeed we have in the north of our *nutag* a great river called Tengis, just as toward the south there is a river called Gün. Halh are wrong in thinking about us as half-Mongols. On the contrary, "Darhad" is a special title that was bestowed on people who were close to Genghis Khan. This is why we enjoy a special protection

3. A popular belief is that the old Darhad Sharnuud clan is an offshoot of the Five Hundred Yellow Darhad Families of the Principal Shrine, who, since Kublai Khan (1226–1294), were protectors of the shrine of Genghis Khan in Inner Mongolia (see Badamhatan 1986, 47–49; Even 1988–89, 106–9). Most scholars would agree with Atwood, however, that "these Darkhad have no relation to the Darkhad of Northern Mongolia" (2004, 162).

from Heaven (Tenger). For example, when a thunderstorm strikes, we cry to Heaven: We are the Yellow People [*Bid sharnuud*]! Then Tenger will protect us from the lightning. This has to do with the story of the five hundred yellow Darhads, who protected Genghis Khan's national *ongon* [ancestor spirit], his armor, and so on.

Before Genghis Khan first came here with his army, it was a wild land [*ezengüi gazar;* lit. "a land without any master"]. The soldiers were struggling to climb the Öl mountain pass. Thick, impenetrable forest covered everything, making passage into our homeland impossible. But Genghis ordered the trees to go away, and a path across the mountain was created for his troops. But one tree refused to obey. Until a couple of years ago, the tree was still there, right at the top. People used to say that every time you go by the Öl Pass, you must stop at the tree and kick it as hard as you can!

This narrative which was related to me by a former teacher of Mongolian history, and which effectively combines well-known historical events with more mythical themes, has an unmistakable message.[4] Around the birth of the Mongol Empire, the virgin land of the Shishged was opened to the south, and this created a passage into the heart of the Mongol nation that has remained to this day, but only because people make an effort to keep it open, as when they remind themselves to punish the disobedient tree.

So if the concept of the black side highlights classic shamanic traits such as crudeness, violence, and witchcraft, the concept of the yellow side offers an alternative image in which the Darhad homeland is conceived as a religious and political center on account of its close association with the Buddhist church and the founding fathers of the Mongolian nation. Yet there is a twist, for Darhads are generally not capable of gaining this important insight themselves. Thus, I was told, Darhads need to be seen in order to see their inner yellowness. Consider this story, told to me in several versions over the years:

Many years ago a Tibetan lama came here. When he reached the Öliin Davaa, what he saw was breathtaking. He exclaimed: "This is a land

---

4. In fact, the name Tengis figures in the opening paragraphs of the *Secret History of the Mongols:* "There was a bluish wolf which was born having (his) destiny from Heaven above. His spouse was a fallow doe. They came, passing over the Tenggis" (Cleaves 1982, 1). The established scholarly convention, however, is that Tengis here refers to a "sea" or "lake," and not to the river Tengis, which flows across the northern portion of the Shishged.

of happiness. White merit [*tsagaan buyan*] emanates from the three White Animals: the Darhad White Sheep, the Darhad White Fish, and the Darhad White Horse." The merit of the White Sheep stems from its tail, which is bigger and fatter than any Halh sheep's. The White Fish has healing powers from the Shishged River: when it is pulled out of the water, it shines like gold. Now to the story about the Darhad White Horse. Once there was a man who was gravely ill. Shamans had been called in, but to no avail. Aware that his friend was about to travel to Urga, the sick man sent for him. "Take this gold and buy me medicine," he said, handing his friend a muddy stone. But no one wanted to sell the friend the medicine when he arrived in the capital city, for all he had to pay with was the stone. Desperate, he went to see the Bogd Khan. The Bogd weighed the stone in his hands, knocked it against the wall, and said: "Yes, this *is* gold. I will now tell you the cure. Back in your home-land there is the Darhad White Horse. Your friend should drink the mare's milk (*airag*) three times a day and eat the mutton of the Darhad White Sheep. Then he shall be cured."

Relieved, the man gave the stone to the Bogd Khan and returned home. Arriving empty-handed, he was scolded by his bedridden friend for not having brought medicine. He delivered the Bogd's advice, only to be told off: his ill friend had already consumed huge amounts of *airag* to no effect. Eventually the friend's health deteriorated further, so he decided to heed the advice nevertheless. And behold, after nine days he did start feeling better, and one month later he had completely regained his health. The other man, meanwhile, had been worried: might his sick friend be dead? Then one day, while he was relaxing inside his *ger,* his children shouted: "Dad, three horsemen are arriving!"

"Oh no," he thought, "this is it. They are coming for me." As he stepped outside, his heart sank still further as he saw three horsemen dismount and approach him. But, wait, it was his old friend who was running to him, shouting: "Look! The cure worked!"

Narratives like this lend themselves to multiple interpretations, but here I want to focus on the fact that neither the Tibetan lama nor the Bogd Khan brings anything to the Shishged that was not already there. The lama only makes explicit in words what existed before he arrived, namely, the blessing of the three Darhad White Animals. Similarly, the Bogd Khan suggests a cure that was already available, the healing milk of the Darhad White Horse. The stone's composite nature of mud and gold carries the same message. Only the sick man (perhaps because he is near death) glimpses its hidden value;

Figure 11. Mörön statue of Prince Chingünjav, eighteenth-century rebel-hero

everyone else needs the Bogd Khan to rub off the mud and thereby make its purity visible.

Attraction and extraction, it thus seems to me, is what this narrative (and several other similar ones) are essentially about. The Darhads were attracting the Buddhists to come, for their land contains a superior whiteness (or yellowness) that was irresistible to them.[5] The attractor, however, is not always aware of its attraction. The Darhads and their landscape in general need someone to bring out their latent attraction, as when the White Fish is pulled out of the water only to flash in the sun, or when a core of pure gold is revealed inside a dirty stone. But it was all there from the beginning. The white blessing was already inside the animals, and the stone was already made of gold; it was only that these hidden qualities had to be extracted by someone with the power to do so. This is the overarching message of the present narrative, as perhaps it also was in the Genghis Khan legend I related.

5. In Mongolia, the color white—symbolizing purity—tends to be symbolically subsumed under yellow, which symbolizes Buddhism.

Inner Topographies into Outer Topographies

As the narratives show, the Shishged landscape has always been a testing ground for the conflict between black (shamanic) forces and yellow (Buddhist/Genghizid) forces, as if these two Darhad "sides" cannot—or at least would prefer not to—meet in an open fight. In that sense, as I shall now demonstrate, the Shishged landscape plays a key role in Darhad concepts of the person by providing an exterior surface onto which the many layers of Darhad minds can, so to speak, be mapped. In a quite literal sense, therefore, moving across the Shishged landscape is akin to unearthing the hidden folds of people's inner topographies.

The opening passages of this chapter described how, for many Darhads, the taiga has the same composition that Darhads have in the eyes of many non-Darhad outsiders, namely, a multitude of concealing layers. The inner complexity of Darhad persons is, so to speak, outfolded onto the taiga, just as the "many different things" that make up the Shishged landscape are enfolded back into themselves in the form of an infinity within. This, I think, is what the so-called influence from nature is about. It certainly is telling that the term *uran* is used to convey the much-feared effects of this influence. Uranium, after all, is known for its instability, and for its harmful effects on its surroundings.[6] *Uran*, I suggest, offers a particularly good trope for expressing an idea shared by many Darhads, namely, that the taiga is a source of transformation, of mutation (of one's vision, for example), and above all, of multiplicity.

Given this background, we may think of the taiga as a "distributed mind," since the source of people's agency is not confined to their physiological bodies but extends into the landscape, as is the case with shells and other valuables exchanged in the famous Kula gift exchange of the Trobriand Islands and in many other Melanesian contexts (Gell 1998). Thus understood, the blueberries and other "radioactive" agents of the taiga emerge as Kula-like objectifications of a shamanic potential residing inside all Darhads. This in turn implies that Darhad persons can, so to speak, exorcise their black side by staying away from the taiga and its dangerous substances.

Indeed, the pancake-flat grasslands that define the Darhad Depression proper are considered the peaceful (*taivan*) place par excellence in the

---

6. In case the reader wonders precisely how the concept of uranium has entered the shamanic imagination in northern Mongolia, I should add that the same hunter who told me about the radioactive blueberries in the taiga took a keen interest in the many articles about science fiction and scientist ideas that appeared in Mongolian newspapers in the 1990s. Indeed, several people compared the Shishged to the world-famous Bermuda Triangle. "Both places are full of invisible forces that cause things to break down," a retired geologist from Mörön once explained to me while trying to fix his car en route to Tsagaan Nuur.

Shishged. It is where the pastoralists nomadize; and it is where the wild predators usually do not go—though not always, as Gombodorj and his family
learned the hard way. And it is where everyone supposedly enjoys a carefree
existence in the short but bounteous (*elbeg*) summer (as long as they are not
interrupted by hordes of drunken youth). Above all, the steppe is not associated with shamans and shamanic spirits as the taiga is. It is true that the taiga
encroaches from all sides, but one does not need to venture there unless one
is a hunter—or a shaman. Of course, children go there with their mothers to
pick berries in early autumn, just as the men go for an occasional hunt when
the first snow falls. But essentially, if one is an ordinary pastoralist or villager,
one tends to spend one's time within the seemingly safe micro-cosmos of the
Darhad Depression, leaving its dubious and dangerous margins (referring
here not just to the taiga but to the urban centers to the south as well) to a
range of marginal personae, such as shamans, hunters, and female suitcase
traders. (For more about these traders, see Pedersen 2006a.)

What makes life on the steppe so relaxed (*chölöötei*) compared to life in
the taiga (and indeed the city) is that things tend to add up. Unlike wild
animals (and wares sold at black markets), livestock (*mal*) can be gathered,
counted, compared, and priced according to the so-called livestock unit or
bod. (One *bod* equals one horse, cow, yak, or *hainag*, a yak-cow hybrid; two-
thirds of a camel; seven sheep; or ten goats.)[7] Even the often Buddhisized
spirits of the steppe can be measured, or classified, according to their position in an encompassing cosmic order, which is what the lamas and the local
leaders who assist them seek to do or affirm in the annual *ovoo* rites held in
some Shishged districts (discussed in greater detail later on).[8]

The problem with the entities of the taiga, by contrast, is that they do not
fit into any such quantification regime, and therefore do not lend themselves
to the same degree of political, economic, and spiritual management. For
example, unlike meat from domestic animals, meat from the hunt (*angiin
mah*) is never sold—or so the hunters say. In this specific sense, it is like the
intestines (*gedes*) of freshly slaughtered livestock, to which the same rule applies, if for the much more mundane reason of preventing it from rotting.

---

7. All herds in the Shishged, along with the corresponding nomadic households, are subject
to biannual counts by *bag* leaders, as they were during the socialist period, when even more frequent surveys were a cornerstone in the ongoing adjustment of production quotas in different
productive units within *negdels*.

8. In that sense, the process of establishing economic equivalence between different species
of domestic animals emerges as analogous to the civilizing process of "straightening out Darhad
people's minds," as described by a wealthy businessman from Arbülag. Both processes seem to
involve a gathering of dispersed entities (animals, intentions) to make them commensurable by
bringing them under a single, quantified scale.

Instead, *angiin mah* and *gedes* are distributed to kinsmen, friends, and neighbors according to the principle of "demand-sharing" that is well-known from many hunter-gatherer societies (Peterson 1993), whereby people simply turn up at the donor's home expecting to receive a share. But whereas the flow of *gedes* over time adds up to a reciprocal, balanced transaction (every household regularly slaughters livestock and distributes *gedes,* and all portions are considered essentially identical), *angiin mah* does not. For one thing, some households never distribute *angiin mah* (perhaps the men do not hunt, or there are no men). Also, no portion of *angiin mah* is similar to another, for there are many different species of game, and no two animals of the same species are identical. Thus hunting meat, like occult specialists and their actions, is considered unique: every portion is an ontological singularity. As in the case of two shamans fighting, the portions of meat passed between households over time (or presented in compensation) are not mutually equivalent, as they retain their *sodon* quality even after the exchange, imbued as they are with unique capacities for curing and for inflicting harm.[9]

In short, the taiga constitutes everything that the steppe does not; but unlike in traditional oppositions between "nature" and "culture" in anthropology, all the implied contrasts between people and animals, and between different kinds of people, are asymmetrical. No entities or persons associated with the taiga—whether shamans, hunters, predators, berries, or spirits—add up to a common point of unity, for every single one of them constitutes a unique entity or singularity, thus defining the taiga as a zone of pure multiplicity. Entities of the steppe, conversely, can be made equivalent to and hierarchically encompassed by one another—like the informal leaders responsible for their management.

It is precisely this asymmetry, I suggest, that allows native Darhads to use the steppe zone to accomplish what moving away has done for the migrant Darhads mentioned earlier in the chapter, namely, to escape from "all the different things" associated with the taiga zone. The steppe provides a spatial refuge where people can live beyond the reach of the shamanic "influence from nature." But how did this refuge come into being? Why is the steppe so peaceful and the taiga so dangerous? To get to the bottom of these questions, we need to explore in some detail the strange and fascinating ecclesiastical

9. The contrast between "wild" and "tame" meat is not as clear-cut as this brief discussion may suggest. For one thing, the meat from domestic animals is divided into categories with specific alimentary and medical properties, many of which are gender- and age-specific (see also Badamhatan 1986, 119–21). Second, pelts constituted an important taxable item in the Ih Shav' period (the unit of equivalence being *seveg,* or "tea baskets"), and this old quantification regime seem to have continued, and greatly expanded, within the *negdel* with the general collectivization of the hunting economy (Badamhatan 1986, 28–34).

institution known as the Darhad Ih Shav', which governed the Shishged and its inhabitants for more than two hundred years. At the same time, this will allow us to take stock of the fate of Buddhism in the Shishged during both socialism and its aftermath.

The Darhad Ih Shav' (1749–1921)

From the mid-seventeenth until the early twentieth century, most of Outer Mongolia was divided into numerous "banners" (*hoshuu*) or princedoms ruled by local Mongolian princes (*taij*) or other noblemen (*noyod*), who in turn deferred to Manchu officials directly appointed by the imperial court in Beijing, in accordance with the divide-and-rule principle introduced by the Qing colonial masters following the loss of Outer Mongolian independence in 1688. In addition to a secular population of pastoralist commoners and slaves, most banners were home to one or more Buddhist monasteries (*hiid*) headed by senior Mongolian lamas, some of whom bore the title indicating holy reincarnation (*hutagt*). While subsumed under the secular imperial-aristocratic order, and while engaged in informal power-sharing arrangements with the local nobles, these Buddhist estates often operated as largely independent economic if not political units, with their own ecclesiastical subjects (*shabinar*), their own herds, and their own administrative structures.

The Shishged, however, differed from this picture in a number of ways. First of all, in deference to its inhabitants' privileged status as subjects or disciples (*shabinar*) within the private estate of Mongolia's leading Buddhist reincarnation, the Jebtsundamba Khutuktu, it fell under the direct jurisdiction of his ecclesiastical administration in Urga, which, among other things, freed the inhabitants from having to provide corvée labor and taxes to both aristocratic and imperial masters; indeed there were no *taij* in the Shishged. What is more, the Darhad Ih Shav' (the Great Darhad Buddhist Estate), as the region and its inhabitants were known, must have been the most important of the Jebtsundamba Khutuktu's estates, and thus a front line in the tense relationship between the Mongolian Buddhist church and the Manchu colonial masters.[10] Indeed, as Charles Bawden notes, the Jebtsundamba Khutuktu "did not control actual territory, apart from the pastures of the

---

10. As Atwood explains: "The Great Shabi of the Jibzundamba Khutugtu constituted the personal subjects of the Great Incarnate Lama.…Shabi 'disciples' was the general term for monastic serfs; the estate of the Jibzundamba Khutugtu, being by far the largest in [Outer Mongolia], was called the 'Great Shabi'" (2004, 210–11; see also 268; Badamhatan 1986, 133).

Darkhat in the far north-west of Mongolia" (1986, 69). Finally, the Shishged was situated inside the politically ambiguous borderland (*hyazgaar*) between the Manchu and Russian empires (Ewing 1981), which, among other things, meant that it was uncharacteristically open to Russian (as well as Tuvinian and Buryat) influences, and that it was virtually sealed off from the rest of Outer Mongolia; indeed without permission from the relevant authorities, it was illegal to cross the border from the four Halh *aimags* to the south (Badamhatan 1986, 26).

So while the Shishged was part of the Qing colony in Outer Mongolia, the Buddhist church was its de facto sovereign for nearly two hundred years. More than anywhere else in Mongolia, this fact allows us to interpret the religious and political reforms imposed by the Mongolian Buddhists in this remote locality in light of the Lamaist discourse of "domestication," which has been discussed at great length in the Tibetan context but hardly at all in any recent writings on Mongolian Buddhism (see Bareja-Starzynska and Havnevik 2006; Barkmann 1997; Blondeau and Steinkellner 1996; MacDonald 1997; Pedersen 2007b; Siklos 1991). I am referring to the norm that, when Tibetan or Mongolian lamas are faced for the first time with what they consider to be a wild yet pristine land untainted by civilization, its inhabitants must be incorporated into the Buddhist pantheon of gods, submit to its ideas of samsara, karma, and rebirth, and become subject to the management of the church and its lamas (Hyer and Jagchid 1983, 88–99; Samuel 1993, 148). As Charles Ramble puts it, "the aspiration of Tibetan religious ideology is to eliminate wilderness by subjugating it" (1997, 133). My aim here is to explore the dynamics of this subjugation in northern Mongolia, and more specifically in the Shishged context.

I suggest that the nearly two hundred–year existence of the Darhad Ih Shav' laid the groundwork for current perceptions of the Shishged steppe zone as a safe haven, for the political and religious interventions of the Buddhist estate not only turned this landscape into one unified space but also made it possible to think of Darhads as a people. As we shall see, with the gradual institutionalization of the Darhad Ih Shav' in the eighteenth and nineteenth centuries, an all-encompassing spatial vantage point came into being, which, for the first time in history, subsumed all its spiritual entities under one cosmological umbrella, just as we may speak of the presence of a single political body that for the first time administered all the different social groupings living in the Shishged.

It is reasonable to assume that the Darhad Ih Shav' was the product of a wider alliance between Mongolia's Buddhist church and its Halh factions toward the end of the seventeenth century with the aim of imposing political stability on the Cis-Hövsgöl region of northern Mongolia, which had at this point suffered from unrest for centuries. More precisely, the 1686 allocation of most of the Shishged territory and its different groupings to the Jebtsundamba Khutuktu at the Khuren Belchir Assembly must be understood in light of contemporary attempts to strike a power balance between the Halh khanates and their Manchu overlords, to whom they had voluntarily submitted in a desperate attempt to halt the advances of their Jungar or Oirat (western Mongolian) enemies.[11]

Since 1668 the Cis-Hövsgöl region had been at the center of the war raging with the Oirats. There is no doubt that the de facto establishment of the Darhad Ih Shav' in 1749 altered life in the Shishged beyond recognition.[12] The very political entity known as the "Darhad people" is a case in point. According to Christopher Atwood, the Darhads "received the[ir] name when the Khalkha Mongolian nobleman Deleg and his lady, Dejid Akhai, gave themselves and their subjects to the first Jibzundamba Khutuktu (1635–1723). From then on they...were exempt from state requisitions" (2004, 132). So, even if we (as some Darhads like to think of themselves) assume that a clan with this name could be found in northern Mongolia before the creation of the Darhad Ih Shav' at Khuren Belchir, it is clear that this group was infused with individuals from other ethnic or political collectivities to become what were called Darhad serfs (*Darhad shabinar*) (Atwood 2004, 132; Badamhatan 1986, 62–63). Indeed it could be argued that the concept of Buddhist domestication is inscribed in the polyvalent semantics of the Darhad ethnonym itself. Among other things, the word *darhan* (pl. *darhad*) denotes someone or something that is "sacred," "protected," "exempted," and—interestingly—"an area set aside for religious reasons or rites" (Hangin et al. 1986).[13]

It is not entirely clear how many monasteries the Darhad Ih Shav' contained at different times in its history. Several monasteries were relocated owing to conflicts with local shamans, or, during the Russian Civil War, with invading warlords from the White Army (Pürev 1980, 46–48). It is, however,

---

11. I specify "most of" the Shishged territory, as the so-called Ar Shirhten Urianhai banner, which comprised the two westernmost *bags* of today's Ulaan-Uul district, fell under the direct jurisdiction of the Qing-appointed governor in Uliastai, and therefore was not part of the Darhad Ih Shav' (Ewing 1981; Wheeler 2000).

12. Apparently the Darhads made a forced migration to the Selenge region in north-central Mongolia during this period (Badamhatan 1986, 25, 44–45; Badamhatan and Banzragch 1981, 13–15).

13. In addition to "sacred" and "protected," the word *darhan* has at least two other meanings, primarily (1) "smith," "artisan," or "craftsman," and (2) "freeman" or "to be free." Thus the term was "traditionally used to refer to those men who had a right to keep plunder that they took personally in war or to keep game that they killed personally. They were not compelled to share as was common" (Jagchid and Hyer 1979, 287–88). According to Atwood, the "Darkhad name means 'Exempt Ones' (cf. Middle Mongolian *darqan*)" (2004, 132).

reasonably certain that the first monastery dates back to 1757. This was the Zöölöngiin Hüree (also known as the Darhadyn, Renchinlhümbe, or Revüü Gerje Gandannamjilan Hüree), which was to become the religious, administrative, and commercial center of the Darhad Ih Shav' for the next 175 years or so. As the tale related by Diószegi more than hints, however, the monastery was relocated a number of times. Initially it was built at the river mouth called Ivdiin Am, which is located in the present-day Soyot subdistrict of the Ulaan-Uul district in the area known as Behiin Suur'. But partly for religious reasons and partly for practical ones, it was later relocated in two stages to Tovogiin and Tasarhain Khash, respectively, finally finding its base northeast of the Shishged's geographical center, near the present-day Renchinlhümbe district center, Zöölön. As the decades passed, this religious and political center grew ever larger, partly as a result of the continual sponsoring of new temples (*aimag, datsan, dugan*) and prayer halls (*hurlyn öröö*) by different patrons, some local men of wealth, and other high-ranking lamas from the capital of Urga/Ih Hüree (now Ulaanbaatar).

From 1788 to 1821 the office of the Jebtsundamba Khutuktu in Ih Hüree governed its Darhad estate as a single *otog* (the ecclesiastical equivalent of the *hoshuu,* the basic administrative unit in Qing Mongolia), which was known as the Black Darhad Shav'. At some point between 1821 and 1855 it underwent an administrative reform which turned it into the Darhad Ih Shav'. It was reorganized into three *otogs,* known as the East, West, and North *otogs,* each administered by a secular *otog* leader (*otogiin darga*), who was ultimately subsumed within the Buddhist ecclesiastical hierarchy in which the *hamba lam* (abbot) represented the local pinnacle (Legrand 1976, 81–82; Vreeland 1962, 11–23). Every year a delegation led by a *zaisan* (a kind of governor) was dispatched by the Jebtsundamba Khutuktu to check on his northern estate (Atwood 2004, 132; Badamhatan 1980, 26).

Not surprisingly, the establishment of this tripartite administrative structure was followed by the introduction of a tripartite monastic structure as well. Thus in 1880 a second monastery was constructed at a place called Tsaram, but was soon relocated to Burgaltai, named after the river in the Shishged of the same name. This monastery was moved once more to its permanent location south of the Hög River, although it kept its former name, the Burgaltai Hüree. In 1890 a third monastery was established, which, around the beginning of the twentieth century, was then also moved to the river mouth of Ivdiin Am. Henceforth this third monastery was known as the Ivdiin Hiid. Finally, two smaller prayer temples (*hurlyn dugan*) were at some point constructed to the north of the Zöölön monastery, namely, the Töhiin Hural and the Mandalyn Hural. For more than a century, then, the Zöölön monastery was the indisputable center of Shishged social life. By its heyday around 1900,

Figure 12. The Zöölön monastery. Early-twentieth-century drawing by Tseveenii Dondiv, from the collection of the late Otgony Pürev; photo by Laurent Legrain

it had grown to accommodate between 700 and 1,200 lamas (Badamhatan 1986, 26–30), most of whom were recruited locally.[14] It was, from all the accounts I have heard, an extraordinary place (for details, see Pedersen 2011). Situated on the extreme northern fringe of the Qing Empire, the Zöölöngiin Hüree was a bastion of Buddhist enlightenment, learning, and the arts, made even more prominent by its association with the Jebtsundamba Khutuktu.

At the beginning of the twentieth century, then, there were five or six Buddhist monastic sites in the Shishged, all located within the territory of the Ih Shav'.[15] If one were to plot them on a map, something resembling a star-shaped figure would emerge. This suggests that there might have been a design behind the location of monastic sites. Of course, pragmatic reasons may account for their location, just as a variety of contingent religious factors should also be taken into account, such as the possibility that the sites were determined by divinations carried out in situ, by the nature of the flow

14. The people I spoke to as well as other sources suggest that most lamas in the Ih Shav' were Darhads, though the Zöölöngiin Hüree was apparently also home to some Buryat lamas (Sandschejew 1930, 24).

15. According to Maidar (1971, 56–61), there was also a sixth monastic site in the Shishged at the time.

of streams, and so forth.[16] Still, one cannot help noticing the similarities with the mandala image or "cosmogram" (Samuel 1993), which plays a key role in many Indo-Tibetan religious and political traditions (Samuel 1993, 235–36; Snellgrove 1997, 198–213).[17] The Zöölön monastery, it seems, was the center of a condensed "yellow" micro-cosmos, and its four adjacent monastic sites were satellites, replicating (if never to a perfect degree) the properties of the center. The question remains, however, whether these satellites had self-similar satellites in *their* vicinities, as one would expect from a proper mandala in the Indo-Tibetan tradition.

A Magic Circle

If the strategic positioning of monasteries was one way in which the Buddhist church sought to transform the Shishged landscape and its "wild" inhabitants in accordance with its overarching goal of domestication, then the tactical incorporation of preexisting sacred sites was another. The written sources and people's accounts make it clear that by the mid-nineteenth century, the institution of the Ih Shav' had taken over the management of most of the prominent sacred sites within the Shishged Depression proper. In particular, the sacred stone cairns (*ovoos*) appear to have represented a prized item of Buddhist subjugation.

Across the Mongolian cultural zone, *ovoos* have since time immemorial been constructed at places believed to be the abode of "land masters" (*gazryn ezed*), spiritual entities that are considered responsible for the natural conditions (such as rainfall, disease, and fertility) on which human and animal life are dependent. The typical *ovoo* consists of a cairn of stones, although in forested regions like the Shishged they are sometimes made from tree branches. *Ovoos* traditionally were associated with the reproduction of different kinship groupings (clans) and administrative units (banners), whose male members performed annual sacrificial rites at *ovoo* sites. They have always been subject to more commonplace ritual acts as well. When people travel, they should ideally stop at any major *ovoo* encountered on the way. The traveler must then pick up three stones and circumambulate the *ovoo* three times in a clockwise direction, each time throwing a stone at the *ovoo* and perhaps

---

16. A. Hürelbaatar, personal communication.
17. A mandala is a series of concentric circles and squares around a sacred center; but within each of these are smaller centers, essentially replicating the properties of the larger one. Mandalas, then, are self-scaling or post-plural entities, which, being a kind of of verticalized fractal, "replicate their configuration...through all changes of scale" (Wagner 1991, 166).

saying a prayer. (For a detailed phenomenological analysis of these spatial practices, see Pedersen 2009.)

With the spread of (Gelugpa) Buddhism in Mongolia, which accelerated in the sixteenth century, the authority to conduct *ovoo* ceremonies was widely transferred to lamas, who took over the ritual roles previously performed by male elders and shamans (Heissig 1980, 103–5; Humphrey 1995; Sneath 2000, 235). The Shishged is a case in point. Badamhatan writes that in 1855 the Ih Shav' contained twenty-six *züünii ovoo* and twenty-four *hiliin ovoo*, the former serving "monastic purposes" and the latter "demarcating the border" to the different political entities neighboring this ecclesiastical estate (1980, 24). We do not know how many of these *ovoos* existed before the Ih Shav', but probably the majority did, as they are bound to have played a vital role in the social reproduction of local clan-like groupings (Even 1991). It is therefore reasonable to assume that as different indigenous as well as migrant groups were incorporated into the administrative structure of the Ih Shav', their places of worship were also domesticated, as lamas took over the ritual roles previously conducted by local leaders at these sacred sites.

As elsewhere in Mongolia (Heissig 1980), the *ovoos* did not lose their pre-Buddhist significance in the process. It seems that a variety of former shamanic cult sites became subsumed under the standardized liturgical forms imposed by the Buddhist church, just as the local leaders were rendered subject to the equally standardized bureaucratic structures introduced by the secular arm of the Darhad Ih Shav'. Consider as an example of this push toward political and religious homogenization the case of the North Otog, where, I was told, a high-ranking lama from the Ivd monastery would preside over all the annual *ovoo* ceremonies that took place within this administrative unit. Given that a whole range of different clans and clan-like groupings must have lived within its territory, the North Otog, like the two other *otogs*, is likely to have contained a large number of *ovoos* as well. This suggests that in the same way the *darga* of this *otog* subsumed under his authority the diversity of humans (households, clans) within its territory, its head lama assumed leadership of the multitude of nonhumans residing within the same territory. In that sense, the North Otog and the Ivd monastery fulfilled the same encompassing role toward the different life forms in its territory as did the center of the Ih Shav' and the Zöölön monastery toward them. Seen in this light, this *otog* constituted a center in its own right with various satellites in its vicinity, thus suggesting that the fractal properties of the mandala were indeed replicated on a smaller scale.[18]

18. No sources confirm that a mandala framework was imposed on the Shishged. Nevertheless, certain indications suggest that it was used as a model for the location of monasteries, such as the fact that there were apparently five such sites (Snellgrove 1997, 201).

Can we conclude, then, that the Buddhist church succeeded in turning the Shishged into "an enclosure, not necessarily circular, which separates a sacred area from the profane world" (Snellgrove 1997, 198)? This would require a point of view from which this encompassment could be seen (or imagined to be seen), that is, a vantage point from where the entirety of the Darhad Ih Shav' could be apprehended in a mandala-like way. Indeed, it appears that the *ovoo* called Jargalant, which is also known as the Zöölön Ovoo, played the role of such an imaginative vista. This *ovoo* was—and still is—located on a hilltop close to the geographical center of the Shishged. As locals never fail to tell visitors, this is "the only place from where it is possible to see the whole Shishged." At this site, I was told, seven lamas from the Zöölön monastery used to perform an important annual ceremony.

First, the lamas would visit a small island in the middle of a holy lake (probably Deed Tsagaan Nuur). Here they would make offerings and read prayers to seven larch trees named for the stars in the Great Bear constellation. They would then climb a nearby hill, on whose peak towered the Jargalant Ovoo. In keeping with convention, only the lamas themselves were allowed to go all the way to the top. The laymen participating in the ritual were left behind on a plateau below (and, in what appears to be characteristic for the time, the women were not allowed to participate in the event at all). The seven lamas then performed an *ovoo* sacrificial rite (*ovoony tahilga*), in which offerings, sutra readings, and beckonings were made for the local land master. Finally, a big celebration (*naadam*) was held on the plateau, in which subjects from across the Shishged region participated.

In much the same way that the invention of the printed map facilitated imagining the European states as unified nations (Anderson 1991), the Jargalant Ovoo played the role of a spatial technology from which the Shishged steppe was imagined as a container of sacred space, as it still is. Charles Ramble has reached the same conclusion in the Tibetan-Nepalese context. He writes:

> Places and divinities [are] organised around [a] central point in the basic form of a *mandala*. But the pattern is not universal, since not everything that undergoes organization by the site conforms to the spatial distribution suggested by this scheme. It is rather as if the pattern that formed around the site were, like a *mandala* in the most general sense, a magic circle that changed everything that came within its perimeter. The changes are thus not uniform but in accordance with *possibilities of form* offered by the nature of the quantities concerned: divinities are ranked hierarchically, stray events find themselves drawn into a unifying narrative, rocks are accorded resemblances to suitable subjects, and wildlife becomes tame. (1997, 134; emphasis added)

Buddhist domestication projects, in other words, do not give rise to perfect real-life mandalas but rather create transformations within already existing "possibilities of form." In fact, if we take Ramble's insight to its logical conclusion, it is in many ways beside the point whether the Shishged landscape was "really meant" to be transformed in this manner or not. What matters first of all is that this particular environment, with its characteristic "hollow" topography, must have presented the Mongolian lamas with perfect "possibilities of form" through which they might carry out their domestication agenda.[19]

The mission was never completed, however. The perimeter of the magic circle drawn by the lamas never did reach into the depths, or even the edges, of the taiga. The frequent relocation of monasteries described in the passage from Diószegi cited earlier serves as an important reminder of this. It is obvious that, had the lamas not met such fierce resistance from the local shamans and associated "demons," monastic relocations like these would not have been necessary. We can therefore understand these monastic movements, and the traces they have left in the landscape, as indices of the shifting balance of power between shamanism and Buddhism in the eighteenth and nineteenth centuries. Diószegi's narrative speaks of the earliest years of the Ih Shav', a time when the only Buddhist institution in the Shishged was a tiny temple inhabited by a single lama, which had to be moved closer to the steppe, as "shamanism was flourishing" where it was first built. Then, as the Ih Shav' became more established, its activities were expanded farther toward the taiga, so that, in the late 1890s, the Ivd monastery was (re)built at the same spot from which the Darhad (Zöölön) monastery had originally been moved.

But this was also to be the maximum extent of the Darhad Ih Shav'. The taiga was mostly left for the shamans and hunters to deal with. Just as in similar cases in Tibet, the Buddhist "domestication" or "subjugation" of the Shishged landscape was never completed. Since then, the relationship between shamans and lamas has been a vexed one, ranging from open conflict to uneasy coexistence. For example, before the 1921 revolution, decades of bitter strife gave way to an occult division of labor between the lamas and the shamans. In particular during the reign of the last Hamba Lam of the Zöölön monastery, the legendary D. Molomdagva (1837–1921),

19. In many ways, the Shishged is a natural whole. Or, one could say, it constitutes a natural hole, namely, the hollow in the taiga within which Darhads live. This is no mere play on words, for the Mongolian term for "basin" or "depression" (*hotgor*) also means "concave," "cavity," or "hollow" (Hangin et al. 1986). Indeed, many people in the Shishged refer to it as *manai Hotgor* (lit. "our Hollow").

an unprecedented degree of accommodation and even cooperation took place between the two sides. Thus the sources are full of cases of shamans who were also lamas (one of whom is discussed in the next chapter), just as they tell of shamans who were living within monastic compounds and even performing their possession ceremonies there (Diószegi 1961, 202; Sandschejew 1930, 52). According to Garma Sandschejew, some lamas even used to seek help from shamans (1930, 57). Conversely, as a shaman explained to me, "where some [shamans] said that Buddhist gods [*burhan*] and the shamanic spirits [*ongod*] do not fit together but are in competition, other [shamans] apparently used to insist that [their relationship] was okay."

* * *

We are now much better equipped, ethnographically and historically, to account for the analogies that many Darhads draw between the topography of their minds and the topography of the Shishged landscape. Even on the assumption that shamans were already associated with the taiga before the creation of the Ih Shav' (a likely possibility), the interventions of this ecclesiastical polity unquestionably served to push the shamans, and the spirits, deeper into the taiga. In this light, the main reason why people are so keen on mapping their layered minds onto the landscape is that in doing so, they are following in the footsteps of their formerly Buddhist—and, as I now turn to argue, communist—masters.

I propose that a general analogy can be posited between the state socialist hegemony of representation (Yurchak 2006) discussed in chapter 1 and the Lamaist Buddhist discourse of subjugation (Ramble 1997; Samuel 1993) discussed in the present chapter. While there are obviously numerous differences between the two, both can be described as highly centralized technologies of "purification" (in Bruno Latour's sense [1993]), which are organized according to strictly hierarchical principles, and whose success is contingent on their ability to relegate any potential threat to the progress of mankind and the cosmos more generally into invisible aporia, or shadow worlds, at their margins. The reason why the socialist period was not remembered as an "age of darkness" could thus be that the communist state, even more so than the Buddhist church, succeeded in hiding away the Darhad shamans and their spirits in the farthest corners of social and psychological life, pushing them as it did not just to the edges of the Shishged landscape but, as we saw in chapter 1, to the margins of language and discourse itself, with the effect that people found it hard to talk, and sometimes perhaps even think, about the world of the spirits.

This might help explain why the Mongolian communists were so obsessed with eradicating all signs of Buddhism in the country, often to an extent that went beyond any "rational" reason, such as the need to curb a possible political threat to their existence. As Bawden notes, the Mongolian People's Revolutionary Party "always paid lip service to the principle of freedom of belief, as a private matter, a freedom which [was] guaranteed by the constitution, but to most of them Marxism and Buddhism were...irreconcilable enemies on all levels, even, at times, that of personal piety. The two could not co-exist" (1986, 25). Recalling the aforementioned analogy between Buddhist and socialist concepts of purification, I tentatively venture that the reason for the deep antagonism between cadres and lamas was not simply, as most of the people involved undoubtedly told themselves and others, that the two were fundamentally different, but also that they, in the very particular and restricted sense I have described, were also essentially alike.

The Fall of Buddhism

Possibly more so in the Shishged than anywhere else in northern Mongolia, the purges of the 1930s achieved their sinister purpose: the annihilation of the Buddhist church. Unlike many other districts in rural Mongolia, the Buddhist church has thus not been successfully reinstitutionalized in the Shishged after socialism. It is true that in the early 1990s a prayer temple was built in the Renchinlhümbe district, sponsored by a high-ranking lama from the Gandantegchenlin monastery in Ulaanbaatar, himself Darhad and born in the Shishged. The temple was closed down in 1999, however, owing, I was told, to a lack of economic support from the locals. When I visited the site in 2000, it was being used to store the caretaker's motorcycle; there was no sign of religious activity.

So while some shamans had been active throughout the socialist period, all that was left from the golden era of Darhad Buddhism by the 1990s were a few former student lamas (*bandi*) from the Ih Shav', who had been spared arrest in 1938 only because of their youth (Pedersen 2006b). This state of affairs was almost universally lamented. Buddhism, as many people expressed to me, was of central importance in their lives, but, they told me, "unfortunately there is no basis for practicing it" in the Shishged anymore. "Ours has become a land without religion [*shashingüi gazar*]," was another often heard complaint. "Look at the temple that was rebuilt in Renchinlhümbe," a man sighed. "Eventually, its lama decided to leave. Not enough donations were given to him. So it was closed. Now, worshippers from around here—and we

Figure 13. The new temple in Renchinlhümbe

are many—have to travel all the way to the monastery in Mörön if we want to attend a prayer meeting [*hural hurah*]."[20]

There is, it is true, an alternative, namely, to pay the lamas to travel the 200 kilometers from the regional capital of Mörön. Nevertheless, not only is this a costly solution, but also it has proved difficult to persuade lamas from Mörön or elsewhere to travel such a long way to a place that is renowned for

20. In the shadow of the near-total annihilation of the Buddhist church as a formal institution in the Shishged, I discovered a sprawling undergrowth of informal Buddhist worship, which had evolved unofficially during socialism. In particular, many people paid regular visits to a few "blessed" (*buyantai*) households in possession of relics from the Zöölön monastery. The most important, a golden statue of Tara, attracted scores of worshippers every lunar New Year, some from as far as Ulaanbaatar. Indeed, I was told, this statue used to be the main protector (*zahius*) of the Zöölön monastery (Pedersen 2011).

being a shamanic stronghold.[21] Contrary to what one might have expected, worry about the demise of Buddhism was not restricted to the respected (*hündtei*) and influential (*nölöötei*) households of Ulaan-Uul—households whose members, like my hosts, would always participate in communal rituals, district meetings, and collective construction tasks, and perhaps even run for local elections (and who, perhaps not coincidentally, all used to be—and indeed still were—members of the Revolutionary Party). Practically everyone I spoke to in the Shishged, including some of the most prominent shamans, voiced concern about the absence of Buddhist lamas in the Shishged. Consider, for example, the heated response from a female shaman from Tsagaan Nuur to the question "Can shamans perform *ovoo* rituals?"

> No way! According to our way of thinking, *ovoo* rites should be performed
> by lamas and by lamas only. In one recent Mongolian film I saw an *udgan*
> participating in *ovoo* worship, wearing shamanic clothes. That is com-
> pletely wrong! Female shamans can participate only because anyone who
> is of middle age or more is allowed to, not because they are shamans. (And
> they should not wear their costumes.) Male shamans cannot perform
> these rituals either. It has to be lamas. Near the source of the Harmyn
> River there is an *ovoo* called Zürhnii Ovoo, where the lamas used to make
> sacrifices. Last spring I saw by divination [*mergelj baihad*] that we ought to
> perform this ritual again. It hasn't been done for many years. Our leaders
> really want it to happen, for there is illness among our livestock, and our
> children are always getting sick. The leaders want these problems to go
> away, but they cannot find anyone to perform the sacrifice. Other sacri-
> fices need to be made for the Gurvan Saihan Ovoo and the Hönhör Ovoo.
> We are in desperate need of lamas who can perform these rites.[22]

To understand why this ritual is considered so necessary, and why it is so important that lamas perform it, let's look at Ulaan-Uul's *ovoo* rite of 1999, following its reintroduction in the early 1990s after the ban on such rituals under socialism had been lifted.[23]

---

21. I have often asked lamas across Mongolia to comment on the state of Darhad Buddhism. They tend to respond with the same harsh judgment: "Darhads aren't Buddhists. They are all shamans!"

22. It is worth noting that my source on the *ovoo* ritual—who was a *bandi* at the Ivd monastery in his youth—emphasized that the Jargalant Ovoo did not exist before the Ih Shav'. This, of course, is something he could hardly know, but the case illustrates the widespread conviction that *ovoo* ceremonies must be carried out by lamas, not shamans.

23. Instead of attempting to destroy the tens of thousands of *ovoos* spread across the Mongolian landscape, the communists rebranded them as road markers, an action that, while not exactly

Human Mountains and Weightless Peripheries

Held on the famous Öl mountain pass, which marks the border between the Shishged region and the rest of Mongolia to the south, the annual *ovoo* rite is the largest and most important ritual in Ulaan-Uul, even though it is by no means the only one. Most *bags* hold their own *ovoo* rites over the summer. Like the majority of *ovoo* rites (re)instituted in Mongolia after socialism, the one in Ulaan-Uul takes place on the country's Independence Day, July 11. Indeed, *ovoo* rituals have helped in forging a new national identity.[24]

Representing what seems at first sight a textbook example of hierarchical encompassment in Louis Dumont's (1980) and Marshall Sahlins's (1985) sense, the Mongolian ovoo rite is meant to summon (*dallaga*) good fortune (*hishig*) from the spirit masters of the land in order to ensure favorable weather conditions and good health in the coming year. Instead of describing the liturgy of the ritual and the complex mediations between human and nonhuman "owners," which have already been described in detail by others (Bawden 1958; Heissig 1980; Sneath 2000), I want to focus on the "eldest men" (*hamgiin*), who play a nonspecified yet vital role in these reinvented rites. More precisely, I suggest that these local leaders personify the yellow side, which is understood to reside within everyone present at the ritual.

It is thus the *hamgiin ah* who, upon their arrival at the Öliin Davaa, are first allocated a place in the middle of the gathering, right in front of the imposing tepee-like structure of wooden poles and prayer flags, which represents the main *ovoo* at the site. (This is flanked by twelve other *ovoos,* one for each year in the lunar calendar.) When the lamas invited from Mörön have finished reading their sutras, the *hamgiin ah* are the first to circumambulate the *ovoo* in a clockwise direction, ever so slowly, while offering libations of milk and vodka on behalf of the Ulaan-Uul community as a whole—or at least the ritual community. Finally, it is the *hamgiin ah,* seated amid a constellation of male leaders competing to take part in this important offering, who cut up the sacrificial sheep into small pieces and distribute the meat to every person in the crowd, women and children included.

While no one has told me so directly (for this is not something that one conveys in words), it is clearly of utmost importance that the *hamgiin ah* should arrive at the *ovoo* site on horseback, not by jeep; they should dismount

---

wrong, deliberately ignored complex interconnections between land, spirits, herds, and herders of the kind described in this chapter.

24. The reinstitutionalization of the *ovoo* rite has typically taken place with reference not to kin-based communities, as was sometimes the case during presocialist times, but to the lower levels of government, such as the district (*sum*) and the subdistrict (*bag*) (see also Humphrey and Sneath 1999, 123–27).

Figure 14. Ovoo ritual at the Öl mountain pass. Photo by Latetia Merli

in a graceful manner, not jumping off like reckless young nomads, and then walk, very slowly but with stout determination, toward the *ovoo*, where they must sit down and remain seated without uttering a word, let alone making any frivolous gesture. They all are dressed in the same inconspicuous manner—dark blue *deels* (herdsmen's gowns), traditional wrestlers' boots (*mongol gutal*), and broad-brimmed felt hats—just as they always seem to carry their worn bodies in the same composed and measured manner. In this sense, their appearance corresponds to that of the many mountain peaks towering over the Shishged Depression in all directions. Like mountains, *hamgiin ah* remain still; like mountains, they are the epitome of solidity; like mountains, they constitute focal points in whose vicinity different life forms are ideally able to gather and coexist on peaceful terms while paying their respects to the elders (Humphrey 1996; Pedersen 2006a).

The *hamgiin ah*, it seems, momentarily become fathers of the Ulaan-Uul community as a whole; indeed their role in the *ovoo* ritual closely resembles that of the master of the household (*geriin ezen*), especially on more formal occasions such as weddings and the lunar New Year. This is not merely a symbolic role. *Hamgiin ah*, I suggest, in their comportment, manners, and clothing, personify what the Darhad yellow side is all about. To recall my discussion of the presocialist rites at the Jargalant Ovoo, these informal leaders momentarily embody what Öl Mountain permanently is: the center of Ulaan-Uul as a whole. By doing so, the "eldest men" enact a certain idea and ideal of what a proper Darhad person, a proper Darhad household, and indeed a proper Darhad community ought to look like, which is to say, a smaller, contemporary, but still essentially self-similar, version of the Darhad Ih Shav'.

But not everyone and everything in Ulaan-Uul is encompassed by the magic circle originally drawn by the Buddhist church in the nineteenth century. One July day, a couple of days after the annual *ovoo* ritual, I asked my host why the master of a neighboring household had not participated. "Why, that man is a thief!" he told me in a dismissive tone of voice. "It is a bad household. People say it is full of flies!" The next morning I went to see for myself. The old man was known as Thief Baatar, a nickname that reflected his reputation as a notorious cattle rustler, but he was also feared for other, much less tangible reasons. Indeed, he sometimes jokingly called himself a shaman, though no one else seemed to agree. He was, however, in possession of various sacred artifacts, and was, at least according to his own boasting, of shamanic descent. "Let me see, where was I yesterday?" Thief Baatar mused mischievously in response to my question, brushing a lazy fly off his ear. "I was home, getting drunk with my sons! Hahaha!"

Not all "eldest men," then, are equally "old." In the *ovoo* ritual, and in many other situations, to be called "the eldest" is a measure of respect (*hündetgel*) more than a measure of biological age (*nas*). As the example of Thief Baatar shows, one may live for many years and still never become "old," in the sense of being imbued with the rock-solid patriarchal credentials of the *hamgiin ah*. Indeed, as has been illustrated several times in this book, in Ulaan-Uul during the late 1990s, a small minority lived their lives outside the yellow totality that was reenacted in annual *ovoo* rituals, some (like Gombodorj) because they were not allowed in, others (like the shaman cited earlier) by their own choice.

Susan McKinnon has convincingly demonstrated how, in certain Melanesian kinship formations, "unified, fixed, weighted centers [are contrasted] to multiple, dispersed, moving, and weightless peripheries" (1991, 33). The important point here is that, were these kinship-based centers to exist on their own, their solidity would become void, for they would have no labile other in whose asymmetrical refraction they could imagine themselves as composed by congruent, commensurable social entities.

In much the same way, the example of the Ulaan-Uul *ovoo* rite shows that if the weighty concept of a centered steppe is to work in the Shishged context, it requires the weightless counterimage of a marginal taiga. The taiga, then, emerges as a zone of pure multiplicity and metamorphosis in asymmetrical opposition to a zone of pure sameness and singularity, the steppe, and this pervasive center-periphery spectacle has come into being through a combination of consecutive political and religious interventions pertaining to the Mongolian Empire, the Mongolian Buddhist church, and the Mongolian Communist Party.

The Darhad Paradox

Like other scholars, Marie-Dominique Even has emphasized how paradoxical it is that "the Darkhad region, [as a] stronghold of shamanic traditions[,] ...was controlled by the Buddhist church" (1991, 200) until the Mongolian revolution. But perhaps it is not so surprising after all. In this chapter I have sought to demonstrate how, with the gradual politico-religious institutionalization of the Darhad Ih Shav' from 1757 to 1921, a whole residual and marginal shadow world came into being, a spatial and existential aporia filled with all the shamanic stuff that could not, and perhaps would not, fit into the new cosmological order imposed by the Buddhist church.

As my historical ethnography of the Buddhist domestication project in the Shishged has demonstrated, the lamas from the Ih Shav' thus needed the Darhad shamans to resist them; for had these shamans not done so, then it would have been hard for the lamas as outsiders to justify, to themselves and others, their self-proclaimed role as protectors of wild Darhads of the north. Indeed, as I have tentatively suggested, the same was the case for their communist successors. For party cadres as for Buddhist monks, flying demons and unruly shamans presented not only a problem to be solved but also, above all, an opportunity to be taken, for without an inner black and shamanic essence within these people and their land, why would they need outsiders to save them from themselves? In a sense, the communists thus simply took over where the Buddhist monks left off, which also explains why it was so necessary for the former to get rid of the latter: one (traditionalist-religious) weighty center was replaced by another (modernist-secular) weighty center, while the weightless (shamanic) margin essentially remained the same.

Thus the Shishged landscape is not just an environment; nor is the study of this landscape a study of the "cultural construction of nature." For this landscape contains vantage points that ground, in a non-arbitrary manner, the two Darhad "sides" as spatio-cum-existential figures in a sort of topographical deixis, whereby everyone and everything Darhad is seen (or imagined to be seen) from particular points of view. This is not to say that the environment "determines" how Darhads see themselves or how they are seen by others. It is only to suggest that the northern Mongolian landscape, like any landscape, offers certain possibilities of form, and that it is from within these forms that the Darhad self-imagination, and the Darhad stereotype, take shape. To study Shishged topographies of the person, then, is to explore how different bodies look from different spatial vantage points—to identify those places in the land from which the two Darhad "sides" need to be seen.[25]

This implies that, if speaking of Darhad identity is to make sense, it must be understood as a fractal or self-scaling phenomenon. Instead of being a single absolute essence (or, conversely, a relative term constructed in opposition to a significant other), a Darhad person is an internally differentiated, post-plural entity whose paradoxical "essence" is to be both self and other at the same time. Darhad identity, in that sense, is an unstable mixture of the wild and the domesticated, the most marginal, shamanic, and least genuinely (Halh) Mongolian, and the most centered, Buddhist, and most genuinely (Halh) Mongolian; for a Darhad person is simultaneously made up of black, shamanic, and taiga-like components on the one hand, and yellow, Buddhist, and steppe-like components on the other.

Thus the yellow side and the black side emerge as immanent in all Shishged social life. Through a complex historical interplay between internal and external forces, and intended and unintended effects, they have become the two substances from which everything Darhad is made. This explains—but does not solve—the paradox of being Darhad in the late 1990s: people were constantly trying to free themselves from the very shamanic "side" that they and others saw as an intrinsic part, an entire half, of who they were. In that sense, one could say that the Darhads did not need any external others to create the divisions involved in the politics of identity, for they were already internally other to themselves.

25. My aim, then, has not been to repeat well-rehearsed arguments about the construction of ethnic identities through the drawing of arbitrary cultural boundaries (Barth 1969; Fisher 2001). Nor has it been to conduct another study of the production of locality, if by this we understand people's symbolic investments in empty spaces in order to turn them into meaningful places (Gupta and Ferguson 1997). More than examining the arbitrariness of the politics of identity, I have explored the production of persons through places imbued with an intrinsic capacity for meaning (see also Green 2005; Ingold 2000; Leach 2003).

4 The Shaman's Two Bodies

One key issue that remains largely unexplored, and therefore still unresolved, in my account of shamanic agency in northern Mongolia in the age of the market is the question of the shamans themselves. Although no one was considered a "genuine shaman" in Ulaan-Uul in the late 1990s, the situation was different elsewhere in the Shishged, as I have noted. The standard complaint voiced by people in Ulaan-Uul was that, because of the lack of shamans in their community, "we have to travel all the way [around 110 kilometers] up to Tsagaan Nuur in order to see a shaman." (Indeed, on the various occasions when I participated in shamanic rituals in Tsagaan Nuur, I recognized several faces from Ulaan-Uul in the audience.) People from across Mongolia seem to think of Tsagaan Nuur as the home of "real Darhad shamans," while places like Ulaan-Uul were awash with people who were "fake" or "half" shamans.[1]

Based on observations of a handful of shamanic rituals in Tsagaan Nuur, on interviews carried out with shamans and their clients in the same district, and on the scattered but quite substantial literature on this topic, this

---

1. In total, I heard of around ten Darhad shamans who were active in Mongolia in 1998–2000, two of whom lived in the Shishged district of Tsagaan Nuur (along with three Duha shamans), while the rest were spending most their time in other parts of the country. Thus two *zaarin* and two *udgan* lived in Ulaanbaatar, while two *zaarin* and one *udgan* moved between Tsagaan Nuur, Mörön, and Ulaanbaatar. In addition, I heard of one *udgan* in the Hövsgöl district of Bayan-Zürh and another in the city of Darhan. The number estimated by Hangartner (2006) during her fieldwork a few years later was much larger. This discrepancy may result from the fact that we talked to different people in the Shishged, or perhaps we had divergent ways of asking about these matters. It could also reflect the astonishing speed by which social life—and perhaps so-called religious tradition in particular—was changing in Mongolia during the period in question.

chapter provides an exegesis of the Darhad shamanic cosmos, with special emphasis on the central role of shamanic artifacts. While this full-fledged shamanic cosmology differs markedly from the quasi-occult beliefs and incomplete shamanic practices discussed in earlier chapters, this difference reflects the situation on the ground in the Shishged in the late 1990s. Thus what follows provides an important, indeed necessary, ethnographic grounding against which my exploration of shamanism without shamans—with its implicit subtext of shamanism *with* shamans—can be taken a step further.

The central point I wish to establish here is that the shamans, much like the *atamans* discussed in chapter 1, are capable of switching their connection (*holboo*) to the spirits on and off, and that this spiritual attachment and detachment is made possible to a large extent by the magical properties of their gowns and other shamanic paraphernalia. Thus the attire donned by shamans during possession séances has a dual purpose in that it simultaneously attracts and deflects spiritual attention. It is in this sense that "genuine shamans," who almost always have costumes, differ from the not so genuine ones, who generally do not. For while shamans are certainly enabled to travel to the spirits by donning their gowns—which is how these artifacts have normally been interpreted by anthropologists—it is also true that they become able *not* to see the spirits, and not to be seen by them, by taking off their costumes. By contrast, half-shamans such as Gombodorj, who lack any means of blocking the spirits, are exposed to their occult agency all the time, without being able to see them fully, let alone control them. In that sense we might say (with some Darhads) that shamans are special in having "two bodies," for they alone can be both yellow and black, weighty and weightless, singular and multiple, and indeed human and nonhuman at the same time.

I start out by telling the story of a famous Darhad shaman already mentioned briefly in chapter 1, Nadmid (also known as Ambii or Dambii) Udgan, a Tsagaan Nuur–based shamaness whom I worked with from 1999 to 2000, and who was probably the most prominent shaman in the Shishged in the late 1990s. After a detailed exploration of the way the spirit world impinged on Nadmid Udgan and her clients, including a description of a possession rite and a consideration of the different shamanic paraphernalia used by shamans and hunters, I return to the work of Viveiros de Castro to present a perspectivist analysis of the traffic in bodily perspectives, which, as I intend to demonstrate, Darhad shamanism is all about. This enables me to reflect further on the question of the different social agencies of genuine and not-so-genuine shamans, and what this tells us about the nature of shamanism in contemporary northern Mongolia

Nadmid Udgan, "Genuine Shaman"

On Nadmid Udgan's death in 2001, writes Otgony Pürev (a Mongolian ethnographer of Darhad descent), "respecting her last words, she was buried publicly on the 27th of August; three mountain passes and three rivers southwest away of her home, in Honhyn Bel, Zöölön Ridge of Renchinlhümbe soum....Eyewitnesses confirm that after the burial, they saw three condors flying around upon this place and the next morning nothing remained of her body, not even a hair or a nail. Only a scrap of white shroud remained" (2004, 159).

According to her own information, Nadmid Udgan was born near the Harmai River in the far northwestern corner of the Darhad Depression some years before the 1921 revolution. I was never able to determine her exact age, but she certainly looked old and frail when I first met her in 1999. Her maternal grandfather was a shaman from the White Huular clan known as Dembee Zaarin, and her teacher was Baljinnyam Lam.[2] As his name suggests, Baljinnyam Lam was "also a lama" (as Nadmid Udgan herself put it), whose own mentor had himself also been a lama-shaman from the Zöölön monastery. While Buddhist lamas loom large in Nadmid Udgan's early life, the string of extraordinary events that made her a shaman represents in many ways an exemplary case of shamanic predestination as described in chapter 2. Just consider her dramatic account of how she was first affected by and later learned to control the shamanic *udha*:

> When I was two years old I fell seriously ill. Apparently my eyes were like a dying person or animal. At that time my family was migrating from Deed Toom to our spring camp at Serjim Tolgoi. My father went to the Ivd monastery on horseback to find Black-Eyed Choijil, who was in charge of the monastery back then. He told the Choijil lama, "My child is gravely ill, so I have come to fetch you." The lama threw his dice and exclaimed: "Yes, she is badly affected. It is necessary to awake a guardian [*sahius bosgoh*] from the white skies. Quick, fetch a *hadag* [ritual silk scarf], she is almost dead. We must leave immediately."
>
> For two days I had not eaten or drunk anything. The lama read spells [*tarni*] and blew over the *hadag,* and I woke up a little. He then demanded that the treatment [*zasal*] continue at a difficult place [*sadaatai gazar*] situated in a hollow on the south side of Hürdtei. Astounded, my family said to one another: "We are going to a haunted place [*güideltei*

---

2. One of the largest Darhad clans, White Huular was always closely associated with shamanism. Diószegi (1961, 197) mentions that he met "about thirty male and female shamans [from] the two *xular* clans" in the 1950s, the other clan being the Red Huular.

gazar, lit. 'a place with paths']. What a strange lama this is, what a terrible thing to do to a child." As the group got closer, noises like those of a really horrible bird [ih muuhai shuvuu shig] were heard, and they thought it was a crow. But they kept going forward. Meanwhile, up front, the lama was constantly throwing his dice.

As they arrived at the hollow, my mother said to herself, "Okay, now our poor child is going to die." But Black-Eyed Choijil calmly said, "Put up your ger, make a fire, and prepare tea." The lama himself was busy blowing into the conch shell and beating his hand drum [damar]. As the fire picked up, the lama said, "Look at the child."

"Oh no, what is happening to her!" my father said to himself, for what he saw was not me but the image of a child wearing a light blue deel resembling the rays of the sky [tengeriin tuya shig], walking on the ridge of the mountain. The livestock became restless (as they always do at haunted places), and there was the eerie noise of children crying at the back of the yurt. But still, the lama was calm and simply said, "Now just relax, eat, and go to sleep."

Black-Eyed Choijil now enlivened [am'luulj tahisan] two or three talismans [ongod]. What came out of them was the Three Hyaryn Things. This is how this spirit [ongon] was made for the first time. One thing was made from the tail of a horse, including the bone. The lama enlivened it, and some very strange things appeared. He drummed and made small statues out of rice and flour, and eventually two more things appeared. At the same time, the sound of the children's crying ceased. Next morning my eyes were much better, and my family was very happy. Eternally grateful, my father presented a horse to the lama.

But the sense of relief was to last only a few years. When Nadmid Udgan turned eight, she was again afflicted by böögiin övchin, the "shaman sickness" (though she did not specify what happened to her), and from then on there was no turning back. That the udha had indeed taken hold of her was verified through divination by a male shaman called Tserempil (or Tseremchil), who passed on the responsibility for nurturing the neophyte shaman to a teacher from Nadmid Udgan's clan, the aforementioned Baljinnyam. Then, when Nadmid Udgan turned fourteen, members of her family prepared a shamanic costume, and she shamanized for the first time (anh böö böölsön). Her completion as a shaman was now accomplished (biyelsen), and she would remain a shaman for the rest of her life, though it does appear that she kept quite a low profile for much of the socialist period.[3]

3. A man in Ulaan-Uul gave me a less flattering account of Nadmid Udgan's life: "Her own mother was a shaman too and it was she who taught her. From the time Nadmid Udgan was ten

Unlike the uninterrupted shamanic patriline of Gombodorj and his fore-bears discussed in chapter 2, Nadmid Udgan's *udha* was difficult to trace back in time, because, as she explained apologetically, "I was adopted as a child." Indeed it is significant that clans (*ovog*) and descent lines more gener-ally play a relatively minor role in her biography. According to the ethnog-raphers who visited the Shishged in the first half of the twentieth century, the consecration of new shamans back then was a strictly clan-related af-fair. Apparently shamans were considered to be of key importance for the well-being of clans, and the cost of the initiation—including the shamanic costume—was incurred collectively by their members (Badamhatan 1986, 185–86; Pegg 2001, 130 37; Sandschejew 1930, 35, 56–57). Some of the Dar-had clans used to organize big annual *tailgan* rituals. These are also known in Buryatia (Hamayon 1990, 637–43), where male shamans shamanized to (re) vitalize (*am'luulj tahih*) the essence of the patriline, while also presiding over the consecration of new shamans (Sandschejew 1930, 50).[4] Among Darhads, wrote Sandschejew, clans were "first of all units of help for the collection of money to make a shaman" (1931, 35). Two generations later, as noted in the introduction to this book, I was left with the impression that "the Dar-had clan system" (if there ever was such a thing) had, to all intents and pur-poses, disappeared. This was reflected in the composition of audiences at shamanist séances, who came from all classes and segments of society, and in the fact that shamans seem to have received their gown and other artifacts from atomized, bilateral kin networks (as appears to have been the case with Nadmid Udgan), or from non-cognate shaman teachers, and not from clan members as in the *tailgan* ritual.[5]

This devaluation of the clan may explain why most of the Darhad sha-mans I met or heard of during the late 1990s were women.[6] It was cer-tainly clear that, in contrast to the situation before the revolution—when women with occult abilities, whether shamans or midwifes, were widely

---

years old, she began to shamanize with drum, gown, and everything. Then, when they [the com-munists] came after the shamans, she hid her outfit in the forest. Some things were even thrown away. She gave birth to two sons, and many years passed, until one day, one of them became ill. She enlivened her *ongod* and started shamanizing. But the son could not be saved, and he died. Some say that this happened because she had thrown away her *ongod*."

4. For details on the initiation, see Badamhatan (1986, 185–86) and Sandschejew (1931, 56–57).

5. It remains to be seen whether future generations of Darhad shamans practicing in the Shishged and beyond will be associated with reinvented clan communities, as seems to have hap-pened among several peoples in Siberia and indeed among shamans in Ulaanbaatar; see, for ex-ample, Merli (2006). Hangartner's work seems to confirm this possibility.

6. Notwithstanding certain exceptions (Humphrey 1996), clan-based and non-Buddhist Mongolian groups have tended toward a majority of male shamans (Hamayon 1984).

considered a threat to Mongolia's patriarchal order (Hamayon 1994)—gender now played a minor role in people's evaluation of shamans.[7] When I once asked a man who was more powerful (*hamgiin hüchtei*), male or female shamans, he retorted impatiently: "Male or female doesn't matter! The only important thing is the wisdom that he or she masters [*ter hünii ezemshsen erdmees bolno*]." Indeed, female shamans like Nadmid Udgan were held in high esteem by locals and outsiders alike, and their ceremonies attracted huge crowds. "When Nadmid Udgan shamanizes," a young woman from Tsagaan Nuur remarked, puffing on a counterfeit Davidoff cigarette, "half the village turns up. It is like a rock concert. Nothing else happens here."

Clients and Their Concerns

All sorts of clients came to Nadmid Udgan and the other Tsagaan Nuur shamans with all sorts of problems. They came because of diseases striking their herds of cattle, because of illness among their children, or because their household was facing insurmountable debt owing to a failed trading venture or a bad loan. As elsewhere in postsocialist Mongolia, ad hoc solutions for such problems were often sought from other experts as well, who might be biomedical professionals, Buddhist lamas, or, to a limited extent, Christian missionaries (who have not had much success in the Shishged, in contrast to more urban settings in Mongolia).

Particular kinds of problems, however, seemed to call exclusively for the intervention of a shaman. Generally, these problems could be described as psychological rather than physiological (in the Euro-American sense), and perhaps for the same reason they were seen as subject to causes that were opaque and suspicious as opposed to transparent and natural. Thus it would be rare for a man to visit Nadmid Udgan after breaking an arm in a wrestling match, whereas he would be more likely do so if he or his relatives were faced with "pressure" (*daramt*) inflicted by jealousy, gossip, and slander, or—as in the case of certain well-known politicians—sorcery (*id shid*), curses (*haraal*), and other forms of black magic (*domyn arga*). Another common reason for visiting shamans was for "insurance" (*daatgal*) purposes. As one

---

7. Apparently, the Shishged was home to many female shamans in the first half of the twentieth century (Badamhatan 1986, 157; Diószegi 1961, 197). Indeed, given that more than one-third of the shamanic spirits listed by Badamhatan (1986, 170) have female designations (such as Eej, "Mother," and Udgan, "Shamaness"), and most such spirits are believed to be the souls (*süns*) of deceased shamans (discussed later in this chapter), this seems to suggest that even further back in history a significant proportion of shamans in the Shishged were female.

woman from Tsagaan Nuur explained, "if you do *daatgal* in the autumn, you will be watched over [*harj avarna*] until spring, when you will have to do it again."

Consider, as an illustration of clients' concerns and shamans' solutions to them, some of the elaborate preparations carried out by Nadmid Udgan before what would be the biggest shamanic ritual I participated in, the biannual "awakening" (*bosgoh*) of the Father of Harmai, a prominent shamanic spirit associated with the White Huular clan. As I entered her house early on the afternoon before the ritual, Nadmid Udgan was busy making protective amulets (*seter, lusyn örgöl*) on her manual sewing machine. Every *seter*, she explained, was *daatgal* for a particular household, who had written their wishes on tiny pieces of paper, which she had subsequently sewn inside each *seter*. The reason why she was so preoccupied was that each *seter* had to be left at the "wilderness talisman" (*heeriin ongon*) of the Father of Harmai prior to the rite, which was located several kilometers to the north, on the banks of the Harmai River.[8]

Later that day, when Nadmid Udgan returned from the site of the wilderness talisman, two brand-new Land Cruisers with Ulaanbaatar license plates were parked outside her place. "Ah, some people from the capital," she observed in an offhand manner, implying that this was by no means an unusual occurrence. Her visitors turned out to be three prominent businessmen, who had driven more than 1,000 kilometers to solicit help against certain "problems" pertaining to their affairs in the capital. To judge from his appearance (he had a grim look on his face, or what little of it could be glimpsed behind the dark sunglasses he would continue to wear for the rest of the day), one of the businessmen in particular was in trouble. Indeed, during the divination session that Nadmid Udgan now initiated, it transpired that he was the victim of a particularly vicious evil tongue (*hel am*) attack and was in need of urgent shamanic treatment (*zasal*, lit. "fixing").

The divination itself took place through the medium of money. (Nadmid Udgan was famous for this technique.) Following the established convention

---

8. The talisman was made up of nine trees situated in a larch grove, each of a different age. Each of these sacred trees (*mönh mod*, lit. "eternal trees")—which, Nadmid Udgan emphasized, had to be either larch or willow—was plastered with small pieces of multicolored cloth (*tsuudir*) and white *seter* from previous offerings. The rite, known as *hangain lusyn daatgal* (mountain spirit insurance), involved a series of sacrificial acts. A smoky fire was lit at the foot of each *mönh mod*. Offerings (candy and so on) were made to the fire, and prayers were said in all directions, especially to the west and north (where the Father of Harmai resides). A libation of milk and yogurt was offered, first to the eternal tree and then in all directions. The shaman then held each *seter* to her forehead as she carefully read out her clients' wishes, after which more prayers were said. Finally, each *seter* was tied to a *mönh mod* and more offerings were made. The same procedure was then repeated until all *seters* had been successfully consecrated.

for visiting diviners in Mongolia, the businessman first (after having finished a cup of tea and introduced himself) presented a variety of gifts for the
shaman, which were also offerings for the spirits: a ritual silk scarf (*hadag*)
in blue, a big brick of tea, some candy, and above all, ten thousand tögrög
in crisp new thousand-tögrög bills. After having first placed the prestations
on the altar below her "household talisman" (*geriin ongon*) in a gesture heavy
with awe and respect, Nadmid Udgan now wrapped the bills inside the *hadag*,
which she then held first to her forehead and then in front of her lips, while
she murmured prayers that clearly were not intended to be heard by anyone
but herself and the spirits. After what (at least for her anxious and impatient-
looking client) seemed a long period of spiritual deliberation, during which
she repeatedly held the *hadag* to her forehead and then brought it back to
her mouth accompanied by more occult murmurs, she carefully unwrapped
the money. Now the actual "seeing" (*üzeg*) could begin. Apparently, Nadmid
Udgan was by this point in an altered state (*hii uhaantai*, lit. "airy mind"), for
she kept asking questions calling for verification, such as "Is it autumn now?"
or "Has the hay been cut?" After receiving confirmation of the season, again
following standard procedure for diviners, she asked in what year (*jil*) of the
lunar calendar the businessman had been born ("the Year of the Rat," he informed her), how many people there were in his household ("four," was the
reply), and what the nature of his work was ("I do trade," he whispered). The
shaman then began speaking in measured, low, and confiding tones, deliver-
ing a verdict to her urban client that was as troubling as it must have been
hard to understand:

> The young man here, he is very rich. But now a problem had arisen: there
> is no income but plenty of expenditure [*orlogyn üüd n' haalttai, zarlagyn
> üüd n' neelttei*]. It is surprising, this problem, for he has never stolen or
> lied [*hudlaa heleegüi, hulgai heleegüi*], but it is there. Humans always
> have problems which make it hard [for them] to live. There is pressure
> from the sky, and there is pressure from the earth [*tenger deerees daraad,
> gazar dooroos hatgaad*], and also the water spirits [*lus*] are pushing. So
> what does this person have to do? He has been subject to the white evil
> tongue [*tsagaan hel amtai*]. The problem must be dealt with by making a
> sacrifice [*tahil örgöh*] for the three gods [*gurvan burhan*] and the ninety-
> nine skies [*tenger*]. It is a very difficult sacrifice, because some very rare
> things [*ih hovor yum*] are needed to perform it: the milk from nine white
> mares, the milk from nine white goats, and the milk from nine red cows.
> (The last in particular is extremely rare, since it can be found only in the
> Darhad *nutag*.) The bigger the problem, the rarer the sacrifice—and this
> man has a massive problem indeed!

Later that afternoon, as I went into Tsagaan Nuur village to secure my own gifts and offerings for the evening's sacrifice, I bumped into the businessman and his Ulaanbaatar friends in the single shop in the ghostly district center. He was desperately trying to collect the items prescribed in Nadmid Udgan's divination. "I need to find the rare things before tomorrow morning!" he exclaimed with a combination of despair and hope, "and the shaman also asked me to come tonight. Apparently, the spirits have not finished with me yet!"

Shamans and Their Paraphernalia

As these examples indicate, full-blown shamanic possession rituals (*böö böölöh*) were by no means the only activity performed by Nadmid Udgan and the other shamans in Tsagaan Nuur. They were also involved in a whole range of lower-key shamanic activities (such as divination sessions for individual clients) in competition with other kinds of occult specialists (diviners and so forth). Yet while such rituals sometimes involved entering into various states of trance (*hii uhaan*), and the magical appropriation of artifacts (sheep shoulder blades, purified paper currency, and the like), they never involved wearing any special outfit. Indeed, possession of a shamanic gown (*böö huvtsas,* also known as *huyag,* which literally means "armor") was the single most important thing that set "genuine" shamans apart from not-so-genuine ones in the late 1990s. As we are about to see, not only did this artifact enable Nadmid Udgan to control her spirits, but also (much as in the *tailgan* rituals of the past) it was proof of the community's affirmation of her shaman status.

Upon entering Nadmid Udgan's wooden house, one was struck not just by the simplicity of the place but by its small size. There hardly seemed to be room for anyone but the shamaness herself. And yet, during large possession séances such as the awakening of the Father of Harmai, her premises accommodated more than forty people. The room was dominated by the altar in the respectful north section of the home (*hoimor*), where her shamanic attire was kept. In most shamans' homes I visited, these highly feared artifacts were kept out of sight under normal circumstances, only to be produced from locked cupboards in the final hours before possession ceremonies commenced. Much the same went for Nadmid Udgan's spirit talisman (*ongon*), which, outside ritual contexts, could be glimpsed only behind its layers of protective cloth in its designated place on the wall of the northwest corner (*baruun hoimor*) of her house. Let me now examine this particular artifact in some detail, as it provides a useful point of departure for my wider exploration of the shamanic spirits and shamans' relations to them.

Figure 15. Shaman's altar with *ongon*

Most of the spirit talismans I saw in the late 1990s consisted of multicolored cotton tassels (*tsuudir*), ceremonial silk scarves (*hadag*), leather strings, odd pieces of metal, as well as fur, teeth, bones, claws, and beaks from wild animals pieced together to form a messy bundle. Many (though by no means all) Darhad individuals and households were in possession of lineage talismans (*yazguur ongod*) or household talismans (*geriin ongod*), which served as both containers of and vessels for attracting different kinds of shamanic spirits. (The talismans kept by most shamans, including Nadmid Udgan, were essentially similar to those kept by ordinary people, only they were bigger and even more intricately designed.) Indeed, "vessel" is an apt translation of the Mongolian term widely used to designate these artifacts—namely, *ongon* (pl. *ongod*). *Ongon* is etymologically related to *ongots,* which means "vessel," "receptacle," or "boat" (Even 1988–89, 387; Humphrey 1998, 427). Notice that the word *ongon* refers to both the shamanic spirits "as such" and their material instantiations in certain artifacts, places in the landscape, or bodies of wild animals. In this sense, Mongolian *ongon* is like Polynesian *mana,* for both challenge the "commonplace assumption that 'things' must necessarily be thought of as ontologically distinct from 'concepts'" (Holbraad 2007, 191).

While all individuals and households may be in possession of spirit vessels, it is the shamans, the hunters, and other occult specialists who tend to worship these talismans most actively. Unlike the household vessels, which must in theory be passed down across the generations through paternal or maternal lines (though they often seem to cross-cut between them), and which ideally must be consecrated by shamans, the so-called hunting vessels (*anchny ongon*) are constructed by the hunters themselves, who, if appropriately gifted, "should automatically know how to make them from their hunting experience," at least according to Gombodorj, who went on to explain:

> A good hunter has many different *ongod,* one for each kind of game. It is important to enliven [*sergeeh*] them in the right manner, and to feed them with milk and other things. The most common thing is to make a hunting vessel before going hunting, but it is also possible to do this after returning, if one has been in contact with a master of the game. The point is to not be hit by the souls of wild animals [*angiin süns*]. Take me, for instance. Because I hunt a lot of marmot, it is inevitable that I sometimes return with some marmot stuff [*yum*]. Upon my return, my marmot vessel will absorb [this stuff] and I will be okay.

The vessel, then, at one and the same time attracts spirits and protects hunters from their wrath. Like a sort of shamanic lightning rod, it shields hunters from the uranium-like energies of the taiga as it is manifested in the form of wild animal masters and other black things (such as blueberries). Small wonder, then, that vessels are cherished objects which hunters and their families do their best to take care of. As another hunter explained: "Each *ongon* has its own psychology [*setgel züi*]. You need to develop a direct relationship [*shuud har'tsaa*] with it." Thus, he concluded, "a vessel is the most precious thing [*nandin yum*] that you can have. It is a container of souls [*sünsnii sav*], which is always pulling you toward where it is. If you lose contact with it, then you will die."

To hunters, then, hunting vessels are shamanic tools that are just as indispensable as other, ostensibly more practical tools for ensuring a successful hunt, such as guns and traps. They always feed these talismans fat and milk before hunts, just as, more generally, households will add new elements (typically *hadag*) to their vessels when significant events occur, such as when a son leaves for the regional capital to sell their animal skins, or when a daughter is moving to the capital to enter university. Because of the "direct relationship" between vessels and people, the latter may be acted upon even in their absence. For example, a hunter's wife will make an effort to remember which offering was most recently added to ensure her husband's hunt, for otherwise she will be unable to call back the hunter's soul in case of trouble with the spirits of the game.

Like the spirit vessels, the shamanic costume itself, which consists of boots (*böö gutal*), gown (*böö deel*), headgear (*böö malgai*), drum (*hengereg/hets*), and drumstick (*tsohiur/orov*), is usually locked away in drawers beneath the altar, only to be taken out in the final hours before a ceremony.[9] This is not surprising, for in Caroline Humphrey's apt phrasing, the costume is believed to place the shaman in a "world-conquering time-machine" (1996, 202). The costume thus enables the shaman to travel to the spirits or, conversely, the spirits to travel to the shaman (to the regret of scholars like Eliade, the direction of this occult movement always seems to be unresolved), a journey that is often depicted in prayer and invocations as riding (*unah*) an animal, which, depending on the spirit, may be a horse, a camel, a goat, or some other creature. The different parts of the costume play distinct roles in this respect: the drum, for example, is conceived of as the mount, the drumstick as the whip, and so on (for further details, see also Diószegi 1961; Dulam and Even 1994; Pürev 1999).

At the same time, the gown is at the very center of a world, or more accurately of many worlds, in its own right. It consists of textures and substances

---

9. For detailed descriptions of these artifacts, including elaborate semantic analyses of the designations used for them, see Badamhatan 1986, 158–69; Diószegi 1963, 57–69; Pürev 1999, 176–267.

that represent a multitude of dimensions, including the taiga and its different animate beings, the ninety-nine shamanic skies (*tenger*), and all the past possessions of the shaman. Its temporal dimension is instantiated by means of knots tied onto cotton tassels (*manjig*) attached to the inside of the gown. Each knot indicates a particular curing event. Clients (or their relatives) tie new ceremonial scarves and streamers (*mog [oi]*, or "snakes") onto the *manjig* during the *zasal* (Pürev 1993; 1999, 176–89; see also Badamhatan 1986, 158–71). As a closer look at the possession rite itself will reveal, the effect of this knotting practice is that the shaman's body becomes a "knot of knots" (Humphrey 1996, 270), that is, a sort of map of the totality of the problems that have prompted clients to solicit help from the shaman in the course of her career.

A Shamanic Ceremony

As we have seen, the day before a big shamanic séance, many clients arrive early at the shaman's premises so that there is time to have individual divinations and perhaps "insurances" (*daatgal*) made prior to the evening's collective ritual. People bring a variety of prestations (*tahil*) to the shaman and her spirits: beer and vodka, cigarettes, bricks of tea, candy, cakes and biscuits, and, invariably, *hadag*. The foodstuffs (*idee*) are displayed on the altar, where they remain until the end of the night's possession ceremony, and the rest is carefully wrapped up and packed away. Quite substantial amounts of money can also change hands if the problem identified by the shaman requires elaborate measures to fix it—and if the clients are rich, as the case of the Ulaanbaatar businessman made clear.

The afternoon and evening pass with the shaman performing divinations and different kinfolk making preparations for the ritual, such as preheating the shamanic drum and arranging the offerings nicely on the altar. In the ceremonies conducted by Nadmid Udgan, two close relatives played important auxiliary roles, not just before but also during the ceremonies. Her eldest son's function was that of "assistant" (*tüshee*); among other things, he was responsible for helping his mother don her shamanic gown. Equally important was an elderly female relative whose job, as Nadmid Udgan's "interpreter" (*helmerch*), was to communicate messages between the spirits and the audience.

Although actual spirit possessions never occur before midnight, the shaman's home is packed with visitors several hours in advance. The majority of these guests may be classified as onlookers. Unlike the clients, onlookers have not presented any money or *idee* to the shaman, so they are unlikely to be "fixed" in the ritual. The seating arrangement seems to reflect this division: the onlookers tend to be seated toward the west (the "guest side") of the room and clients toward the east (the "family side"), where the shaman's assistants also sit, alongside other close relatives, including children. The clients, in other words, are spatially incorporated into the shaman's household during the ceremonies.

Eventually, as the ritual is set to begin, only two areas remain unoccupied: the central *hoimor*, which is where the shamanizing will take place, and the area around the entrance (*üüd*), which is the direction in which the "poison" (*horlol*) that has entered the clients will be expelled by the shaman. As with the shamanic gown, each element of the possession ritual is saturated with significance, not only in terms of what is being said (as well as sung, chanted, and grunted), but also in terms of the shaman's and other central ritual persons' gestures, although there is by no means agreement, even among shamans, about precisely what is significant and how and why this is so. None of these elements will be explained fully here (see Badamhatan 1986, 163–90; Even 1988–89, 317–80). While the literature on Darhad shamanism is rich in information on its more liturgical aspects, it remains remarkably silent on what actually takes place when the spirits are supposed to be present in the shaman's body. But the shamanic audiences I encountered, whether composed of locals, outsiders, or both, did not travel up to several hundred miles just to listen to pretty songs and beautiful poems. They came to solicit solutions to their problems from the spirits and to see shamans possessed. For this reason I describe in some detail the three phases of the ritual sequence, since this offers a good sense of what actually happens in the course of a Darhad shamanic ceremony.

During the introductory phase, spirits of all sorts are invited to participate in the gathering, to enjoy the "precious bits" (*deej*) offered on the altar, and so on. The shaman sings a variety of praises (*magtaal*), prayers (*daatgal, zalbiral*), and invocations (*duudlaga, tamlaga*). Some of these are performed only on certain occasions; others—such as calling the "Nine Guardians of the Otog" (Otgiin Yösön Sahius)—are an indispensable element of all ceremonies. During this phase the shaman offers libations of milk and vodka to the altar, to her spirit vessel, to the fire, and in the direction of the ninety-nine skies. Crucially, she is not considered to be completely without consciousness (*uhaangüi*) at this stage. Instead, the shaman's normal sense of the world is understood to "come and go" (*oron garan*) and to "deteriorate" (*muudah*) slowly, implying, in this particular context, that things are becoming increasingly hazy. This idea of gradual possession is also reflected in the way the costume is put on. The shaman begins by purifying the shamanic boots over the smoke of burning juniper (*arts*), and then addresses some silent prayers to the sacred footwear, after which the assistant puts them on the shaman's feet. After a while, the shamanic gown is subjected to a similar purification, but this time it is the assistant who repeats the prayers, since the shaman's consciousness has already "deteriorated" further. Finally the headgear is put on, and the shaman is ready to become possessed. The shaman at this point makes three violent jumps, picks up the drum and the drumstick, is offered a large sip of vodka by the assistant, and the actual shamanizing can begin.

In the middle phase the shaman makes personal invocations to and is possessed by her own *ongod*. Each such spirit has its own songs, characterized by intricate symbolism and poetic style (see Even 1988–89 for a discussion of these songs). The moment of possession is marked by the shaman drumming faster and faster, while making vomiting (*böölöh*—"to shamanize"— connotes "to vomit"—*booljiih*) and animal-like sounds (grunts, snorts, or squeaks), and occasionally laughing in a most eerie manner. Then follows the "words uttered" (*heldeg üg*) or "what is sung (by the spirit)" (*duudag n'*). This, together with a variety of requests, "spirit autobiographies," exclamations, and verdicts, is what constitutes the divine message from the spirit to the audience. It is at this point that the interpreter must prove her worth, for there is no obvious sense to this message, let alone any explicit formula for its interpretation. Clearly this constitutes more than just an anthropological problem: most people in the audience are also at a total loss as to what is going on. For this reason it is the interpreter who has the final word regarding who is to be "fixed" by which spirit (each *ongon* will call only one client).[10] When each individual session ends, the spirit leaves (*garah*) the shaman's body, something that is marked by her making a single, and very loud, drumbeat. In this way, several hours pass. One by one, new *ongod* are invoked, so that the shaman may eventually become possessed by all the spirits that he or she masters. Sometimes the spirits are not keen to arrive; on other occasions they come in very quick succession, one after another. During the ritual, the shaman may also take a rest from the spirits, and the drumming, singing, and dancing drop to a lower level of intensity, but without stopping completely.

The end phase is marked by the shaman throwing the drumstick violently into the corner of the room. The assistant must now rush to begin undressing her (headgear first, followed by the gown, and finally the boots), because it is extremely dangerous to wear the shamanic attire while not drumming. Then, as the shaman slowly becomes herself again, she begins to make prayers,

---

10. The client's identity is revealed at the beginning of the "words uttered," when the shaman sings a song in which the birth year (*jil*) (in the twelve-year lunar calendar) and household size (*am bültei*) of this person are mentioned. This leaves room for considerable interpretation. Occasionally, several persons in the audience make a claim to being called on, but it may also happen that no one present is found to fit the bill.

offerings, and libations very similar to those of the introductory phase. Eventually she grabs a portion of *idee* from the altar and offers it to the fire. Then she sits down, lights a cigarette (smoking seems to be an occupational hazard of shamanism), and is offered tea and snacks. Relatives distribute the remaining *idee* to everyone present, and fresh tea is served. The vodka is handed out, more cigarettes are lit, and everyone has a good time. Then, at sunrise, the gathering disperses.

The Knot of Knots

The care with which the assistant helps the shaman put on and take off the gown points to the central role performed by this artifact in the shamanic possession ritual, if not in Darhad shamanism as a whole. As her indispensable "armor," the gown protects the shaman by "absorbing" (*shingeh*) the "souls" (*süns*) of both people and spirits into its many "layers" (*salbagar*), so that they do not "pierce" (*tsooloh*) her body too deeply. At the same time, however, donning the gown also exposes the shaman to the potentially lethal risk of becoming lost in the world of the sprits and never returning to the world of human beings, which is exactly what is feared to happen when a shaman suddenly stops drumming at the peak of possession.[11] Unlike an ordinary nomad's gown (*deel*), which contains its wearer in a protective enclosure with a minimum of openings (Lacaze 2000), the shamanic gown—which is not worn with the otherwise ubiquitous sash (*büs*), and from whose baggy exterior multiple cotton knots, strings, and flaps extend in all directions—is a sort of hyper-surface, which, far from patrolling the shaman's bodily and existential boundaries, invites maximum intervention. In that sense, as I shall demonstrate in further detail below, the gown may be said to enact a vista of multilayered dimensions, momentarily making the otherwise invisible spirits visible.

This is why, as the spirits are invoked at the beginning of the possession ceremony, the shaman's own soul (*süns*) cannot resist being ensnared in the alluring maze of layers upon layers and knots upon knots that makes up his or her shamanic gown. For just as, in Nadmid Udgan's words, the spirits are "absorbed" into this multidimensional plane of proliferating textures, so also does her own person "deteriorate" into disparate elements, not unlike an exploding haze of gas. (Recall that the term for trance—*hii uhaan*—literally

11. A Duha woman told Benedikte Kristensen that "when she was a kid she had once touched her granddad's shamanic dress without his knowledge, which made her feel 'like being drunk' and 'very dizzy'" (2007, 286).

means "gassy" or "airy" mind.) That also explains why the direction of the occult journey between the spirits and the shaman is an unresolved issue in discussions of Darhad shamanism (Badamhatan 1986, 167; Diószegi 1963, 63; Sandschejew 1930, 44). Instead of the shaman's traveling to an otherworldly realm inhabited by spirits, or the spirits' traveling to a this-worldly realm inhabited by humans, the world of humans and the world of the spirits are simultaneously collapsed from both sides onto the hyper-surface of the gown.

Apart from their being indispensable magical tools that enable shamans to travel to the spirits, what effect do these artifacts have on the Darhads' idea of themselves as a people imbued with a latent and invisible black side? Humphrey has convincingly argued that the personhood of old Daur Mongolian men (*utaachi*) was qualitatively different from that of Daur shamans (*yadgan*). More generally, traditional Daur social life evolved around two contrasting social ontologies: a chiefly ontology of eternal sameness, solidity, and rigidity expressed in the solidity of mountains and the bone-dry imaginary of the patriline (*yas*); and a shamanic ontology of perpetual metamorphosis, malleability, and fluidity expressed in the unpredictable movements of wild animals and the inchoate trajectories of the shamanic spirits. So, whereas the agency of *utaachi* inhered in their capacity for personifying the bone-dry ontology of the dominant Daur patriarchal order, *yadgan*—whether male or female—were imbued with political and religious prominence insofar as they personified the labile ontology of endlessly roaming predators no less than restless spirits (Humphrey 1996, 29–64, 183–93).

I suggest that the contrast many Darhads draw between a yellow side and a black side, and indeed a yellow religion and a black faith, results from similar divisions in the Shishged context, and that the shamanic gown is vital for keeping these in place. More precisely, we might think of the shamanic ritual as one sustained-ground reversal, in which the ordinary conventions of social life are flipped upside down, or rather inside out. Through a temporary reversal of what is visible and invisible, inner and outer, the performing shaman exposes the otherwise hidden "layers" (*davhar*) of persons' minds. (Indeed the fact that possession is marked by shamans making vomiting sounds suggests that their insides are being turned inside out as the spirits enter.)

Given this background, we can conceive of the shaman as a weightless black margin to the weighty yellow center of the old men discussed in the previous chapter. For shamans are not imbued with the unified, encompassing bodies of the "eldest men" who play a central, informal leadership role in the annual *ovoo* rituals. On the contrary, their bodies are black to the core (inasmuch as it makes sense to say that a possessed shaman has a core, or for that matter a body at all), for during ceremonies shamans like Nadmid Udgan are invaded by a plethora of heterogeneous spiritual beings that are irreducible to any concept of sameness. Recalling that each problem fixed by the shaman is memorialized ("knotted") onto her gown, I suggest that this artifact acts as a sort of occult microscope through which people in the shaman's audience gain momentary access to the normally invisible intentions of fellow human beings. By wearing people's misfortunes on her skin in the form of *hadag* attached to her gown, the shaman makes visible what cannot normally be gauged from a person's appearance, namely, his latent propensities for trickery, cursing, and violence.

Thus understood, the possession séance, and specifically the materiality of the shamanic gown, divides the shaman's ritual community into potential perpetrators and potential victims of misfortune. While the latter are always present at rituals as clients who are afflicted with *horlol*, the former may not be, but the black impact of their layered minds (maledictions, *hel am*, and so forth) is nevertheless rendered visible in the new *hadags* and knots that are fastened to the shaman's gown in the *zasal*. This, by the way, also explains why people in Tsagaan Nuur took such an interest in memorizing the design of Nadmid Udgan's gown, for it provided them with an updated map of the distribution of misfortune in the village, a very useful thing at a time when accusations of witchcraft proliferated.

* * *

A Darhad shaman, then, may tentatively be defined as a person with the capacity to personify as many relations as possible, both in the external sense of having unique access to the spirits, and in the internal sense that she alone is capable of making people's hidden intentions visible by turning their dark interiors inside out. The shaman is, then, the knot of knots in the community, unlike the "eldest men," who are the centers of centers; there is no limit to the number of humans, and nonhumans, that Darhad shamans can embody.

But note: if the "genuine" shamans in that sense personify the black side of Darhad persons, how are they different from the not-so-genuine shamans, who in the previous chapters were found to play precisely the same role in Shishged social life? For example, is that not what I concluded that Gombodorj, the living trickster, does: embody all the violent, cunning, and black capacities that his fellow Darhads are so keen on projecting onto the taiga? This conundrum suggests that if a fundamental difference exists between the personhood of genuine shamans and that of not-so-genuine ones, it must lie in the ways in which they relate to the shamanic spirits. To explore this possibility, we need to take a further look at the Darhad shamanic cosmos, for only by digging deeper into the question of what a shamanic spirit is, and what kind of agency it has, can we return to the theme of shamanism without shamans and try to solve this riddle.

Economies of Spirits

Across North Asia, indigenous (as well as sometimes less-indigenous) people are engaged in a plethora of interactions with different kinds of spiritual entities (Hamayon 1990; Humphrey 1996; Ingold 1986; Pedersen 2001; Vitebsky 2005; Willerslev 2007). Perhaps we can group these interactions into distinct "economies of souls." As Roberte Hamayon argues in her sweeping comparative study of North Asian shamanic societies (1990), as one moves from the forests of Siberia to the steppes of Mongolia, patrifiliation takes over from alliance as the dominant mode of kin relatedness; the breeding of domestic animals gains importance at the expense of the hunting of wild ones; and an otherwise "horizontal" spirit world is slowly elevated into a more an cestralized, and therefore verticalized, cosmos composed of beings that are mostly "ontologically different from the human soul" (Hamayon 1994, 87; see also Ingold 1986). Mongolian shamanism, Hamayon maintains, is thus generally characterized by "a preference for transmission within the world of the self rather than exchange within the world of the other" (1994, 81). By contrast, shamans in Siberia maintain affinal relations with the spirits of wild animals in order to ensure the availability of game for hunting (see also Willerslev 2007). The closer one moves toward the stratified, pastoral societies of Inner Asia, the more tangential the role of shamanism becomes, according to Hamayon's argument, so that eventually it "fragment[s] into a series of separate practices carried out by the marginal specialists" (1994, 88).

In many ways, the Darhad case is positioned right at the midpoint of this comparative axis. Not only are many Darhad shamanic spirits simultaneously zoomorphic and anthropomorphic (Dulam and Even 1994), but also, to paraphrase Hamayon, Darhad shamans are "concerned with relationships within society" as well as "with its natural environment" (1994, 87). Thus, whereas Daur Mongols had "no name...for the unknown place[s]...where [the shamanic] spirits dwell[ed]" (Humphrey 1996, 122), most Darhad *ongod* have a "definite and unchanging abode" (Diószegi 1963, 72), which corresponds to the burial site of a dead shaman. Upon the death of a shaman (or, to be more precise, three years after it), her soul (*süns*) turns into a shamanic spirit soul (*ongon süns*), which, over a period of about three years, is then slowly absorbed into (*shingeh*)—and eventually becomes master (*ezen*) of—the locality in question.[12] Among the places "owned" by prominent *ongod*

12. While all dead shamans turn into shamanic souls (*ongod süns*), and while all these *ongod süns* are "absorbed" into the burial sites of shamans, not all are "masters" of equally prominent places; for there is, after all, only a limited expanse of land for them to be "absorbed into." The general picture seems to be that in a given shamanic line (*udam*), the oldest *ongod* serve as

are mountains, but also trees, lakes, rock formations, and rivers. Indeed, the abodes of *ongod* seem to be clustered around the mouths of rivers, or in the zone between the steppe and the taiga, which, incidentally, is also where many shamans live (for a map, see Pürev 1999, 342–44). Some of these spirit loci have been remembered for centuries, and the literature on Darhad shamanism suggests that they once played a role in the legitimization of hunting and pasturelands of different patrilineal and—ideally—virilocal clan groupings (Badamhatan 1986, 171–72; Diószegi 1963, 72–75; Dulam 1992, 12; Dulam and Even 1984, 136–38; Sandschejew 1930, 59).

Borrowing Humphrey's useful terms (1995), we may thus speak of a subversive "shamanic landscape" which challenges the dominant "chiefly landscape" of patriarchal elders and the Buddhist church. The shamanic burial sites delineate an alternative spiritual geography, or soul economy, in which people can relate to occult entities in a way different from the asymmetrical manner of the lamas and male elders. On the one hand, we have a spiritual economy promoting "vertical" (unbalanced) sacrifices and prayers to transcendental divinities at places of worship (*ovoos*) located mostly in the steppe zone. On the other hand, there is a shamanic spiritual economy, which promotes "horizontal" (balanced) propitiations and prestations to a more immanent category of spiritual entities—namely, the souls of shamanic ancestors—whose abodes are predominantly associated with the taiga (Ingold 1986; Pedersen 2001).

But if one takes a closer look at the shamanic spirits themselves, then it turns out that many of the contrasts that, on the larger level, seem to distinguish the shamanic spirits from the more Buddhist or chiefly ones, begin to reappear on the smaller level as internal differentiations among the former entities. Each *ongon* is thus known to belong to one of two partitions, the partition of the fifty-five "western skies" (*baruun tenger*) or "white skies" (*tsagaan tenger*), and the partition of the forty-four "eastern skies" (*züün tenger*) or "black skies" (*har tenger*). This division figures not only in the design of the shamanic paraphernalia (see Badamhatan 1986, 158–61, 190–91) but in many shamanic invocations, too (see, for example, Even 1988–89, 101–75). In other words, the contrast between black (shamanic) spirits and yellow (Buddhist/chiefly) spirits suddenly reappears *within* the former category, in that *ongod*, from a point of view inside the shamanic cosmos itself, are divided along the same axis of differentiation according to which they map onto one or the other pole from an external

---

"owners" of the most prominent abodes (major rivers, prominent mountains, and so forth). But the younger spirits still have abodes in their own right; only their fields of power are not as extensive as those of the older ones (Even 1988–89, 113–14; Pedersen 2009).

perspective. Indeed, as we shall see, this fractal quality of the shamanic spirits is manifest not only in their location on the Shishged landscape but also in their degree of genealogical proximity to well-known Darhad clans and descent lines.

According to Nadmid Udgan, most of her "ten or so" *ongod* come from the black skies. Some, however, are blacker than others, namely, those that cannot be traced back to any shamanic lines. Unlike the rest, these *ongod* are not referred to as Father (Aav), Mother (Eej), or other consanguinal terms; nor are they ever called Hairhan (Precious One), the designation sometimes used for the most powerful spirits, such as the legendary Zönög *ongon*. Instead, these spirits are known by more vague and anonymous names, above all, the apparently neutral "Thing" (Yum). Representing, as it were, the orphaned, proletarian alternative to the Fathers and Mothers of the black skies, the *ongod* referred to as "things" are clearly among the least prestigious in the internal pecking order of shamanic spirits, for they lack a respectable shamanic pedigree, so to speak, in terms of the degree of ancestralization that can be traced in any given spirit. Thus, despite the latent conflict between shamanic and patriarchal imaginaries, there seems to be a sense in which "the strongest" (*hamgiin hüchtei*) Darhad shamanic spirits—but not necessarily shamans—are associated with long descent lines of *zaarin* (the so-called Fathers) or similarly unbroken matrilineal generations of *udha* (the so-called Mothers).

Turning now to the spatial distribution of shamanic spirits' abodes, we notice a clear tendency: as the distance between their location and the steppe zone increases, the more black and amorphous the spirits become. A good example is Ders Shig Yum, the only one of Nadmid Udgan's shamanic spirits belonging to the black skies that did not have its abode in the Shishged. Instead, she explained, "Ders Shig Yum originally comes from across the border, in Tuva." The terms used to describe this spirit suggest that its distant origin outside the Shishged offers little spatial or genealogical anchoring, for Ders Shig Yum seems to be perceived as ultra-fluid and supra-multiple. Among other things, the word *ders* is used to denote something grassy (thus Ders Shig Yum = Grassy Thing), and I have heard several tales in which shamans "became many as grass" (*dersnii toogoor bolchihdog*) in the face of encroaching dangers from the outside, such as Buddhist lamas or the Red Army.[13]

A very different picture appears at the other extreme, among those of Nadmid Udgan's spirits that belonged to the partition of the fifty-five "white

13. According to Nadmid Udgan, Ders Shig Yum first arrived in the Shishged "when a prince called Da Noyon went to Tuva and brought it back with him." The first shaman to have mastered Ders Shig Yum was apparently Günge Zaarin from the White Huular clan (Diószegi 1963, 73; Pürev 1999, 272).

skies." All of these rank high in the internal hierarchy of her *ongod,* but the highest in the spiritual pecking order was the only one of her *ongod* that, as she put it, did "not originate from a human [a shaman], but from the heavenly sky [*hünees garaagui, tenger sansraas garsan*]." This is the Darhad Ivd Hyaryn Steppe Thing (Ar Darhad Ivdiin Hyaryn Talyn Yum). Hyaryn Yum (as we may call it) is considered to rank above other shamanic spirits, for, as Nadmid Udgan enthusiastically explained to me by making a graphic gesture upward to the sky, alone among *ongod,* Hyaryn Yum resides in Heaven (Tenger)—far, the implication seemed to be, above the "maximum" height that can be attained by any soul of a dead shaman, ancestral or not. Unlike the hyper-black Ders Shig Yum, Hyaryn Yum, from Nadmid Udgan's perspective, was a supremely "white" or "yellow" spirit. Indeed, as we saw earlier, it was first "enlivened" by a lama-shaman to protect her against the shamanic illness.[14]

Both of these facts—that some *ongod* are more ancestral than others, and that some *ongod* are more human than others—suggest that shamanic spirits are imbued with a complex, some might say multiple, or even contradictory ontology. Not only are the spirits divided into the two "morally" different partitions of either black or yellow *ongod,* but also they exist in (at least) two qualitatively different states at the same time.[15] For, as we have seen, while most of a given shaman's spirits are "absorbed into" concrete physical sites in the Shishged landscape in the form of the sacred burial places of dead shamans, the same spirits also exist in the more abstract and immaterial dimension of the skies (*tenger*), even if some spirits (such as Hyaryn Yum) are more immaterial than others, while still others (such as Ders Shig Yum) are so immanent that they are not "masters" of anything in particular. This raises the question of what the cosmological role of the skies is. Why is it not enough that shamanic spirits are "owners" of different places and animals on the land?

14. Ironically, this most "Buddhist" of Nadmid Udgan's spirits is known to originate from the old Ivd monastery—the very place where, according to lore and as described in chapter 3, the lama pioneers from the Ih Shav' were attacked by "flying demons" (Dioszegi 1963). Instead of representing a hyper-black entity positioned at the margin of the Buddhist zone of influence in the Shishged, which presumably must be how the lamas would have though of it, Hyaryn Yum, from the shamanic perspective, was the most "white"/"yellow" and "Buddhist" of Nadmid Udgan's *ongod.*

15. While it would be an oversimplification to see such dualisms as the result of external influences alone—after all, the partition between the forty-four black skies and the fifty-five white ones also can be found in Mongolian contexts where the Buddhist church has played little or no role (see, for example, Humphrey 1996, 122–26)—the Darhad Ih Shav' undoubtedly served to increase their importance in local cosmological thinking.

(On next page: Figure 16. Shaman tree)

One Sky and Many Skies

Sky concepts are very common in Mongolian shamanism (Hamayon 1990; Heissig 1980; Humphrey 1996). Indeed, the concept of *tenger* played a key role in Mircea Eliade's famous—but, as we are about to see, flawed—thesis that all "archaic forms of ecstasy" involve an "ascent to the sky" (1964). Unlike some Mongolian and Western scholars (Even 1988–89; Pürev 1999), I am not concerned with whether or not the sky concept is properly shamanic—or for that matter properly Darhad. I am interested in the apparent paradox that shamans conceive of *ongod* as immanent and transcendental at the same time, that is to say, as spiritual entities that are both materially present in the landscape and yet immaterial and latent somewhere up in the sky. In that sense, I suggest, *tenger* may also (like the notion of the person) be described as a fractal or "post-plural concept," for it is simultaneously a many (as in "the ninety-nine skies") and a one (as in the "heavenly sky").

At first glance, it appears that Darhad shamans do think of their "ecstasy" as an "ascent to the sky" in Eliade's sense. Badamhatan writes, "With regard to the appearance of the spirits at the moment when the shaman incorporates them, the Darhad shamans do not mention…animal forms or concrete conceptions: the majority of them report that spirits arrive as a ray of light" (1986, 185). Similarly, in her book on Mongolian folk culture, Caroline Pegg cites Nadmid Udgan as saying that, when invoking the spirits, she "feels that she leaves the earth and travels to the sky" (2001, 133). What Eliade and numerous subsequent scholars of northern Asian shamanism seem to have overlooked, however, is that, with a few exceptions (such as for instance Hyaryn Yum), shamans like Nadmid Udgan do not conceive of their worship as a traveling to one single Sky (*Tenger*) in perfect unity and harmony, which often—say, in Mongolian heroic epic and Chinese imperial mythology—is conflated with the physical sky. Instead, to judge from what I have been told and heard in northern Mongolia, the concept of *tenger* in Darhad, and perhaps in Mongolian shamanism more generally, is irreducibly multiple, for it denotes a series of parallel or more precisely "slated" realms, like overlapping tiles on a roof, that the shaman must pass through during a given possession in order to be fully embodied by her spirits, and thus be fully accepted as a shaman.

The concept of the skies, I suggest, makes possible a necessary stretching of the shamanic cosmos, which allows shamans to interpolate an unfathomable distance and thus separation into the otherwise radically immanent and seemingly "flat" (horizontal) spirit dimension of shamans' souls and animal masters. I attribute this notion specifically to shamans, since ordinary Darhads do not seem to give much thought to the skies. Thus, whereas the concept of *tenger* features very prominently in shamans' invocations, which shamanic audiences generally find quite uninteresting, the subsequent "words uttered" by the possessed shaman—clearly the highpoint of the shamanic ritual from the point of view of laymen in the audience—contain little or no reference to the skies (Even 1988–89; Hamayon 1994).

During shamanic possessions, the *ongod* are generally understood by the laypeople to be "here," which is why it would be quite illogical to speak of (and *to*) these spiritual entities as if they were somewhere "up there," in the skies. For the shamans, by contrast, it makes good sense to add an additional, overlapping dimension to the occult realm of the spirits so that their journey is rendered, as it were, sufficiently extraordinary. Somehow it would just not be as impressive if the Darhad shamans "merely" traveled to the Shishged taiga and were possessed by the restless soul of a dead shaman; indeed, as we have seen, this might happen to practically any Darhad person, albeit usually very much against his or her will. Not only would establishing a purely horizontal and this-worldly connection to the shamanic spirits seem just a little too easy, but also it would ignore the fact that many *ongod* are ancestral spirits, which marks them as positioned "above" (*deed*) the living. Indeed a common term for ancestors is *deedes*, or "the above ones."

In sum, I believe that the concept of *tenger* serves a double purpose in the Darhad (and perhaps the larger Mongolian) shamanic cosmos, a purpose that is at once ontological and sociological. Not only does the sky concept render the shaman's journey much, much longer by installing an irreducible gap between shamans and their spirits, and more generally humans and nonhumans, but also it makes the shamanic spirits appropriately "vertical," as ancestors should be. It is thus necessary to qualify Eliade's old and much-cited idea that shamanic possession involves an ascent to the sky, in the singular. Instead, Nadmid Udgan and other Darhad shamans operate according to a concept of multiple skies—in the form of an overlapping or, as I have called it, "slated" arrangement of ninety-nine parallel transcendental realms—as one among several steps in a series of occult dimensions which they must pass through during prayer and possession. In that sense the shaman's journey emerges as both horizontal and vertical—or, more precisely, as neither horizontal nor vertical—for what happens during possession is an enactment of a transversal vector, a shamanic line of flight that takes both verticality and horizontality to their limit.[16]

---

16. See also Holbraad and Willerslev (2007) and Swancutt (2007).

Spirit Guardians and Spirit Helpers

Ongod, then, exist simultaneously—or transversally—as actual things in the landscape, as virtual hypersurfaces made visible in the design of certain sacred artifacts, and on the transcendental plane of *tenger*. And yet this is not all there is to say about the exceedingly complex ontology of these entities. In fact, as the story of Gombodorj showed, perhaps the most vital thing about *ongod* is that they are conceived as distinct persons, each of whom is endowed with known spirit biographies, if not personalities. To understand better this aspect of the agency of shamanic spirits—the fact that every such nonhuman being is imbued with traits that are just as multifaceted yet just as recognizable as in the case of individual human beings, if not more so—we need to explore the distinction between spirit guardians and helpers, which can be found in many shamanic traditions.

A spirit guardian—or, as they are sometimes referred to in the literature on Mongolian shamanism, spirit protector—is a named shamanic spirit (such as Ders Shig Yum) that is mastered by one or more shamans. As we have seen, each (or nearly each) spirit protector was originally "absorbed" into the burial place of a certain dead shaman, from whose soul it derives. It has its own material objectifications on vessels and gowns, is the target of specific invocations, and may (if those invocations are successful) take up temporary residence in shamans' bodies during possession rituals. Shamans master a limited number of spirit protectors, ranging in the handful of cases about which I collected information, between five and twenty—in Nadmid Udgan's case, "around ten." These may be "clan spirits" (*yazguuryn ongod*), *ongod* from other groups often acquired from shaman teachers, or shamanic spirits that are not associated with any human ancestors (typically designated as "Things").

Spirit helpers, conversely, are all the different bodies or objects in which a given spirit protector may manifest itself. They are known by a range of designations, such as "metamorphosis" (*huvilgaan*), "escort" (*daguul*), "light body" (*höngön biye*), and "path" (*jim*). Often, spirit helpers take the zoomorphic form of a wild animal, whose species-specific capacities are then appropriated by shamans according to their particular purposes, such as when they undertake journeys to places and people on behalf of clients (as in assault sorcery, for instance). Nadmid Udgan listed six animals that she presented as her spirit helpers (*zarts*): wolf, bear, fox, raven, lark, and magpie. These helpers, she explained, may be identified during séances by the specific animal sounds (grunts, squeaks, and so forth) shamans utter when they become possessed by them. Spirit helpers, however, may also take the form of non-zoomorphic entities in the landscape (such as blueberries or idle power stations) or inanimate natural phenomena (such as rainbows or rays of light), or they may be manifested in social phenomena as ephemeral and omnipresent as the flow of gossip in a community.

In other words—and crucially for the point I am making about the nature and efficacy of shamanic agency—a given spirit guardian (*ongon*) comprises a potentially infinite number of spirit helpers. In a detailed study of Darhad shamanic invocations, Marie-Dominique Even reaches the same conclusion. She writes: "The multiplicity of *ongon* rests upon the adjunction of the ancestral shamanic *ongon*'s auxiliary spirits, the different forms it can adopt, which in shamanic terminology are often known as 'servants' or 'metamorphoses'" (1988–89, 115). Much like the postsocialist Mongolian state discussed in chapter 1, a shamanic spirit (that is, a spirit guardian) can be defined as an inherently multiple entity irreducible to any singular form, which moves along an unpredictable path of perpetual and unpredictable becoming or transition. This allows, indeed compels, it to absorb ever more forms and substances as it departs from others in its restless journey from one body (or spirit helper) to the next.

Instead of thinking of *ongod* as single and stable entities, it is therefore more accurate if we conceive of them as inherently labile and capricious assemblages of heterogeneous elements. Indeed there is a sense in which the shamanic spirits simply *are* movements, more than they are discrete entities imbued with the propensity *to* move (Holbraad 2007). Shamanic spirits, then, are not representations of change, whether economic, political or social; nor are they products of change. Instead, a given *ongod* is a *sui generis* enactment of change or "transition" in a particular ontological register that might be called occult or spiritual. To flesh out this key point, it is useful to consider Gombodorj's reply when I once asked him, "Where does a spirit master go when it is not present in the game animal anymore?" He cut me off with "I have no idea," clearly annoyed by my question. "I guess it just goes here and there [*iish tiish yavna biz*]." Answers like these suggest that spirit helpers are thought of as visible traces left by the invisible movements of spirit guardians, each new metamorphosis being like a shadow cast by the *ongon*'s travel across the duration of time. Thus, the only way to get a glimpse of *ongod* is through their absence, for because of their labile ontology, the spirits can be seen only by *not* being seen. All that is ever made visible of a guardian is the empty gap or interval between any two of its helpers.

This enables me to posit a further ontological displacement of the shamanic spirits akin to the one between the singular and plural forms of *tenger* discussed earlier, a no less paradoxical relationship between *ongod* "as such" and their material objectifications in sacred artifacts, which, do not forget, are also known as *ongod*. The "bundle-like" design of the shamanic talismans, I propose, may be interpreted as nonrepresentational instantiations of the spirits' relentless transmutation from one form to another. Thus understood, people's offerings to their family vessels and clients' knotting of shamans' gowns are inherently doomed attempts to depict, within the visible realm of extensive things, the invisible movement of spirits within the intensive realm of occult change. Seen in this light, the shamanic artifacts emerge as imperfect mappings of the spirits' movements, like the hazy trace left behind by particles moving through a vapor chamber in a physical experiment.

This challenges dominant Euro-American conventions concerning the hierarchy of being and becoming, or stability and change, which are based on the Cartesian premise that transcendental entities such as the Christian God or the Hegelian state exist in a supra-stable and hyperunified form to which human access is limited only to fleeting sensations that may at best assume an unstable and heterogeneous form. In many ways, as I have just demonstrated, *ongod* present an obverse "problem of representation." As in a Cartesian nightmare, in which Plato's cave analogy is uprooted and flipped 180 degrees, the Darhad shamanic spirits, as indeed the postsocialist Mongolian state turned out to be, are not absolute and atemporal entities, which humans (and other worldly beings, such as animals) are reduced to seeing only as shadows that are too contingent, too capricious, too fleeting. On the contrary, *ongod* are labile *an sich,* and people's "representations" of them are inevitably too stable, too ideal. As swarmlike assemblages of human and nonhuman affects, *ongod* move through time and space, land and sky/skies, words and things, along transversal lines drawn by their incessant jumping from one body to the next, as manifested in unpredictable "strokes" (*tusgal*) of misfortune and luck.

Too Many Bodies

With this exploration of the shamanic spirit cosmos in mind, we can now return to my overarching question concerning the agency of the "genuine" Darhad shamans and how it differs from that of their not-so-genuine counterparts. Let us begin by taking a fresh look at the spirit vessels and their properties as "containers of people's souls," as the hunter I quoted put it. Now, apart from being objects of worship, these artifacts are imbued with the capacity to change the appearance of hunters' bodies. Indeed, the same hunter confided to me, this is "the deepest of shamanic secrets" (*böögiin shashny hamgiin nuuts yum*), for it entails the most "dangerous implications" of all. He went on:

Let us say that I want to be a good wolf hunter. Then I must make a wolf *ongon.* If I make an *ongon* that looks like a wolf out of sheep's wool, then the wolf will think that *I am* a wolf. The point is that I will become like a wolf [*chono shig bolno*]. A person who has thus nearly become a wolf [*barag chon bolchihson*] will not be recognized as a human [*hün*] by the wolf. So I can kill it easily. This is what is called a hunting *ongon.* They all have this purpose.

The primary purpose of Darhad hunting vessels, in other words, is to enable the hunter to take on (or at least approximate) the body of his prey so as to get close enough to kill it. My question now is whether the same goes for the Darhad shamanic gowns. Are they also a sort of extra skin, which the shaman puts on to trick the spirits into thinking that she is one of them?

As Benedikte Kristensen was told by a Duha shaman, "when he dresses in his shamanic costume, his own mind disappears and he starts to see 'through the eyes of the ongons' and 'fly and fight like them'" (2007, 287). Another Duha shaman once bragged that he "has two bodies"—one being his ordinary body, and the other his "shamanic body" (*böö biye*).[17] Yet crucially, these two bodies cannot be divided into one singular non-shamanic body and another equally singular shamanic body. Rather, as we saw earlier, shamans are equipped with a singular human body on the one hand and a multiple nonhuman body on the other. The shaman's first and singular body—which the Duha shaman referred to as his ordinary (human) body—is made up of all the "yellow," vertical, and commensurable relations that shamans are involved in along with everyone else; whereas the second and multiple body, which he referred to as his shamanic body, consists of all the "black," lateral, and noncommensurable relations, which in principle only shamans should have. So if the hunting vessel momentarily endows the hunter with one additional skin and thus one nonhuman body (a wolf body, say), the shamanic gown equips the shaman with a whole series of extra skins or bodies, one for each spirit guardian that the shaman masters.

We are once again reminded of the perspectivist or deictic conception of the cosmos as being divided into a multiplicity of discrete bodies, which all share the same will to see and be seen, that is, the capacity to be (as opposed to have) a point of view (Viveiros de Castro 1998a, 1998b, 2004, 2007). In the Amazon, it takes another body to see another world, and this is just what Amerindian shamans—and only they—have, since, in Viveiros de Castro's formulation, "they alone are capable of assuming the point of view of

---

17. Alan Wheeler, personal communication.

Figure 17. Making a shamanic drum

[nonhuman] beings and, in particular, are capable of returning to tell the tale" (1998a, 472). The shamans can do this because, as noted earlier, their bodies are seen not as unified and fixed physiological forms (as bodies are in dominant Western traditions), but as always changing "affects, dispositions or capacities which render every different species unique" (1998a, 478).

My central contention, then, is that both hunting vessels and shamanic gowns provide their Darhad Mongolian users with nonhuman perspectives, which, by facilitating a momentary transformation of their bodily "affects, dispositions, and capacities," enable hunters and shamans to cross otherwise unpassable ontological divides and return unharmed afterwards. Small wonder, therefore, that Gombodorj and other potential shamans were found (by both themselves and others) to be desperately in need of shamanic costumes, for this artifact essentially enables the shaman to determine when to take the perspective of her spirits and when not to. Thus, paradoxically, the gown can be said both to attract and to deflect spiritual attention. If the shaman is caught by the occult thrust of the *ongod* affect-swarm by donning her gown, she is also capable of arresting this virtual movement by taking it off. By removing her gown, Nadmid Udgan stepped out of the spirit flux and was made still, just the way an ordinary Darhad person is meant to be.

In a peculiar, roundabout sort of way, the genuine shamans thus emerge as *less* shamanic than the fake shamans are, for whereas the latter are in permanent continuity with the fluid ontology of spirits, the former are transformed into labile assemblages of affects only upon donning their shamanic gowns. If in donning their gowns, Darhad shamans like Nadmid Udgan become ordinary persons turned inside out, they are conversely turned back into (relatively) ordinary persons by taking them off again. Much as the *atamans* were found capable of being within the realm of politics in chapter 1, shamans are simultaneously stable, singular, and yellow (as ordinary humans are supposed to be) and fluid, multiple, and black (as spirits are supposed to be).

This, then, is why and how the social agency of a "genuine" shaman from Tsagaan Nuur such as Nadmid Udgan differs fundamentally from that of not-so-genuine shamans from Ulaan-Uul, such as Gombodorj. For lack of any material (or immaterial) hinge to separate them from—while at the same time connecting them to—the world of *ongod,* the potential shamans are destined to remain within permanent potential reach of the spirits. Thus Gombodorj's problem is not merely that he is not shamanic enough but that he is at the same time too shamanic. As someone who has "too little body insofar as [he] possesses too many bodies" (Viveiros de Castro 2007, 161, emphasis omitted), Gombodorj is like an overcharged thundercloud that is desperately seeking an object on which to release its pent-up energies. Predestined to remain suspended among too many bodies, he needs a different kind of body, a composite body comprising his own singular and human body plus the multiple and nonhuman body afforded by a shamanic gown. Only when equipped with this artifact, along with a ritual community (a village, a clan, or at least a family), will his capacity for metamorphosis become balanced between stability and movement in a way that is neither too shamanic nor too little shamanic, as that of Nadmid Udgan, a "real" shaman, was.[18] Until then, he and other half-shamans

18. An analogy may be drawn to newborn Mongolian babies, who are also considered in need of an extra skin to slow down their innate propensity for metamorphosis. There are many techniques for doing this, such as feeding the infant and the mother mutton soup (*har shöl*) to render their bodies sufficiently "dry." Indeed there is a general sense in which Mongolian children are not considered fully human until they have reached a certain age and have undergone various rituals, such as the first cutting of the hair, which typically takes place around the age of three (Park 1997, 128–34; Empson 2010).

must remain neither fully singular nor fully double, whose fate is to be the impossible forms giving the forces of ceaseless transition a (post)human body.

Shamans without Shamanism

The goal of this chapter has been to offer a full-blown anthropological exegesis of Darhad shamanism as a coherent cosmology imbued with a distinct logic, and thereby fill out the hitherto largely empty ethnographic ground with regard to this book's overarching theme: the not quite shaman. It might be objected that by expressing myself in this manner, I place myself within an antiquated culturalist paradigm, whereby a "Darhad shamanic cosmology" is assumed to exist as a system of shared cultural symbols whose meaning it is the anthropologist's role to decipher. My reply to proponents of such a "social constructivist" critique (if it is fair to call it that) would be to ask them to question their own epistemological blind spots. As has recently been pointed out by a growing number of anthropologists and social theorists, it is now increasingly social constructivism itself that comes across as stuck within an obsolete paradigm that understands humans as constructing the same world differently, according to their cultural "worldviews" (Henare, Holbraad, and Wastell 2007; Ingold 2000; Jensen and Rödje 2009; Latour 2002; Law and Mol 2002; Viveiros de Castro 1998b). If, however, one takes as the theoretical premise of one's ethnographic analysis the possibility of a "multinaturalist" ontology of many worlds that all exist *as* construction (or becoming, or transition), as I have tried to do in this chapter and the rest of the book, then cultural exegesis no longer depends on a representational theory of symbols, meaning, or context. If things are not distinct from their meanings, but are rather meanings in a certain form, and if immaterial things are not less (or more) real than material things, but simply real in another (and possibly more virtual) ontological register, then their interpretation does not require a conventional social or political-economic context, for as postplural entities, they contain the potential to act as their own scales (Strathern 2004), and thus potentially to serve as particular kinds of concepts in their own right (Holbraad and Pedersen 2009b).

This methodological point is vividly brought out in the account I have given of the shamanic costume, which, as I tried to demonstrate, is precisely a thing that *is* its own meaning and indeed acts as its own context. As a cultural artifact that already contains all the dimensions that are needed to explain it (Riles 1998), the gown that is worn by the performing Darhad shaman does not need to be interpreted (at least in the conventional, hermeneutic sense of the term), either by local clients or by foreign anthropologists, for this object and the specific manner of its display already constitute what Strathern calls an "indigenous mode of analysis" its own right (1988). To paraphrase Roy Wagner (1986), we may in that sense think of the shamanic costume and the ritual practices associated with it as a theory that stands for itself: it is simultaneously an enactment of the shamanic cosmos and an analogical extension of it.

One of the nice things about such objects of self-analysis is that they do not require many "shared meanings" on the part of the people interpreting them in order for them to "make sense." Instead of being carriers of underlying symbolic meanings (which is how Mongolian shamanic artifacts have mostly been understood by anthropologists and other scholars), the assemblage of material indexes that I have called the shamanic hypersurface is, as it were, all that people need to know—or rather to see—in order to get "the meaning" of the ritual and the world of spirits generally. Thus, when Nadmid Udgan was possessed by her spirits, what people in the audience saw (myself included) was essentially what they got. We walked away from the event with neither more nor less cultural knowledge than what was made visible to us in the spectacle itself. Neither they nor I was in need of an elaborate "web of meanings" in order to decipher the "hidden code" of the spirit cosmos as a whole, for the logic of shamanism (in so far that it makes sense to speak of an emergent form in such seemingly culturalist terms), was directly imprinted on the extra-bodily skin of the dancing shaman.

Put in more concrete terms, all that the ritual community and the shamanic worshippers more generally need to know is that each *hadag* knotted onto a *manjig* was another act of *horlol* made visible, and the remaining components, scales, and dimensions of the world of spirits literally fell into place on their own.

Perhaps that is why, in northern Asian shamanic contexts, the same term is often used for shamanic spirits and their different material instantiations (in the Darhad case, *ongod*). In a non-representational universe, it does not make sense to think of talismans as attempts to depict spirits. Rather, we may think of such artifacts simultaneously as products of and vehicles for shamanic auto-exegesis. The artifacts are, at one and the same time, contexts for and theories of themselves. By recursively comprising all the scales needed to describe them, they also constitute a peculiar kind of latent concept—one which was never made by anyone in particular with any specific practical or symbolic purpose, and which was not developed within the confines of a single mind, but which nevertheless is imbued with power and beauty far surpassing those of many concepts forged out of words alone as part of a deliberate plan. We may, then, speak of the shamanic gown (and many other artifacts) as being imbued with intrinsic and distinct "conceptual affordances" (Holbraad, n.d.), and these potential and largely incidental (un-willed) concepts may (or may not) be extracted and used for different purposes by local nomads, urban elites, and foreign scholars. Accordingly, we may think of Nadmid Udgan's shamanic gown, and the plethora of sacred paraphernalia found in Darhad households and the Shishged landscape more generally, as vital transmitters of shamanic knowledge in an often hostile political environment, where seventy years of communist repression—and, before that, more than two centuries of Buddhist dominance—have led to a situation in which all the "genuine" shamans have been marginalized, if they haven't disappeared altogether. Because of the capacity for such post-plural artifacts to act as their own contexts and indeed perform their own auto-analysis, it is they, above all, that, during socialism if not before, made—and continue to make—it possible to be a client, and indeed a specialist, of Darhad shamanism without being in possession of any elaborate body of knowledge "about" the spirits and the shamanic cosmos as a whole. Shamans without shamanism, as it were.

Could this explain the consistently negative or even angry responses I received when asking people in the Shishged to spell out the precise nature of the shamanic spirits? Even specialists like Nadmid Udgan tried to dodge my questions, often telling entertaining if not downright comical stories about *ongod* instead. As I argue in the next and final chapter, seemingly negative answers like these express not epistemological doubt about the existence of the spirits (as anthropological convention would have it) but rather an irreducible ontological uncertainty about their precise mode of being and positioning in a given time and space. Might it be because *ongod* are defined by an inherent capacity for change that people refrain from trying to pin down their manner of being?

5 Mischievous Souls

"These people joke about everything, so it is impossible to know when they are telling the truth [*ünen*] and when they are telling a lie [*hudal*]." These were the words of a young man from Ulaanbaatar, in whose brand-new Russian GAZ jeep I once traveled to the Shishged. It was his first visit to Hövsgöl province. As we approached the Shishged, he began to express a number of practical concerns about going further, for the area is renowned for its truly awful roads and flooded rivers. It soon became clear, however, that his worries also stemmed from more intangible fears. "Is it true that the Darhads are prone to curse you?" he kept asking. "It is true that there are many shamanic spirits in the Darhad Depression?"

That afternoon he joined me on a visit to a friend of mine. A former director of a collective farm, and since 1990 chairman of the Ulaan-Uul branch of the Mongolian People's Revolutionary Party, my friend was at this point a respected leader in the Ulaan-Uul community, renowned not only for his informed views on politics but also for his staunchly materialist worldview. But of course the young driver from Ulaanbaatar knew none of this as we entered my friend's *ger*. All he knew was that the old man was a Darhad and "looked terrifying with his huge, bushy beard," as he later described his first impressions.

After going through the obligatory greetings between host and guests, my friend directed his attention toward the rather timid-looking driver. Issuing some general warnings about the always imminent danger of *haraal*, he added, in the mock-patronizing tone that is characteristic of some elderly Darhad men: "You must watch out while you are in the Darhad lands. The wilderness is full of restless souls and hungry bears. Shamans are abundant." Giggling, he then whispered, "In fact, I am myself a shaman!" At first my driver took this lightly. After all, the old nomad was laughing, so, as he told me later, he figured, what was the big deal? But then, as the warnings became more explicit, my driver (and increasingly I myself) became less certain. Was our Darhad host pulling our leg, or was he being earnest? This is (roughly) what he said:

> So, I gather that you are going to sleep at Har Us [Black Water, a river pool]. You'd better watch out for that place. It is full of *chötgör* [demons]. People avoid going there after dark. Once, a guy passed through in the middle of the night. Suddenly his horse froze stock-still, but its head was dragged to the side, as if being pulled by something. When he saw that the same thing was happening to his dog, he understood that a water demon must be present. Humans can't see them, but animals can. Why, you don't have a dog with you? Oh, I must lend you one of mine for the night. *Chötgör* are dangerous; they eat people's souls!

When we arrived at Har Us, just as the sun was setting over its dark waters, my driver exclaimed that he was too frightened to sleep there, and I found myself quite ready to agree with him. This was despite the fact that, shortly after having issued his warning, our host had exploded into a fit of laughter: "Hey, I am lying!" (*hudal, hudal*, lit. "lies, lies"). The problem, however, was that it never became clear to my driver (or to me) what, exactly, our host had been joking about; that is to say, we were unable to determine precisely when our host had begun, and when he stopped, telling his shamanic "lies."

"I just can't get my head around their minds [*uhaan ül hüreh*]," the driver, a Halh man, later complained over tea, echoing remarks I was to hear again and again from non-Darhads. As mentioned in chapter 2, the notion that Darhad persons are inveterate jokers is inseparable from the equally wide-spread idea that they are imbued with dark and cunning shamanic powers. For, as the example illustrates, it is because Darhads are experienced as "always lying" that it is so hard to discern any "straightness" (*shuluuhan*) coming from their "layered minds." This suggests that joking and "lying" have acquired a life of their own in northern Mongolia in the form of a shadowy potential, similar to the invisible black side residing within people, things, and events. In practices of joking, it seems, crude ethnic stereotypes merge with little-understood intricacies of shamanic cosmology, and a pristine space of analysis is laid bare.

* * *

At the earlier stages of my research in northern Mongolia, I still considered Darhad joking practices, and the ethnic stereotype associated with them, as a convenient place to begin my exploration of the nature of shamanic agency after socialism. Back then, joking still seemed to me a neat point of entry for unearthing the secrets of shamanism; it was the icing on the occult cake, beneath which waited layer upon layer of esoteric cosmology. As my work progressed, however, I was slowly learning to understand that, far from representing derivative or even frivolous aspects of the shamanic cosmos, joking, play, and irony are constitutive of it. Instead of providing an easy way of explaining shamanism, mischievous shamanic practice is what needs to be explained—more so than shamanism in earnest. For in a context of shamanism without shamans, the displacements inherent in humor become emblematic of shamanic practice and shamanic agency.

This chapter treats the decisive role played by joking and irony in the revival of Darhad shamanism in the late 1990s.[1] In fact, the preferred manner of talking about shamanism in a shamanless place like Ulaan-Uul often seemed to be through joking. Not only did people deny the presence of shamans, but also, as we just saw, they kept making jokes about people who were clearly not shamans, endlessly pointing out to me this or that person (children included) while exclaiming, with suppressed giggles, "Watch out, Morten, he is a shaman!" In many ways, this "shamanic humor" (as I call it here) is the ultimate mode of shamanism without shamans. As we are about to see, this contention must be understood both in the general sense that joking and "lying" are prominent manifestations of the black side of Darhad people, and in the more narrow sense that joking performs a certain job in the shamanic cosmos, in that it instigates particular effects. In a community scarred by the past purges of its lamas and shamans, joking has acquired shamanic efficacy in its own right, and studying it not only tells us something about the revival of shamanism in northern Mongolia since 1990 but also reveals something about the lasting impact of socialism on the world of the spirits itself.

Anecdotes and Joke Songs

In the late summer of 1999, accompanied by a local friend, I spent a few eventful weeks on horseback traversing the already snow-clad hills of the western Shishged in pursuit of legends (*domog*) and anecdotes (*onigoo*). On more than one occasion immediately after a successful visit to a nomadic *ail*, I would exclaim, "What a good storyteller that man was!" To which my

1. Humor and joking have been the subject of numerous studies in anthropology, theology, and philosophy (see, for example, Apte 1985; Berger 1997; Bergson 1999; Carty and Musharbash 2008; Douglas 1968, 1993; Freud 1991; Kierkegaard 1963, 1989; Morreall 1983, 1999).

friend would retort, "A bloody liar, that's what he is!" The man we had visited, I was then lectured with no little passion, had made it all up, for "as everyone knows, he is a totally ignorant person!"

Good anecdotes, I was given to understand, are told only by people who know what they are talking about. It is not enough just to have a good imagination, for to imagine something is dangerously close to telling a lie (*hudal*), which is universally frowned upon—the case of Gombodorj providing a good example. Instead, a good storyteller is someone who, precisely by knowing what he is talking about, is able to communicate this knowledge in an entertaining way. Perhaps that is why I failed so dramatically on the few occasions when I tried to tell a joke. The problem was not just that my (Danish or British) jokes were nearly impossible to translate. Even when I succeeded in conveying their meaning, people did not find them funny; indeed they were quite taken aback by their blatantly fictional nature. I was, sadly, seen not as a subtle joker (*shogch*) but more like a crude liar (*hudalch*), because instead of dramatizing a real event that might have happened to someone, I was conjuring up something that could never have happened to anyone.

Thus, I was told, a proper *onigoo* always builds on a true (*ünen*) and concrete (*bodit*) event, which may well be delivered in a detailed (*nariin*) and hyperbolic (*hetrüülegtei*) fashion, but cannot contain any purely fictitious (*zohiomol*) or untrue (*hudal*) content. For the same reason, the concept of jokes in the Euro-American sense does not exist among Darhads; only anecdotes do—humorous narratives based on real events or on events that can be imagined as real.[2] Also the structure of the *onigoo* differs substantially from Western jokes. While jokes (as I know them) are built up to facilitate explosions of sudden laughter at a specific point in their narration (the punch line), the typical *onigoo*—several examples of which we have already encountered in earlier chapters—is delivered with the aim of eliciting a continuous trickle of mirth throughout its narration.

As in the case of gossip, a strong normative if not downright hostile undercurrent runs beneath the telling of anecdotes: they often include an element of critique, a certain "evaluative component" (Bergmann 1993, 8). Thus most *onigoo* involve a person or a group of persons who at some point did something wrong or stupid, of which the anecdote serves as a (not so) gentle reminder. This was made clear to me when I once asked a Darhad friend to tell me all the anecdotes he knew. "Morten," he said, "there is no way I can do that. Most anecdotes I know are about people who are living around here,

---

2. According to Berger (1997, 153), "East Asian cultures, though they are full of the comic, have not cultivated the joke as has been the case in Europe and the Middle East."

and imagine if they found out that you had been recording me telling these things about them!"

Let us now consider the joke songs (*shog duu*) or mocking songs (*hoshin duu*),[3] described in several works on Darhad cultural traditions (Badamhatan 1986, 145; Legrain 2001, 2007, 2008a, 2008b; Pegg 2001, 230–31). Most people claim to know at least a couple of joke songs, and it is said that more than one thousand circulate in the Shishged (Tsegmed 1992). Indeed, if you ask a person to talk about Darhad culture, he or she is most likely to tell you about these songs, or about shamanism. Joke songs are used as entertainment at festive occasions such as weddings, public holidays (for example, International Women's Day), and the lunar New Year. They are rarely heard outside such contexts; indeed alcohol consumption seems to be a necessary prerequisite for their performance.

Most Darhad joke songs consist of two verses, each four lines long, with alliteration as the dominant principle of composition. Compared to other Mongolian songs, joke songs are short, and their performance is characterized by an unusual degree of speed in the intonation. Supposedly, much of their wit inheres in their subtle play on words as well as their clever alliterations. Still, practically all the joke songs I heard recounted the story of one or several existing persons who once did something embarrassing, stupid, or just plain wrong, and this anecdotal aspect clearly contributed to their wittiness.

Darhad joke songs, then, are funny not only because of their poetic form but also and especially because of their derogatory content: someone is always being laughed *at* when a joke song is performed. In that sense we can think of them as a sort of congealed gossip: each verse in a joke song corresponds to a certain piece of gossip that has been transformed into a fixed poetic form. Namdagiin Tsegmed, a well-known Darhad intellectual and journalist and the author of two collections of joke songs, explained to me:

> In Halh songs, things are said directly [*shuud helchihej baigaa*]. Darhad songs, on the other hand, always have a hidden meaning [*dald utgatai yum l daa*]. If you speak in an open manner, it is inappropriate. For example, instead of telling someone that his shirt is dirty, we will sing a song about it. Not directly to him, but to someone else, and then the song goes round and round, so that eventually, that person will learn about it. Such are the Darhad joke songs. They may seem to be folksongs [*ardyn*

---

3. For a collection of joke songs collected by the Belgian ethnomusicologist Laurent Legrain presented by singers from Renchinlhümbe, find the compact disc *Chants du peuple Darxad*, Collection musiques populaires, Col CD 111, Colophon Editions, 2001.

duunuud], but they always have authors who must, however, remain unknown. If you were to ask, people would reply, "Huh, I think I heard it at a wedding." This may appear to be a superficial form of expression, but under the surface there is a deep truth.

During my time in the Ulaan-Uul district in the late 1990s, I spent considerable time and energy searching for the "many old people" who, I had been told, knew "hundreds of joke songs." I never found them. On the few occasions when a person did agree to perform a joke song for me, he or she would usually look for a printed version in order to "remember the words correctly." (Copies of Tsegmed's books can be found in practically every Ulaan-Uul household.) In fact, new Darhad joke songs, which "under the surface" recall the (mis)deeds of contemporary persons, seldom seem to be composed anymore; people instead tend to reproduce the existing repertoire, often by seeking explicit guidance in Tsegmed's books, which include detailed explanations of the songs' origins in local lore.

This and other experiences led me to conclude that, at least in the Ulaan-Uul community, the joke song does not play the key role it once did in the organization of everyday life.[4] Rather than referring to a recent past lived and experienced by the speakers, as gossip always does (Bergmann 1993, 39), joke songs are increasingly being associated with more distant temporalities. Not only have a growing number of their victims passed away, but also there is a sense that, while the actions of these persons have by no means been forgotten (or forgiven), today is not the time to assign guilt for mistakes carried out in a different era (*üye*), namely, under socialism. Having slowly ceased to be a dominant form of "social control" (Douglas 1968, 1993), the practice of joke singing has evolved into a professionalized and somewhat stale mode of remembering how life was a generation or two ago.

These are well-known developments in the postsocialist world. As demonstrated by Bruce Grant (1995), one of the cornerstones of Soviet cultural politics was the classification, reification, and celebration of different "nationalities" within the state socialist polity (see also Hirsch 2005). In the Mongolian version of this folklorization process, the so-called song tradition of each tribe seems to have played a central role (Bulag 1998, 27–41). One outcome of this process was the formalization of the role of the singer (*duuchin*). In every rural district, one found—and still finds today—a handful of people thus designated, who are the proud owners of medals and diplomas earned

---

4. Still, the joke song tradition was apparently thriving in the Bayan-Zürh district south of the Shishged during the late 1990s (Gaëlle Lacaze, personal communication), just as it is alive and well in the Renchinlhümbe district, too (Laurent Legrain, personal communication).

in song competitions held in Ulaanbaatar and sometimes even Moscow during the socialist period.

The specific point to make here is that, in the Shishged and elsewhere in socialist Mongolia, these officially sanctioned ambassadors of indigenous culture were expected—and today are very much still expected—to perform mainly *local* songs, including, in this case, joke songs (as well as, interestingly, Duha songs). The outcome of all this, it is now clear, is that the joke songs—along with shamanism—became emblematic of Darhad culture. Across Mongolia (and even outside it, among Soviet and Hungarian ethnographers), for someone to be recognized as a real Darhad subject necessarily involved the mastering of joke songs. Indeed, one senses that the more songs a person knows, the more Darhad he or she is deemed to be.

In this regard, Tsegmed's publications, as well as the self-conscious attitude toward the joke songs expressed by the people I spoke to, are products of a cultural reification process whose specific style originated in state socialist cultural politics (including the power-knowledge effects of Soviet-style ethnography) as much as in a specific cultural tradition. In that light, it is clear that joke songs may be employed as an effective "weapon of the weak" against the powers that be. Indeed many of the joke songs that were made up during the state socialist period carried politically sensitive "hidden meanings" (to use Tsegmed's words), thereby serving as an anonymous medium for expressing political critique.

Today, however, such explicitly subversive and unmistakably political appropriations of the joke song have more or less disappeared. Small wonder; for if some Darhad joke songs from the socialist period contained "hidden transcripts" that served to express veiled political sentiments (Humphrey 1994b; see also Scott 1990), today there is little reason to hide one's opinion about politics anymore. But conversely, as we shall see, the songs seem to have gained a new occult role in shamanic possession ceremonies, where a sort of ritualized mocking, strikingly similar to joke singing, is gaining prominence.

Speaking Lies

A distinct variety of Darhad joking that has received less scholarly attention than joke singing, but in my view is imbued with more social and political efficacy in postsocialist life, is "speaking lies" (*hudal yarih*).[5] This sly and

---

5. Darhads do not themselves classify "speaking lies" as a distinct form of joking. *Hudal yar'!* ([you are] lying!) is simply the exclamation one makes when suspecting that one is the victim of it.

Figure 18. Going hunting

mischievous form of joking, which we have already encountered on several occasions in this book, is part of the larger discursive field of lying, which comprises both proper lies (utterances that are represented as truths but interpreted as lies) and more playful lies (utterances that are represented as "lies" and whose truth value therefore is ambiguous). It is predominantly the latter I focus on here, especially the common practice of "lying" about the shamanic spirit world.

It is quite striking how often Darhad occult specialists, when conveying their shamanic knowledge, do so in a joking manner. For the same reason, perhaps, it is common for people (including anthropologists) to emerge from consultations with diviners, shamans, and so on more confused than they were before they went in. More precisely, this joking among specialists keeps other people mystified about two things: (1) the esoteric knowledge on which these persons' authority is based (that is, shamanism in its broadest meaning), and (2) the "layered" constitution of specialists' minds. In that sense, joking emerges as a distinct technology of power, which, as a prevalent mode of occult communication, plays a vital role in the reproduction of the specialists' authority. Indeed it seems to me of considerable importance that Ulaan-Uul's occult specialists could often be heard talking about shamanic matters by adopting this playful "way of speaking" (Hymes 1974) rather than, say, a more symbolic one. Certainly this playful "lying" about the spirits is a far cry from the respectful ways of speaking—prayers, beckonings, and so forth—used by local leaders and lamas alike to address "land masters" and other spiritual entities during *ovoo* ceremonies and other "Buddhist" rituals in Ulaan-Uul.

Consider the following paraphrase of a conversation I once overheard in Gombodorj's forge. Two visitors were present, a young herdsman and an elderly driver, both locals. Gombodorj was busy polishing a knife when this exchange took place:

HERDSMAN: I just went hunting. Returned today.

DRIVER: Where did you go?

HERDSMAN: To Mungarag Taiga.

GOMBODORJ: Mungarag Taiga, huh. Did you kill something?

HERDSMAN: Actually, I did. A roebuck.

DRIVER: Well, well, that is good.

GOMBODORJ [in a serious tone]: Mungarag Taiga is dangerous.

HERDSMAN: Yeah?

GOMBODORJ: It is full of *ongod*. I do hope the roebuck wasn't female.

HERDSMAN: It was...!

GOMBODORJ: Female roebuck are very dangerous to hunt. You need to know how to distinguish between those with a master [*ezentei*] and those without one. If

Figure 19. Darhad herdsman

you happen to kill the one with an *ezen*, it could be very bad for you. The *ezen* may become angry and cause trouble for you and your family!

HERDSMAN: It is true that my father used to tell me that Ulaan Taiga has many *ongod*. But I always thought that Mungarag Taiga was different.

GOMBODORJ [still serious]: I know this better than your father. Mungarag Taiga is full of *ongod*. Watch out if the roebuck stares back at you. It happened to me once. I was so afraid.

DRIVER [laughing]: You must be kidding! [*Hudal, hudal,* lit. "A lie, a lie"].

GOMBODORJ [now smiling cunningly]: It is true. It means that it is cursing you! You must then kill it in a clean shot or face the *ezen*'s wrath. This is why only skilled hunters should prey on the roebuck. For others, it is too dangerous.

HERDSMAN: I never heard that before!

DRIVER: Hey, don't worry; he is just making fun [*shogloj baina*].

GOMBODORJ [laughing now]: Mungarag Taiga is full of *ongod*; female roebuck are extremely dangerous.

[THE herdsman now looks even more perplexed.]

(*Right:* Figure 20. Moving to spring camp)

GOMBODORJ [deadpan]: You'd better visit a shaman now! Perhaps the roebuck
cursed you! Don't sleep with your wife.... Hahaha...I am just talking lies!
[*hudal helsen yum aa*].

DRIVER: It is true, though. Once, when I was driving out in the east, I met a man
who told me...[and here he began another story about masters].

What is going on here? On the one hand, Gombodorj cannot fully mean
what he is saying, for if that were the case, why would he tell his interlocutors
that he is "lying"? On the other hand, his wish cannot be to lie, either, for
then why did he not hide this fact? A lie, after all, "only succeeds if the other
participants do not know that it even happened" (Barbe 1995, 117).

Gombodorj, it seems, did not *not* mean what he was saying (Willerslev 2004;
Schechner 1985). Or, to be more precise, he was being ironic. According to the
classical (Aristotelian) definition, to speak ironically is to say the opposite of
what one means: the speaker "figuratively" means the opposite of what he "literally" says (Barbe 1995, 62). But while this definition applies to those instances
of irony in which two opposite meanings can be identified in the semantics of
a sentence, it neglects what linguists refer to as the pragmatic context of utterances, which often must be taken into account in order to identify ironic intent:
the tone of voice, the conversational implications, the relationship between the
speaker and the listener, and so on (Barbe 1995, 34–59; Sperber and Wilson
1981). Indeed much of Gombodorj's "lying" was conveyed through nonsemantic cues (the cunning laughter and smiles noted in brackets in the extract), which
served pragmatically to differentiate some of his utterances from others.

Another problem about classical rhetorical theory is that not all ironic utterances have opposite meanings. To overcome this problem, so-called radically pragmatic approaches play down the distinction between the figurative
and the literal and focus on the propositional attitude of ironic utterances:
the speaker's attitude toward what he says and his interlocutor's ability (and
wish) to detect this attitude (Barbe 1995, 73–92). According to this analysis,
then, the interpretive task of those of us at the forge was not to decipher the
meaning of what Gombodorj said but to detect his intentions in saying it. His
ironic attitude made it impossible to decide whether he was "using" or "mentioning" his utterances about the shamanic spirits; that is, we were unable
to determine whether he was pretending or was sincere (Barbe 1995, 45–51;
Clark and Gerrig 1984; Sperber and Wilson 1981, 315).

Shamanic Humor I

I can now theorize the social efficacy of "speaking lies." For what happens
when someone ends a series of ironic utterances by saying, "I am lying," but
says that itself in a playful manner? The result is that, instead of demarcating

its end, this statement itself becomes part of the irony, so that a "bisociation" (to use Arthur Koestler's term [1964]) occurs between playing and lying. Thus, to cite Marike Finlay, "the first interpretation follows if the [phrase] 'I am lying' [is understood] according to a meta-linguistic level of enunciation; the second if we [understand] the phrase according to an object-level of enunciation. The choice between the levels is irresolvably ambiguous" (1988, 235).

This in turn calls to mind Gregory Bateson's concept of the play frame. Play, Bateson argued, requires a "degree of meta-communication…which [carries] the message 'this is play'" (2000, 179). Given that Gombodorj's statement "I am lying" (along with various nonsemantic signals) clearly fulfills this criterion, let us try to put his propositions about the shamanic spirits in Mungarag Taiga into Bateson's famous model:

> All statements within this frame are untrue
> ("I am lying")
> There are *ongod* in Mungarag Taiga
> There are no *ongod* in Mungarag Taiga
> Female roebucks curse hunters when meeting their eyes
> Female roebucks do not curse hunters when meeting their eyes

The ethnic stereotype of Darhads, we see again here, contains more than a glimmer of truth. The concept of the play frame, along with radically pragmatic theories of irony, confirms the prevalent stereotype among Halh people that Darhad joking, and more specifically the particular kind of playful "lying" that relies on the use of ironic mention, do indeed make the speaker's mind "layered" (*davhar*) from the point of view of the listener (see chapter 2). Arguably the effect of Gombodorj's joking is to initiate a so-called sequential paradox, whereby his ironic attitude sets in train an infinite regress in the listener's search for the speaker's intention in the utterance at hand: "the ruling that [Gombodorj is earnest] satisfies a criterion for ruling [this ruling] false; that finding satisfies a criterion for finding it true; and so on, *ad infinitum*" (paraphrasing Honderich 1995, 643–44).

Many Darhads are themselves quite aware of this distinct "way of speaking" (Sherzer 1983) and its effects. As Tsegmed explained to me:

I have traveled all over Mongolia, but nowhere do people speak the way they do around here. Darhads speak poetically. We use metaphors [*züirlel*] and alliteration [*tolgoi holboh*] a lot. We always joke in secret [*dalduur shoglodog*]. It has to do with our character [*zan chanar*] and the nature here. The Halh lands stretch from Lake Uvs in the west to Lake Buir in the east, but our *nutag* is squeezed in between the Öl and

Örög passes. Everyone knows one another: the taiga surrounds us on all sides. This place is like one big stomach: everything takes place in a roundabout way.

In positing an analogy between the land surrounding him and a stomach, Tsegmed confirms the general totemic or "fractal" relationship between concepts of the land and concepts of the person that appear to prevail in the Shishged context (Pedersen 2001). His words convey an unmistakable sense of the different scales on which similar relationships are replicated: the inner landscape of Darhads ("our character") takes the same "roundabout" form as the landscape in which they live (their homeland). More specifically, Tsegmed's description of the sociological and political implications of the Darhad inclination to "always joke in secret" may also be said to offer a vivid image of social life in northern Mongolia—a deeply unpredictable and yet claustrophobic sensation of a repeatedly suspended near-collapse, which may be compared to being confined, Jonah-like, in the stomach of a huge beast. Everyone and everything is moving about within the limited perimeters of a narrow and intense enclosure, at constant risk of bumping into one another. Within the confines of this "outside inside"—the multinaturalist forest, the postsocialist state—everything that looked before like a unified and stable whole (the steppe, the community) is instead a haecceity, a hole.[6]

All of this suggests that Darhad joking practices, like shamanic gowns and collapsing infrastructure, are perceived to render their black side visible. As when the shaman dons her gown, the person who performs a joke song or who "speaks lies" is transformed into or exposed as a fractal person imbued with a porous body and a layered mind, a person capable of entertaining several perspectives at the same time. This has far-reaching implications for my study of shamanic agency in northern Mongolia. Is it possible that what Gombodorj "lied" about in the forge can *only* be said in a playful way, for this is the very premise of shamanic phenomena such as spirits? In order to address this important question, the time has come to consider the role of humor in more ritual contexts.

---

6. I borrow the concept of an "exterior inside" from Mark Mosko's inspiring work on spatial terminology and conceptions among Mekeo people in the Papua New Guinean Highlands, whose villages are "described as an 'outside' place in opposition to the bush, which is 'inside'" (1985, 21). For the Shishged to appear "as a stomach," the taiga cannot be considered the margin of a central steppe, as it is in the patriarchal ideal of a Darhad community discussed in previous chapters. Instead, the taiga must assume the very central properties otherwise associated with the steppe, and thus become an exterior center, asymmetrically opposed to an "interior margin" occupied by the village.

From Praying to Playing

On a number of occasions I participated in the daily prayer ritual (*hural*) at the Buddhist temple (*süm*) in Mörön.[7] As always in such temples, the atmosphere was one of meditative introspection. The only sound was the lamas' monotonous reading of sutras, interrupted only by the occasional blowing of a conch shell (*lavai*), the clashing of cymbals (*tsan*), and, on one memorable occasion, a misplaced and very revealing joke by a junior lama.

Seated on an elevated platform along two parallel wooden benches were the lamas. The highest ranking sat to the northwest and the youngest apprentices, or *bandi,* to the southeast, essentially replicating the (ideal) seating pattern in the *ger.* The laymen were seated along the southern walls, waiting for the reading of the sutras they had requested. When someone started reading, he or she would circumambulate the temple in a clockwise direction, kowtowing (*mörgöh*), praying (*zalbirah*), and making offerings to the *burhan* statues and other paraphernalia lined up along the northern walls.

It was in this context of carefully maintained tranquility that the following incident took place. Visibly bored, a middle-ranking lama leaned over toward a *bandi*—a timid-looking boy about seven years old—and demanded, "Hey, you, go to the *daa lam* and tell him that we shall now read the *sudar.*" It is common practice to relay this sort of information to the participating laymen because, as the prayer language is Tibetan, they have no way of recognizing the sutras themselves. This *bandi,* however, was instructed to inform the most knowledgeable person present, the *daa lam, who* leads the *hural* from his high chair next to the entrance. Small wonder, then, that the boy's first response was to refuse. Only after having been repeatedly urged to obey the request did the *bandi* walk over to the *daa lam.* At first the *daa lam* looked confused. But as he could not help noticing the suppressed giggles from the benches, he understood that he was the victim of a prank. A few angry glances killed the laughter on the spot. Later, when the prayers were over, came the rebuke. "Lamas are not meant to make fun of reading *sudar,*" the *daa lam* barked. "On the contrary, you are supposed to set an example for our *bandi* during prayers!"

The unscheduled laughter provoked by the student's comical intervention serves as a reminder of the more generally troublesome relationship between hierarchy and humor, which sparked the old structural-functionalist interest in "joking relationships" in Africa and elsewhere. Thus, according to A. R. Radcliffe-Brown's classic definition,

---

7. This monastery was (re)built in 1990. In 2000 its congregation (*sangha*) numbered thirty lamas, including novices (*bandi*). In addition to a prayer hall, it comprised a temple dedicated to the worship of Mörön's protector spirit (*sahius*), Choijil (Tib. Ch'ökyong).

what is meant by the term "joking relationship" is a relation between two
persons in which one is by custom permitted, and in some instances required, to tease or make fun of the other, who in turn is required to take no
offence. It is important to distinguish two main varieties. In one the relation
is symmetrical; each of the two persons teases or makes fun of the other. In
the other variety the relation is asymmetrical; A jokes at the expense of B and
accepts the teasing good-humouredly but without retaliating; or A teases B
as much as he pleases and B in return teases A only a little. (1968, 90)

Radcliffe-Brown's analyses have often been criticized for being overly rigid,
but in this case it is precisely this formalism that allows us to identify two
humorous practices that have not been considered so far (see also Pedersen
and Willerslev 2010). The first—in his terminology an "asymmetrical joking relationship"—is the more or less customary teasing directed downward
from senior to junior members of the household, in particular from parents to their children, but also from elder to younger siblings, and from the
mother's brothers to her children. The second and more "symmetrical" joking relationship is the seemingly obligatory banter that takes place between
equals, particularly friends (*naiz*) and acquaintances (*tanil*), but also others
of similar (*chatsuu*) age and status, such as colleagues and former members
of the same army regiment or school class (*neg angi*).

The thing to notice here is the lack of a third variation, in which a junior
or inferior (*dood,* lit. "lower") person "is by custom permitted" to tease a senior or superior (*deed,* lit. "upper") person. When I asked him whether *dood*
persons may joke with *deed* ones, Tsegmed responded: "No. It always goes by
order of age [*nasny erembeer*]; the direction is from up to down. Just as in the
saying *aavdaa avgai avahyg zaana* [instructing father to get a wife],[8] juniors
are not supposed to speak jokingly to seniors. This is an unwritten law [*he-
blegdeegüi huul*] in our custom [*yos*]."

We are now in a better position to understand what took place during the
prayer session in Mörön. If we put the naughty lama in the shoes of a boy in
a nomadic household, and if we identify the *bandi* with his younger brother
and the *da lam* with their father, then we see how the prank performed in
this context would, at least according to *yos*, give rise to a similar response.
In both cases we are faced with joking circumventions of an established hierarchy, which explains their lack of sanction: they go against the grain of
asymmetrical relationships considered natural, proper, and good. One can,
of course, imagine all sorts of situations in which this "unwritten law" is

---

8. The denotation of this saying is "that which one must not do" (such as instructing one's
father on how to get a wife).

broken, but the *da lam*'s harsh response (as well as Tsegmed's reflections) still points to the general ethnographic fact that social hierarchies are emphasized when patriarchal (and monastic) units are put on external display. So while a son (or a lama) may easily get away with such joking in the presence of other family members (or lamas) alone, it is clear that he would not be able to do so in front of outsiders visiting the household (or temple).

To whom, then, were the lamas displaying themselves? For one thing, it was the laymen, who, while participating in the prayer service, were ritually encompassed by the lamas' own hierarchy. (Arguably even a *bandi* is "above" all laymen.) But then, of course, there were also the *other* others to whom the lamas displayed themselves, namely, the various divinities present in the temple. This suggests that the absence of joking in the prayer ritual cannot be reduced to a sociological question but involves the very concept of the divine in Mongolian Buddhism. Just as one is not supposed to joke "upward" toward one's seniors in the household, it seems that one should not laugh at Buddha in the temple.[9]

In fact, given that Buddhist divinities are known to belong to a realm that is infinitely more pure and perfect than that of ordinary perceptions, why, and how, should one laugh at them? If God is perfect and humanity imperfect, then he may have his reasons for laughing at us, but surely not the other way around. The "unwritten rule" is therefore not just that one should not laugh within the temple; it is also that one simply *cannot* do so, for there is nothing to laugh at. After all, if God stands for a state of perfect order, for a total lack of contradiction, then he is not funny, since humor, as we saw earlier, always involves an element of contradiction, of imperfection, of incongruity (Koestler 1964).

Since much of Buddhist aesthetics amounts to celebrating symmetries and congruities, it therefore makes sense that its discursive and material manifestations should not—indeed, cannot—be laughed at. But this also implies that another aesthetic geared more toward the destruction of symmetry and unity, toward revealing rather than concealing incongruity, might allow for the comical to become an intrinsic part of its makeup. I propose that precisely such an aesthetic can be found in Mongolian shamanism.

In Darhad shamanic ceremonies, people do not display themselves as they otherwise do. During all the séances I attended, the audience was seated not in accordance with conventional age and gender hierarchies (as they were during, say, Buddhist prayer sessions or visits to nomadic *gers*), but

---

9. As an Ulaanbaatar lama responded, with a horrified look on his face when I told him about the incident: "Lamas should not joke like that! They should respect that the laymen are experiencing great suffering in their lives." After all, as an ancient Buddhist saying goes, "How can anyone laugh who knows of old age, disease, and death?" (Gilhus 1997, 109).

according to a dispersed principle that turned established spatial and social forms inside out. Thus, households were twisted out of shape as the performing shamans—and, to some degree, their interpreters—occupied the most honored section, to the north (*hoimor*), where, under normal circumstances, the master of the household (*geriin ezen*) and (male) guests of honor would be seated. Certainly, during Nadmid Udgan's ceremonies, for example, local leaders and other men of power (including businessmen and politicians from Ulaanbaatar) were not seated as befitted their status, but were scattered according to a first-come, first-sit principle whereby latecomers end up sitting, quite literally, on top of one another.

All this leads to the question: *What kinds of others* are meant to see a constellation of persons like this? If we use the same logic as in the analysis of the Buddhist prayer session, these must be others whose own internal composition is homologous with the composition of that which they are intended to "see," in other words, a constellation of others who are also internally dispersed among themselves. Indeed, what we learned in the previous chapter about the multiple and heterogeneous nature of the shamanic cosmos supports this hypothesis, for, just like the people in the audience, shamanic spirits are dispersed in all directions, like the expanded surface of a balloon.

We may in that sense speak of space itself as a potential shamanic modality or vehicle of occult orchestration: the spirits are actualized *qua* a certain property of space, namely, its capacity for distributing relations in a particular way (Corsín-Jiménez 2003). But can we also think of joking along similar terms? That is, might the humorous also be imbued with distinct and identifiable occult capacities? Certainly, as Hamayon has pointed out, if praying is foregrounded in Buddhist (and Christian) ritual at the expense of playing, then in shamanic rituals it is the other way around: playing is here primary, even if praying is always to some degree present.

> The notion of playing is widely used to qualify the shaman's or the possessed individual's action towards the spirits, the latter's action towards the former, or both (Yakut *oyun*, Buryat *naadaxa*, Korean *nolda*, Hindi *k(h)elna*, etc.). All religious or ritual playing has been condemned by world religions on account of [its] being opposed to praying. The notion of play encompasses the main features of the shaman's ritual behavior, while also indicating that he acts out a role, and is both "conscious and dupe" of this role. (1993, 21–22)

Buryat shamans used to have a whole pantheon of "play spirits" (*naadamy ongon*), which, in the words of M. N. Hangalov, were invoked in shamanic rituals mainly for "entertainment purposes." One liked to "collect" people's noses, another their hats, and a third variety took a special interest in wom-en's breasts. Yet another spirit, known as Dobogoo Ovogoo (Strict Old Man), was looking for his wife, who he feared was sleeping around. And he was rightly concerned, for the wife, Samsakhai, questioned every man in the au-dience about the size of his "stick" (Hangalov 1958, 476–82).

The Darhads I spoke to had no such pantheon of play spirits; indeed, I have never come across this particular concept in the Shishged. Nevertheless, there is a lot of play—and joking—in Darhad shamanic rituals.[10] Not only do some spirits occasionally make fun of clients and the audience, but also people may sometimes laugh at the spirits. When asked about these matters, Nadmid Udgan tried to downplay the significance of this practice. "It is the spirits themselves—not the shamans—that make people laugh," she stressed, because, as she elaborated with a stern look on her face, "a real shaman will be without consciousness after the spirits come [*Ongon oroh üyed jinhene böö hün uhaangüi baina*]."

According to Nadmid Udgan, spirits that "like to say funny things" are col-lectively known as the "gossip spirits" (*hovch ongod*). To give a sense of what the gossip spirits do, let me now recall one of the shamanic rituals in which I participated in Tsagaan Nuur, the biannual "awakening" of the Father of Har-mai *ongon*.

The Gossip Spirits

It was well past midnight on a summer night, and as usual, Nadmid Ud-gan's place was packed with visitors. Several spirits had already possessed her, and a corresponding number of clients had been fixed (*zasal hiilgesen*). Vari-ous amusing (*ineedtei*) incidents had already taken place. At one point, one of the businessmen mentioned in the previous chapter, the poor man who had come all the way from Ulaanbaatar to expel an attack of malicious gossip (*hel am*), had been summoned by the Father of Harmai himself, and much mirth had arisen from this city-dweller's ignorance in dealing with the spirit. Despite the fact that the man was visibly distraught—he was, it may be re-called, found to suffer from "big problems"—he was not spared. In fact, the more concerned the man looked, the more people had laughed.

While the previous spirits had all differed in their manifestations in Nadmid Udgan's body, it was the present one that would stand out from all the rest. This was Ders Shig Yum, the restless *ongon* from Tuva, briefly

---

10. Humor is not identical to play (Huizinga 1970, 24–25) but could be called a subset of it: while all humor seems to be playful, not all play is humorous (Morreall 1983, 89–91).

mentioned in chapter 4. Rather than holding her drum in the common up-right position and dancing in slow, repetitive semicircles, Nadmid Udgan, when seized by Ders Shig Yum, awkwardly pushed the drum away from her body horizontally and began rotating around and around while drumming ever more violently. This, to judge from people's response, was extremely funny. Meanwhile, the shrill and rather menacing voice of the spirit filled the air, communicating the name of the person in the audience it was looking for. According to the "interpreter," who listened to the "words spoken" for a good while, this person was a timid-looking adolescent girl, seated behind her parents in a far corner of the room as if hiding.

Plainly terrified, the girl was now guided to the center of the *hoimor*, where the obligatory drumstick divination (*zaya töörög üzeh*) was initiated. The shaman is supposed to throw her drumstick three times onto the seam of the kneeling client's *deel*, using the side (*tal*) facing up as a tool for determin-ing the client's destiny (*zaya*). Each time, the client must hand the drumstick back to the shaman while saying the words "*töörög, töörög*." In this particular case, however, not a sound was uttered. The girl's family and others tried to encourage her ("Come on, now, just say '*töörög, töörög!*'"), but to no avail. In response, the shaman/spirit started pecking, birdlike, at the sulking figure on the floor, as if confused about what do to with such a recalcitrant per-son. Everyone was laughing except the girl herself. Eventually she managed to whisper the required words. The mockery, however, was far from over. The shaman/spirit now bent down and, by provocatively putting her ear right next to the girl's mouth, made it clear that the latter had not spoken loudly enough. So the girl repeated the words, this time somewhat louder but also more hysterically. This made the shaman jump up, begin rotating and drum-ming again, and scream, in mocking imitation of the girl's quivering voice: "*töörög, töörög*, HI HI HI, *töörög, töörög*, HA HA HA."

Finally, the *zasal* proper could begin. Forcing the girl's head down into praying posture (*dooshoo mörgöh*), Nadmid Udgan howled, "*baahan, baahan bartsad baina aa!*" (big, big obstacle!). The poor girl was now subjected to a sustained whipping with the drumstick, which was followed by the shaman/spirit complaining loudly: "How can someone like you, who is so young, al-ready have lost five years of your life? To an old person, even five days are precious, and now look at you! *Baahan, baahan*." The girl was weeping as she was led away. Everyone else was overwhelmed by laughter. And the fun was not over, for Ders Shig Yum now started insulting people in the audience at random (or so it seemed). One of its songs, for example, insinuated that two people from the Tsagaan Nuur village had been "taking walks in the hills" to-gether (had been having an affair). As one might expect, this sparked another explosion of laughter in the audience, especially since one of the purported lovers was sitting there with them, accompanied by his increasingly angry-looking wife. Soon after, the spirit departed from Nadmid Udgan.

Apparently Ders Shig Yum always behaves in this way. According to Nadmid Udgan, the spirit likes to stick its nose into everything (*yumny dunduur oroh,* lit. "to go between things"). Or, as she described it with an apt image, Ders Shig Yum "is a bit like a tape recorder. It stores people's conversations and then replays them elsewhere." This, indeed, is what all gossip spirits do: they "imitate people's bad things" (*muu yumyg l duuraina*), having previously recorded and "stored" (*tatah avah*) them under different and more private circumstances. Ders Shig Yum, in other words, is an obscene figure. Like Gombodorj's obscene banter with his in-laws, Ders Shig Yum confronts people with strongly tabooed matters that are never talked about, and this, not surprisingly, produces laughter.

Although gossip spirits like Ders Shig Yum are considered "light" (*höngön*) in comparison with more "heavy" (*hünd*) ancestral spirits, and although people may therefore laugh in their presence, they can be invoked for serious and sometimes sinister purposes. For example, a family may ask a shaman to send a gossip spirit to the home of their affines (*nagats*) to see how their newlywed daughter is faring. Or if you happen to be a shaman yourself, you might want to send a gossip spirit to the home of another shaman to spy on the secret things that may be taking place there. In either case, the spirit will "store everything exactly as it takes place" and then later copy or imitate (*duuraina*) it for you, just as Ders Shig Yum did. Finally, gossip spirits may also interfere directly in relationships, for example, by manipulating people's attraction to one another.[11] Indeed, said Nadmid Udgan giggling, they sometimes cause married couples to separate and then form new pairs, "just for the fun of it."

On several accounts the gossip spirits take the prize as the most plastic of all *ongod.* For one thing, they are at the very bottom of the ancestral hierarchy of shamanic spirits: the fact that they are designated as "things" (*yum*) indicates that they lack the pedigree of clannish "Father" and "Mother" spirits. Second, most gossip spirits, like the shamans mastering them, are gendered female. Finally, a factor inseparable from their non-ancestral and feminized characteristics, gossip spirits are imbued with a hyper-fluid nature, for unlike other *ongod,* they are truly omnipresent. Thus gossip spirits do not need the bodies of zoomorphic spirit helpers in order to travel, as other spirit guardians do. They move around entirely freely. In fact, perhaps we should think of these occult entities simply *as* gossip, for just like gossip, and for that matter joke songs,

---

11. Incidentally, the term for "gossip"—*hov*—is related to *hovs,* which means "magic" or "witchcraft" (Hangin et al. 1986), which is sometimes highlighted by shamans (Dulam Bumorchir, personal communication).

they consist of detachable units of authorless talk in constant movement from one social realm to another. It is true that, like other shamanic spirits, they can speak only through the bodies of shamans (who act as "loudspeakers," as it were). But as Nadmid Udgan told me, again giggling, "there is always the possibility that a gossip spirit is listening to what you are saying!"

Let us think back to how, when we were discussing the gossipy personality of Soli Yum, Nadmid Udgan jokingly remarked, "So, the name of this *ongon* reflects what it does!" She was probably referring to the polysemic term *solio*, which means "exchange," "barter," "mixture," "insanity," as well as, indeed, "rotation" (Hangin et al. 1986). Also think again of Ders Shig Yum's dance. When possessed by this spirit, Nadmid Udgan spun around and around, as if to emphasize that what it *said* had the same "insane" form. Ders Shig Yum was rotating because that is what this and other gossip spirits are felt to be: forms of exchange, or *solio*, whose essential mode of being is to be always moving (like the postsocialist market), and in so doing reconfigure their surroundings by "causing new things to mix" (as Nadmid Udgan put it), as when couples dissolve to form new partnerships, or secrets (and daughters) flow from one domestic unit to another.

What is funny about gossip spirits, then, is inseparable from their plastic way of being. Indeed, people think of them as having obscene "personalities": like the Buryat play spirits, the gossip spirits happily break the strongest taboos, just as they unashamedly let the worst and most embarrassing secrets out into the open. But there is also a deeper sense in which gossip spirits are comical. Consider again Ders Shig Yum's funny (*shogch*) manifestation in Nadmid Udgan's body. The reason why people were laughing, I suggest, is that this particular performance constituted an "impossible form." Ders Shig Yum's possession of Nadmid Udgan was comical not only because gossip spirits, as the most marginal *ongod*, say and do funny things, but also because it made visible within one realm of reality (the shaman's body) what is otherwise restricted to another realm (gossip). Thus understood, Der Shig Yum's dance was "necessarily funny," for a comical shape was the only possible—or, one might say, impossible—form this fundamentally capricious and permeable entity could assume in a body. In short, this and other gossip spirits emerge as ritual instantiations or performative visualizations of what gossip might look like.

A Play World

Like children who laugh when they see something for the first time, I could not help smiling when I first saw Nadmid Udgan shamanizing. Yet there is a thin line between laughter and fear. Both arise from sudden affective and cognitive shifts brought about by a novel, unexpected, or alien experience. What distinguishes fear and laughter is the extension of space between subject and object: if the subject feels that the new, unexpected, or alien phenomenon is too close to him, whether physically or metaphysically, then he is likely to fear it rather than find it funny. (Just as, conversely, if he feels the phenomenon to be too far away, he is likely to pay only limited attention to it.) Mirth happens only when the world is apportioned into the right kind of relations; it requires a certain "safe" distance between the subject and object of the laughter (Pedersen and Willerslev 2010). Indeed, as I gradually became less of an observer and more of a participant in Nadmid Udgan's shamanic séances, I ceased laughing. On many occasions, I learned to fear instead.

What was the new, alien, and thus sublime object of my fear and laughter? I have argued that when Ders Shig Yum possessed Nadmid Udgan, her dance was a paradoxical attempt to arrest something that is fundamentally non-arrestable, namely, the relentless flow of gossip. I now suggest that this applies to all spirit manifestations, whether material, performative, or discursive, for they all offer a comical view into the inherent paradoxes of the shamanic cosmos; they are in that sense a sort of objectified joke.

Shamanic spirits are comical almost by definition. Far from revolving around a mandala-like reduction of dimensions surrounding a focal point of balance, as in the case of Buddhist aesthetics as discussed earlier, shamanic art seems to be all about the explosion of dimension and the proliferation of asymmetries through deliberate acts of unbalancing and decentering. Instead of trying to hide the fact that any depiction of the spirits would necessarily amount to an incomplete version of their ephemeral nature, shamanic art, like comedy, aims to make this incongruity—this "failure of representation"—as apparent as possible. Thus understood, it was not just the comical dance of Ders Shig Yum but *all* the spirits possessing Nadmid Udgan's body during rituals that were impossible forms, for all were deliberate attempts to "represent" the fundamentally nonrepresentational nature of *ongod*.

It is in this sense that one can speak of all Darhad shamanic spirits as "theoretically funny." Because of the inherently motile nature of these invisible presences, any effort to make them visible will automatically "encrust something mechanical on the living", in Bergson's apt formulation (1999, 39), and, like a sort of punch line in a cosmic joke, reveal the paradoxical nature of *ongod*. Thus the laughter (and fear) that I experienced in Nadmid Udgan's house was not the result of imposing a comical frame of "make-believe" upon a ritual frame of "let-believe" (as in Kapferer 1991) but a genuine conjuring act through which a funny reality was elicited from the world, namely, the labile state of play in which *ongod* exist. (For a more elaborate version of this argument, see Pedersen and Willerslev 2010.)

The role of play in Darhad shamanism, then, is not just a matter of shamans playing the role of their spirits as actors do, nor is it simply a matter of certain "light" spirits playing tricks on the audience as comedians sometimes do. Play is what shamanic spirits essentially *are:* inherently multiple and labile agents of change, which exist in a state of perpetual transformation. Quite unintentionally, Badamhatan makes a comparable point in his discussion of the Shishged fishing economy. "The Darhads," he observes in a side comment, "use the term 'play of the fish,' *zagasny naadam,* for the migration of the White Fish, which goes upstream in groups to mate in September and returns to the lakes in October or November" (1986, 92). This, I suggest, is exactly what *ongod* do as well. Like fish swimming, the shamanic spirits move around by "playing" (*naadah*) with the dark and unknown forces of an omnipresent but invisible liquid, as if the Shishged valley had been flooded by an occult lake whose life forms every human and nonhuman were forever after forced to deal with.

Shamanic Humor II

I have now discussed the central role of joking in Darhad shamanic rituals. Yet as we saw earlier in this chapter, joking also plays a key role in more everyday contexts, in which occult specialists often "lie" when talking about the spirits. This "shamanic humor" represents a considerable methodological and epistemological challenge. If people like Gombodorj are joking when communicating their occult knowledge, what is the status of this knowledge from an anthropological—and from an indigenous—point of view? Is it true or is it false? Do such utterances reflect people's beliefs? That is, did Gombodorj mean what he said in the forge? And, more specifically, what can this popular practice of mischievous "lying" tell us about the nature of shamanism without shamans in northern Mongolia after socialism?

I suggest that as an occult "narrative without closure" (Holmberg 1989, 169), shamanic humor transports the esoteric play frame of possession ritual into the mundane play frame of everyday life (Handelman 1990, 70). While the jokes that occur in a Darhad shamanic ritual are finite in nature (as in the example of Nadmid Udgan as naughty interpreter), the basic paradox involving the plastic nature of *ongod* is suspended ad infinitum, as the spirits' playfulness spills into daily life with the clients' departure. They take with them the basic shamanic enigma: Are the spirits here or are they not here? Eventually this enigma is played out again as people like Gombodorj begin to "lie" about the spirits, at which point the one big shamanic joke is broken down into many smaller ones.[12]

The question remains, however, what is the epistemological status of these jokes? For cognitivist anthropologists such as Dan Sperber, the answer might be that shamanic humor, like symbolic forms of language more generally, conveys different degrees of belief on behalf of the speakers (1985, 1996). Ironic utterances, according to this so-called radically pragmatic interpretation, are thus not genuine propositions but "semi-propositions." Instead of representing the world, irony is all about representing other representations, hence turning ironic utterances into tools for communicating one's beliefs about (or attitudes toward) other beliefs. If, for example, someone makes the sarcastic remark "How democratic!" in response to a blatantly authoritarian decision, then this should be analyzed as an indirect citation (or "echoic mention") of a real or imagined scenario in which someone "uses" this utterance to make a genuine proposition (express a belief).

This kind of interpretation represents a fashionable solution to the so-called problem of belief, which was the subject of a famous anthropological debate in the 1960s ("are twins birds?") but still represents a key source of disagreement among anthropologists, cognitive psychologists, and historians of religion. For Sperber and other naturalists, counterintuitive propositions such as "twins are birds"—or, for the sake of the present discussion, "the female deer is a shamanic spirit"—are not, as cultural relativists would have it, products of a different cultural logic or worldview. Instead, this and other meta-representational forms of speech reflect a natural (cognitively hardwired) skepticism about the purported existence of all such metaphysical entities (see also Boyer 1994).

Now, if we take this interpretation to its logical conclusion, it would seem to imply that Darhad shamanic humor is not about the shamanic spirits at all but only about communicating a certain attitude toward other people's claims about the (im)possibility of their existence. I find it unlikely, however, that when "speaking lies," Darhad specialists are simply expressing beliefs about other people's beliefs. This would imply that people like Gombodorj do not take shamanism at all seriously, and that is clearly not an accurate description of his highly intimate but also very reflexive relationship to the world of *ongod*. A more culturally sensitive and therefore satisfactory

---

12. As David Holmberg explains in his study of shamanic possession rites ("soundings") among the Nepalese Tamang (1989), the Tamang shamans (*bombos*) are essentially "instruments through which enigmas resound." This is so because "although soundings clearly have boundaries and a ritualised closure—figured in the bombo's mastery of possession—large portions of a sounding are suspensions that lack narrative closure" (1989, 169). Indeed, Holmberg notes, "bombos often laugh at direct questions about their practice....Although often deadly serious [events], some [bombos] joke that their soundings are deceptions" (1989, 160).

interpretation would be to say that when Darhad occult specialists "speak lies" about the spirits, they are both representing a genuine belief in (making a proposition about) these metaphysical entities *and* communicating a meta-representational attitude toward (making a semi-proposition about) this belief. On this interpretation, then, shamanic humor is a tool for communicating relative beliefs in occult phenomena, for by reflexively referring (as "echoic mention") to themselves while also denoting (as "propositional use") the shamanic cosmos, Gombodorj's "lies" about spirits in Mungarag Taiga inserted a nested doubt into his utterances.

We may distinguish between two kinds of such shamanic doubt in the Shishged, both of which are connected to the dramatic social, cultural, and political changes that northern Mongolia has been subject to over the past century or more. On the one hand, the foregoing chapters have pointed to a widespread doubt about shamanism as a body of cosmological knowledge, inasmuch as the present-day Darhad shamans are not considered particularly knowledgeable, let alone particularly trustworthy. On the other hand, some people (such as my hosts) also harbor doubts about whether the shamanic spirits exist or not. In the latter sense, Darhads' skepticism about shamanism calls to mind Henrietta Moore and Todd Sanders's observation that "pentecostalists in Malawi often understand witchcraft as being about humor or irony, which thus carries connotations of skepticism" (2001, 5).

While such skepticism is hardly new in the Mongolian context (Humphrey 1996, 361–64), both forms of shamanic doubt seem to have proliferated during socialism. In fact it is likely that state socialist cultural politics encouraged (if not forged) the very ironic attitude toward the shamanic spirits that is expressed in contemporary Darhad practices of "speaking lies." After all, the "primitive and cunning shamans of the past" were always among the most popular targets of satire in the propagandistic plays about Mongolia's "reactionary" and "feudal" history that were staged by state-sponsored theater troupes in the "houses of culture" (*soyolyn töv*) found across rural Mongolia during the socialist years, even in a remote district like Ulaan-Uul (Marsh 2006).[13]

Inspired by Bruce Kapferer's classic study of Sinhalese exorcism (1991), we may think of these performances as socialist exorcism rites, whose explicit aim was to subsume the Darhad shamanic cosmos under a ritual play frame of propagandistic "make-believe," so that yet another "backward people" could contemplate the false nature of their religious beliefs.

---

13. Apparently in Soviet Siberia "antireligious authorities considered the words *shaman* and *deceiver* to be synonymous" (Balzer 2006, 85).

Compelling as this interpretation is, it fails to take into account that cultural politics of this sort may engender novel and often unintended forms of agency rather than simply resulting in a lack of them. This is precisely what seems to have happened in the case of Darhad shamanic humor. Ironically, the staging of propagandistic satire in Ulaan-Uul's "house of culture" thus represented the only public space in which shamanism could be practiced during socialism. In a remarkable ethnographic film (Merli 2000), a Darhad shaman recounts how, back then, he was part of a traveling theater troupe that performed politically correct cultural shows across the Mongolian countryside. Because of his background, he was always assigned to play the role of a stupid and egoistic shaman, who would lose his wits and go into trances. But actually the man was not acting, for he *did* become possessed while on stage; indeed the only way he could respond to his shamanic calling was by pretending to pretend that he was a shaman.[14]

The example of the double-playing shaman confirms that not only can irony be used in the interests of those in power (to make fun of the "stupid" and "superstitious" shamans) but also the other way around. On this interpretation, then, shamanic humor emerges as a subtly distorted version of—or play on—state socialist propaganda's own satirical message that shamanism is false. As demonstrated by the Darhad shaman who pretended to pretend, the ironic format of political and religious satire may thus be used to express not just a skeptical (semipropositional) attitude toward beliefs about spirits in line with official state discourse, but also genuine (propositional) beliefs in them, disguised as mockery.

But we are still not quite there. For what if people simply stopped being aware, or at least ceased to care, whether they believed in the propaganda or not? "Virtually [everyone] had a double life," observes Humphrey (1994b, 25), for the only way—or at least the most common way—of trying to remain sane in the face of mounting contradictions between ideology and practice was to assume the characteristic dual perspective that became a trademark of the last Soviet generation, whose everyday paradoxes have been so aptly described by Humphrey (1998), Ssorin-Chaikov (2003) and Yurchak (2006), among others. The result, as "native" social theorists and philosophers such

---

14. Not only were the satirical plays staged in Mongolia very similar to the shows devised in the Soviet Union, but also they seem to have given rise to the same unintended shamanic effects. In his moving account of reindeer breeders in Yakutia, Piers Vitebsky describes how, "in theatres across Siberia, shallow re-enactments of shamanic trances were staged as a special set piece in dramas. There were professional actors who specialized in this, and one of them told me how he sometimes felt dangerously on the edge of real trance, which he would not have been competent to handle" (2005, 231–32).

as Slavoj Žižek have suggested, was that the average citizen in state social-ist societies stopped being aware of the fact that he was pretending. As this "cynical reason" (1993) became routinized as a way of life, people started to forget when they were pretending and when they were not. In effect, people not only stopped believing but also stopped disbelieving.

If we apply these findings to the Darhad context, then a number of new riddles arise. For one thing, if the specialists did not know whether they were pretending or not during socialism, how can they know now if they were pretending or not back *then*? Also, and even more disturbingly, how can specialists know if they are pretending or not *today*? My attempt to ex-plain shamanic humor as an expression of relative belief has, it seems, been caught up in the same infinite regress that characterizes ironic signification as a whole.

The Truth of "Lies"

One possible way out of this impasse is to turn the question of relativity on its head: perhaps it is not people's beliefs about the shamanic spirits that are relative but rather the organization of the shamanic cosmos itself. In order to explore this alternative possibility, let me once again consider Bateson's con-cept of the play frame, which, it might be worth recalling, denotes a separate dimension of reality whose logic is qualitatively different from the conven-tional logic associated with the dimension of non-play (2000).

What is the status, and the effect, of the play frame? Is it, as scholars such as Kapferer and Sperber seem to imply, a dimension that is added onto a real-ity existing independently of play? Or could it be a dimension that, by virtue of its very playfulness, offers a view of otherwise invisible sides of reality? On the first interpretation, specialists' ironic semipropositions (which are neither true nor false) in the form of shamanic humor ambiguously refer to proper propositions (which are either true or false) in the form of genuine beliefs about the world outside play. On the latter interpretation, conversely, Gom-bodorj's playful "lies" bespeak an occult dimension of reality that cannot be talked about by means of propositions of the kind used to represent people's earnest beliefs. This occult dimension of the shamanic spirits is a play world, and the point of shamanic joking—and laughter and play more generally—is to stage tiny temporal play frames within this play world so as to participate in the great eternal cosmic game (*naadam*) that the spirits play.

So which is it? As Johan Huizinga demonstrates in *Homo Ludens* (1970), the issue boils down to which of the two dimensions, play and earnest, en-compasses the other:

The signification of "earnest" is defined by and exhausted in the negation of "play"—earnest is simply "not-playing" and nothing more. The signification of "play," on the other hand, is by no means defined or exhausted by calling it "not-earnest" or "not serious." Play is a thing by itself. The play concept as such is of a higher order than is seriousness. For seriousness seeks to exclude play, whereas play can very well include seriousness. (Huizinga 1970, 65)

Here the dimension of play is "larger" than the dimension of the earnest, which for Huizinga is relegated to a subset that is logically contained by- -as opposed to subsuming, as in, say, Sinhalese exorcism—the things of play. On this alternative perspective, then, Gombodorj's playful "lies" should not be analyzed through a conventional (positivist) model of representation, according to which propositions (at least in ideal terms) are supposed to be either true or false. Instead his shamanic humor emerges as a form of discursive play whose truth-status should be compared with other, nondiscursive forms of play, as opposed to, as in the case of Sperber, the truth-status of more earnest forms of discursive non-play.

At first glance this interpretation of shamanic humor resembles a rather different body of writings about similar phenomena. For Michael Taussig, whose brilliant work on shamanism and political power in Latin America has explicitly included the question of laughter (1987, 1993), the case of shamanic humor would probably represent a good example of "epistemic murk" (1987, 121). For him, the poetic language employed by shamans does not suffer from the "fixity of meaning," which, according to "Western fictions," is required to form "true propositions." Unlike the liturgy-heavy rituals of the Catholic Church, the "sorcery-centered religious mythology" of Amerindian shamans celebrates the irreducible fluidity of all signification processes by staging "Dada-like pandemonium[s] of the senses," during which there "is no way of separating the whirling confusion of the prolonged nausea from the bawdy jokes and teasing elbowing for room in the *yagé* song's irresistible current, with neither an end nor beginning nor climactical catharses but just bits and pieces in a mosaic of interruptedness" (1987, 412).

Indeed, humor and irony were always pet topics of critical cultural studies, for these phenomena so obviously challenge the "grand narratives" of modernism, naturalism, and positivism. Not only is there no fixity of meaning in irony, but also there is no fixed speaker either, for the enunciators of ironic utterances evaporate into a discursive "everyman's land" (Finlay 1988, 229). For the same reason, there are no such things as genuine beliefs or proper propositions here, for the speaker is himself a product of a sort of discursive "everyman's land" rather than its author. Here, "lack of fixity of meaning" in an ethnographic phenomenon such as Darhad shamanic humor therefore emerges as an end in itself. Irony renders the perspectives of different persons or groups of persons mutually relative, for the multiplication of points of view implicated by the explosion of the enunciator's subject are all equally valid representations of the same world.

In that sense, we could say that, according to the theoretical position advocated by Taussig and many other performative anthropologists, the truth-status of shamanic humor is posited as relative in an "epistemological" way: all the different points of view are positively true, but only insofar as each such perspective is confined negatively, or solipsistically, to a singular speaker or group of speakers. Conversely, according to the alternative interpretation that I advocate here, the truth of shamanic humor is posited to be relative in an "ontological" way: the different points of view brought about by "speaking lies" are all equal in their failure to represent the spirits, yet this negativity bespeaks positively, or deictically, the existence of multiple worlds. That is why, on this analysis, talking about the shamanic spirits logically takes a playful form, for such is also the impossible form these entities take themselves.

Irony, Søren Kierkegaard wrote many years ago, is "infinite absolute negativity. It is negativity, because it only negates; it is infinite, because it does not negate this or that phenomenon; it is absolute, because that by virtue of which it negates is a higher something that still is not" (1989, 261). This "negative" definition of irony calls to mind the way in which shamanic humor—like certain shamanic artifacts—was found in the previous chapter to render the shamanic spirits "negatively visible." By instigating an infinite regress in the listener's (and the speaker's) mind, "speaking lies" compels people to take an "infinite absolutely negative" stance toward the enigmatic shamanic cosmos. In the same way in which hunting vessels and shamanic gowns are "impossible objectifications" of the spirits' will to move, the discursive genre of shamanic humor renders it all too apparent that the spirits cannot be spoken about by means of ordinary representational language.

Thus understood, shamanic humor must be theorized not as a way of communicating degrees of belief (and therefore doubt) about occult phenomena but as a particular actualization, in the medium of language, of their inherently plastic and capricious mode of being. Indeed, given that the Darhad shamanic spirits are playful "as such," it makes perfect sense to speak about them in a way that is also playful in form. In that sense, the phenomenon of "speaking lies" is not a question of representation at all. Indeed, it would not make very much sense if shamanic language were to take the form of conventional utterances, which seek to represent a certain (degree of) belief about this or that thing. On the contrary, it makes perfect sense that shamanic humor takes the ironic form it does, for this "impossible form" of speech, and this genre alone, is isomorphic with the plastic way of being of the shamanic spirits as perceived by my Darhad friends. In that sense, to communicate one's knowledge about the spirit world quite logically calls for the use of playful discursive genres such as joking and "lying," for playful (*naadah*) is exactly what these spirits are themselves. Instead of expressing doubt about the spirits, shamanic humor thus emerges as an "impossible" discursive orchestration of them: the radical pragmatics of ironic speech replicates the virtual form of the *ongod,* which is movement itself.

It is here that my interpretation of shamanic humor departs from a number of the approaches described earlier. In my account, the lack of fixity of meaning in ironic discourse is an occult means rather than an occult end. Instead of resulting in Taussig's "epistemic murk," shamanic humor offers a unique opportunity for instantiating in language that it is the cosmos itself that is relative, not people's representations of it. This shamanic concept of relativity does not involve a conventional (Western, cultural relativist) decentering of truth, whereby all perspectives are seen as equally valid in epistemological terms. Rather, we are faced with a concept of "natural relativism," which, once again, calls to mind Viveiros de Castro's theory of Amazonian perspectivism (1998a, 1998b, 2004). In Darhad practices of "speaking lies," the lack of a fixed center is positivized, while the simultaneous enacting of multiple points of view becomes a way—in fact, the only way—of grasping a cosmos that is inherently labile and multiple. Rather than doubt about the existence of spirits, then, what is nested within shamanic humor is the deictic, post-plural nature of the spirits themselves.

The shamanic enigma that spills over from possession rituals into more everyday contexts through the practice of "telling lies" is thus not so much the question of *whether* the spirits exist but more a question of *where* these invisible beings are at a given moment in time or a given point in space. After all, as we saw in the analysis of Nadmid Udgan's possession rituals, the spirits are true only in play, and shamanic humor can in that sense be interpreted as a concerted attempt on behalf of the enunciating subject to express through the medium of irony the fundamentally paradoxical (playful) nature of the cosmos. So, to return to the example from Gombodorj's forge, what he was conveying was that Mungarag Taiga is not either haunted or not haunted but both haunted and not haunted. On the one hand, had I believed that it is always haunted, I would have made the same mistake as many Halh visitors to the Shishged, who—not unlike the constructivists—take the latent nature of things to be always equally present. Had I, on the other hand, assumed that the place is never haunted, I would have made the opposite (naturalist) mistake of overlooking the fact that in the Shishged, anything is potentially more than it seems. Had I taken his joking seriously as irony, however, then perhaps I might have realized that all Gombodorj was trying to tell us was that the *ongod* are always on the move, floating from one place, thing, or person to the next, like ocean foam caught in the wind.[15]

In that sense, the fact that specialists like Gombodorj so often "lie" when speaking about the spirits not only is a methodological problem but an analytical possibility as well, for "lying" is what shamanic agency seems to be all about. More specifically, such shamanic humor allows us to theorize the labile makeup of selves, bodies, and communities in the "age of the market." And that, surely, is at the heart of the matter when it comes to understanding the nature of shamanism without shamans in northern Mongolia.

Humor as the Incognito of Shamanism

In closing my analysis, I want to emphasize that I take very seriously the possibility that "speaking lies" reflects a semiconscious internalization of state-orchestrated cultural politics, for this certainly is plausible in light of the complex relations between the socialist (and, before that, Buddhist) rulers and local shamanic actors. This "postsocialist" account of shamanic humor and the "perspectivist" account I gave earlier may be considered complementary as opposed to mutually exclusive: each may be said to provide the invisible theoretical subtext needed for the other to work. It follows that the question is not how to make a (false) choice between "shamanist" and "postsocialist" explanations of phenomena such as "speaking lies," but how to hinge together or stitch up contrasting analytical perspectives without reducing the one to the other. In that sense, an ethnographically and theoretically satisfactory account of Darhad shamanic humor must be one that is able to demonstrate that this practice is indeed an outcome of northern Mongolia's recent political history, while in the same breath making it perfectly clear that the deeply postsocialist nature of "speaking lies" does not make this practice any less shamanic.

Kierkegaard famously wrote that in certain situations, humor is the "incognito" of religion (1963, 177–99). In fact he went so far as to maintain that "there is nothing as faithfully guarded by the comical as the religious" (1963, 167). As this chapter has demonstrated, there are (at least) two ways in which

---

15. In adopting this particular metaphor, I have in mind Henri Bergson's observation that "laughter indicates a slight revolt on the surface of social life.…Like [ocean] froth, it sparkles.…But the philosopher who gathers a handful to taste may find that the substance is scanty, and the after-taste bitter" (1999, 178–79).

joking had become the incognito of shamanism in northern Mongolia in the late 1990s. The first sense involves the fact that many occult specialists tended to joke when talking about shamanic affairs, especially in a place like Ulaan-Uul, with its lack of "genuine shamans." But there is also another sense in which joking became the incognito of Darhad shamanism in postsocialist Mongolia, namely, insofar as the specialists, without being aware of it, remained socialist subjects to a certain extent, in that they kept on pretending to pretend to believe in the spirits, even if there were no communist cadres to order them to do so. In both senses, the Mongolian postsocialist legacy, through a complex amalgamation of intended and unintended effects, has enhanced the power of the Darhad shamanic spirits by rendering them even more labile, and ever more multiple, in perfect anticipation, as it were, of the times of permanent transition to come.

Instead of instigating doubt about the spirits, "speaking lies" has allowed Darhad shamanism not merely to reinvent itself in a time of postsocialist transition but in a sense to become more powerful than ever before precisely *because* of its awkward relationship with socialism. For what emerges on the other side of this chapter's ethnography of what may seem to be linguistic details and cosmological oddities is a much larger message: that joking (like drunken violence or shamanic gowns) is an occult modality in its own right. As a result, every Darhad person in effect becomes endowed with shamanic potential.

"Telling lies," then, is the realization of shamanism without shamans in its ultimate sense. In a community where no one has the capacity to be a genuine shaman, everyone is a potential shaman insofar as he or she makes amusing jokes about this very lack. A quintessentially postsocialist ironic genre in which everyone (but especially the occult specialist) is quoting real or imaginary others, shamanic humor repeatedly undermines people's sense of what, where, and indeed whether the shamanic spirits are. Yet, paradoxically, it does so in a way that only serves to strengthen the spirits' grip on their lives.

Conclusion

"**M**ORTEEEN! WHERE ARE YOU? I AM GOING TO KILL YOU!" Over and over again the threat was hurled across the boggy grasslands of Baga Bilüü to the muddy pit that served as my hideout. The words struck me like a hammer to the head. It was the perfect summer night, and a productive day of field-work had been drawing to a close when I found myself being chased across the steppes by an *agsan*-afflicted man wielding a Kalashnikov.

I began this book by recounting an iconic event from my time in Ulaan-Uul in the late 1990s: a village community besieged by bands of roaming men afflicted with drunken rage and leaking souls, forcing angry fathers and anxious mothers to hide the elderly and the youngest away after having dis-patched their older offspring to the nearest rooftop as lookouts. I now close my exploration of contemporary Darhad shamanic agency by recalling an-other key ethnographic moment from my stay in the Shishged, which, for a final time, reminds us that a postsocialist phenomenon like *agsan* cannot be explained away by straightforward socioeconomic reasons such as poverty, alcoholism, and unemployment. By recounting how I ended up in this pre-carious situation, and by considering some of its rather unexpected conse-quences, I hope to shed conclusive light on the social agency of Ulaan-Uul's potential shamans and, therefore, on the nature and efficacy of shamanism without shamans in northern Mongolia after socialism.

It was just after dinner, and a lazy atmosphere had settled over the tiny wooden barn that my hosts used as their summer residence. I was sitting in my favorite corner between the fireplace and one of the two metal beds, sip-ping salty milk tea and smoking endless "rollies" while half-listening to the lively chitchat between the wife and her thirteen-year-old daughter. Except for two smaller brothers and myself, no man was present in the house, for the husband had left that morning on one of his weeklong trips to the a national park. The daughter was in a happy and exited mood—a lot was happening in Ulaan-Uul these days, for it was the time of the annual *naadam* games, which takes place in conjunction with Mongolian Independence Day on July 11. Finding her daughter's energy infectious, the wife enthusiastically tried to add to the excitement, sharing with her daughter and myself a number of "secret" anecdotes of the sort that wouldn't normally have found their way outside the more established chains of gossip.

I do not know whether it was because it was common knowledge that the husband was away, or if it was pure coincidence, but at some point we received a rather unusual group of visitors: three women, none of whom was accompanied by her husband or children, and all of whom were in a fairly advanced state of tipsiness. We had already been alerted to their arrival by their unusually noisy approach. In rural Mongolia, visitors are supposed to approach a household in a manner appropriate to their age, gender, and position. In the case of women, and especially married ones, this implies that they should not make any flamboyant gestures, let alone speak too much or too loudly, and should generally try to avoid attracting undue attention. This particular trio of women were making little effort to conform to any of these rules. They barged through the door with broad smiles on their faces, accompanied by a typically masculine aroma of cigarettes, vodka, and horse sweat, and quickly filled the room with animated laughter, bawdy jokes, and friendly insults.

Soon my hostess and I had been enrolled in the small party, though we never quite managed to catch up with the elevated mood, or for that matter with the level of intoxication, of our three guests. One of them, the youngish wife of an officer in the local branch of the border army, seemed to be having a particularly good time, as witnessed, for instance, by her suggestion that we should all take turns singing our favorite songs (a common practice on festive occasions in rural Mongolia); "but not," she insisted, "those songs about Mother and Nature that we always sing, but our dearest *love* songs!"

So it happened that I found myself in a small wooden barn with four women putting their heart and soul into the performance of Darhad love songs—songs that, since I was the only man present, were directed toward me as a representative of my particular sex and gender, even if they were not addressed to me personally. This went on for a good while, during which the vodka kept flowing, until suddenly my own performance was (thankfully) disrupted by the door being flung open as a male figure barged into the room, bursting with pent-up anger. It was the spouse of the youngish woman, the officer, who had been on his way home from duty when, much to his surprise, he had spotted his wife's gelding outside the barn. Surprise soon turned to anger when, sitting on the doorstep with his own bottle, he heard what was taking place inside; and this anger eventually spiraled into *agsan* when he overheard his wife's performance.

It is never nice to be the target of an *agsan* person's wrath, especially if he happens to be armed with a semiautomatic rifle. Before long I was lying in a ditch, panting heavily after a narrow escape from the house. The women had made a valiant effort at holding the man back. One of them, the rotund wife of a senior official, tried to obstruct his path, and the wife in my host family, who was famous for her height and fearlessness, gripped him from behind in an effort to restrain his arms, while she desperately shouted: "RUN, Morten, RUN RIGHT NOW!" This gave me the few seconds I needed to escape. The angry husband never managed to catch up with me, and the fact that it was a moonless, overcast night ensured that he never managed to find me either, although I kept picking up fragments of the threats hurled from atop his horse for a long time to come.

The next day it was my turn to be angry. Returning early in the morning to my hosts' place after a night spent at a safe haven provided by the nearby *ger* of the grandmother, I immediately poured forth my outrage about the events of the previous evening. "That man is totally crazy," I shouted, waking the family from their cozy slumber. "He threatened to kill me for something I did not even do! I had to hide in a ditch for half the night!" The fact that my anger was met with total silence and embarrassed glances only agitated me further. Perhaps, I thought, my hosts were ashamed about what had happened, though they obviously should not be. "Of course, it wasn't your fault," I reassured the wife. "He alone is to blame. What that crazy guy did was unacceptable, and even more so in light of the fact that we are talking about an armed officer returning from duty. In fact, I feel that the incident must be reported to the man's superiors so that appropriate disciplinary measures may be taken. At the very least, I demand an apology from him!"

To judge from the perplexed expressions of amusement mixed with bewilderment that greeted this righteous tirade, my host family did not quite share my view of the situation. Indeed, as it later dawned on me, it was not so much the drunken army officer and certainly not the family themselves in their role as hosts who were the source of embarrassment—it was me. At this point, however, I was still under the impression that our divergent understandings of the situation were the result of a mere communication failure (maybe it was my use of the Mongolian language?), that I simply needed to express the reasons behind my outrage in a clearer way for my hosts to realize how right I was. Eventually the husband, who had just returned that morning, heaved a great sigh and went off on his horse to find my adversary, whom he somehow

Figure 21. Border military personnel

managed to persuade to come back and offer me an apology, in spite of the enormity of his (as well as his wife's) hangover.

What followed was as revealing as it was awkward. As the officer forced himself to mumble an excuse to me, he was totally unable, or indeed unwilling, to suppress a cheeky grin. It hit home how staged the whole excuse exercise was. Clearly the man did not mean what he was saying, and what was even worse, neither he nor my hosts made any real effort to demonstrate that there was a valid reason why he should apologize to me, or indeed why he should be remorseful at all. My response to this came as a shock to everyone. Absorbed by an ever-growing sense of frustration and self-righteousness, I informed my hosts that I would be leaving for the capital that same evening "to take a few weeks' break." While there was nothing new about my traveling to Ulaanbaatar—I had been talking about doing so for some time—my hosts obviously (and correctly) linked my imminent departure with the events of the previous night. The fact that people took it as a sign of fear on my part only added to my frustration. Why could they not understand what seemed to be the most obvious thing in the world: that the officer had erred and that he should take responsibility for his actions?

That people found these events hilarious became clear upon my return to Ulaan-Uul several weeks later. After a reunion with my hosts ("we thought you would never come back"), a bottle of vodka was opened, and a small group of relatives and neighbors gathered for an impromptu welcome. Ever so subtly, the topic of the *agsan* officer and my own (over) reaction was brought up. The younger brother of the wife turned to me and said, "Do you know, Morten, you are famous now?" Without waiting for me to respond, he continued with a wide grin: "Of course, many people around here knew about you before, but after what happened the other week we are sure to remember you for years to come. For something big has happened to you, something that only rarely happens with locals even in the course of their entire lifetimes: a joke song has been composed about you!" Accompanied by several others in the room, he then went on to hum the first notes of a song, which had the unmistakable melodic form of all Darhad joke songs, and whose lyrics, equally clearly, were centered on the events that night on Baga Bilüü and my ensuing "escape" from the barn.

I never heard a full version of the song. (As I have mentioned, such songs are seldom performed in the presence of the person who is the object of ridicule.) But the fact that a brand-new song had been composed in my questionable honor finally revealed to me that it was *my* behavior, and not that of my adversary, which was the source of embarrassment—and, now that an appropriate period of time had passed, of laughter too. For just as throughout my stay in Ulaan-Uul it was considered perfectly acceptable to hide the truth from someone afflicted with *agsan,* it was also expected that one would refrain from moralizing about his behavior when he stopped being *agsan* and regained his usual self. To do otherwise (which was precisely what I had done) was not merely naïve and pointless; it was embarrassing and wrong. For in demanding an excuse from the hung-over officer and then leaving in anger, I had collapsed two (ideally) separate domains of life into one: the invisible, labile realm of the black side and the visible, stable realm of the yellow side.

This is not to say that *agsan* persons are not held accountable for their actions (as Gombodorj's predicament makes amply clear); but they cannot be morally blamed for their violent drunken behavior, or expected to express, let alone feel, any remorse. This is so because, along with various other phenomena associated with the "age of the market" (such as "lying," gossip, and greed), *agsan* is perceived to be a proto-shamanic condition, one in which the afflicted person's mind and body have been temporarily (and in a few cases permanently) invaded by affects other than his own. So instead of being wholly human or wholly nonhuman, my *agsan* adversary that night on Baga Bilüü was an incomplete shaman: a postsocialist agent of excess both more and less shamanic than a complete shaman, with all the existential, social, and indeed political ramifications this entails.

Not Quite Shamans

What does it mean for us to think about postsocialism through the prism of shamanism? I use the word "prism" and not (say) "lens" here, for one could surely not make an encompassing study of every postsocialist aspect of social life in the Shishged in the late 1990s, however much one were able to "focus in" on it. Instead, in keeping with the plastic and capricious nature of the spirits, I have tried to write about the revival of shamanic agency in northern Mongolia in the age of the market in a "prismatic" way that has refracted my account into several, partially connected ethnographies isomorphic with the other "impossible forms" found in a world of shamanism without shamans.

In trying to make this "lateral" (Maurer 2005) or "recursive" (Holbraad 2008) analytical move, which reflects a theoretically reflexive attempt to extend postplurally the form of the object of analysis to the form of the analysis itself, the present study may be seen as part of a broader trend in current anthropology and related fields, in particular science and technology studies. As the editors of *Thinking through Things* (2007) note, the writings of Gilles Deleuze and Bruno Latour, along with those of anthropologists such as Roy Wagner, Marilyn Strathern, and Eduardo Viveiros de Castro, make it possible to take more seriously—or, put more modestly and in my view more precisely, to take seriously in a new way—the concepts brought about through ethnographic fieldwork. They write:

> What is exciting about such an approach is that, instead of just adapting or elaborating theoretical perspectives—often pillaged from other disciplines—to reconfigure the parameters of "our" knowledge to suit informants' representations of reality, it opens the way for genuinely novel concepts to be produced out of the ethnographic encounter....On this view, anthropological analysis has little to do with trying to determine how other people think about the world. It has to do with how *we* must think in order to conceive of a world the way they do. (Henare, Holbraad, and Wastell 2007, 8–15)

What "genuinely new concepts", if not exactly new worlds, emerge from the present study? In so far as a novel analytical concept may be said to have been created in my encounter with my Darhad friends (and foes), the most likely candidate is, I think, the indigenous notion of not quite shamans itself, along with its necessary conceptual corollary of shamanism without shamans. It is, or so I would like to think, quite new in an anthropological context not only to identify but also to maintain persistently as one's primary ethnographic and theoretical focus throughout one's work this "wrong" side of shamanism "proper"—the shadowy world of "half" shamans, who, as we have seen, are in some ways more shamanic than the "real" ones, and who, as we have also seen, are in many ways emblematic of the postsocialist predicament in northern Mongolia as a whole. Yet I can take only limited credit for identifying this new anthropological concept, for the importance of the potential shamans and the distinct agency associated with them was literally forced on me by others; indeed, for a long time, even after having returned from Mongolia and while writing the first drafts of this book, I did my best to resist it. Above all, the concept of not quite shamans stems from the lost generation of potential shamans themselves. It was people like Gombodorj, along with the irritated and sometimes terrified people around them, who forced me to take shamanism without shamans seriously.

As a final illustration of this point—that some concepts, like spirits and their bodily manifestations, impose themselves on people (including anthropologists) often against their will—let me briefly return to the case of my ex-adversary, the *agsan* army officer. For while I never had the pleasure, or otherwise, of meeting him again, word of his deeds reached me in the winter of 2001 when I was involved in making a documentary film in Ulaanbaatar. One cold January day as we were filming at one of the city's bustling black markets, I bumped into a Duha acquaintance at a shoe stall, where he told me the following—and to me surprising—news: "You remember that guy who once threatened to kill you? Well, he is now the mayor of Ulaan-Uul. He won the local election last summer in a landslide!"

The strange thing about this final twist to the story is not so much that the same man who once attacked me in a fury of drunken violence could later become the head of one of the Shishged districts. The odd thing was rather why I should be so surprised to hear about his newfound political career in the first place. After all, as this book has shown, there is nothing particularly unusual in this *ataman*-like ascent to power. On the contrary, his example underscores one of the central points I have been trying to make in this book, which is that in northern Mongolia after socialism—and perhaps elsewhere in the postsocialist world—occult agency and political efficacy, shamanism and postsocialism, were mutually imbricated. Both operated through endless moral transgressions, bodily metamorphoses, and conceptual extensions. *Atamans* as much as shamans both assumed their power and exercised it by making themselves double or even triple, bouncing as they did between multiple bodies and in the process taking these forms to the limit so as to make themselves visible to different audiences of human and nonhuman spectators. In the late 1990s, and possibly still today, agency above all was in the hands of persons imbued with the shamanic capacity to change in accordance with the changes of transition itself, while at the same time retaining a semblance of form.

I have aimed to demonstrate in this book that the imbrication between shamanism and postsocialism is not about the inscription of different "worldviews" onto a fixed and passive worldly substrate. Rather, their imbrication results from the coming into being of a genuinely new world in northern Mongolia after socialism: a radically emergent cosmos known by names such as the "age of the market," the "transition," or the "age of darkness." It would, for the same reason, be inaccurate to label Darhad shamanism an "occult economy" in the sense discussed in the introduction to this book. An occult economy it may well be, but only as long as this is understood in "ontological" (posthumanist) terms and not "epistemological" (humanist) ones: contemporary Darhad shamanism as occult economy, not in the sense people make of transition but in transition's sense of them, and, so to speak, its sense of itself. For indeed, is that not precisely what a shamanic spirit is: an actualization of transitional "self-awareness"—the attempt of an always changing world to analyze itself? Thus shamanism without shamans emerges as the "impossible" form taken by the shamanic cosmos after socialism; it is, simultaneously, an indigenous theory of societal transition, and the most recent actualization of transition as a virtual ontological state.

Shamanic Agency in Transition

My argument in this book has rested on the key observation that moving in and out of human and nonhuman bodies to assume their perspectives and to acquire their assemblages of affects is what Darhad shamanism is about. Shamans such as Nadmid Udgan go beyond the visible world—not by renouncing it as some world religions do, but by plunging deeper into it. As a multinaturalist, perspectivist activity, shamanism is all about exploring the blind spots of the immanent rather than seeking to escape the world through transcendence. Far from trying to attain a more spiritual, less material state, shamans try to take the perspective of as many bodies (that is, to be as material) as possible. In doing so, they see things—and make things be seen—in ways that are otherwise restricted to nonhuman beings. Thus shamans make worlds (not views) visible that cannot normally be seen, such as those of wild animals, dead ancestors—or postsocialist states.

Yet as this book has demonstrated, the real trouble—and therefore also the real fun—begins when the shamanic spirits are no longer confined to particular minds, bodies, and artifacts. This is what happens when the "genuine" shamans are all gone, and when the hunters (or their wives) have stopped feeding their spirit talismans. And it is what happens when there has been a perceived collapse of stable institutions (whether Buddhist or state socialist) to rein in, if not repress outright, the labile forces of transition to ensure that the lives of ordinary people can still unfold within the stable shelters of *ail* and *negdel.* The result, as I have demonstrated, is that individuals, households, communities, and sometimes entire nations and polities have been turned inside out, subjected to the ever-changing will and still more fleeting perspectives of multiple nonhuman agents, ranging from singular persons like Gombodorj to polities like the postsocialist Mongolian state, which in many ways has emerged as an *ongon*-like sovereign.

One of the most important lessons to be learned from focusing on shamanism without shamans—apart from the ethnographic contribution to the anthropological literature—is what it can tell us about social agency in contexts of rapid political, economic, and cultural change. As the anecdote about the army officer demonstrates, the overspill of form associated with northern Mongolia's potential shamans is not just a negative thing. However annoying and dangerous they may be felt to be, by local people and anthropologists alike, it is they more than anybody else who can capture, embody, and therefore also manipulate the unpredictable path of flight instigated by rapid transition. As I have tried to show over the preceding chapters, the potential shamans, and they alone, are imbued with a hyper-shamanic capacity to mold, extend, and apportion emergent social, political, and economic realities into new impossible forms, making it possible to ride on the edge of change.

Bibliography

Abaeva, Liubov L. 1992. *Kult gor i buddizm v buryatii: evoliutsiaa verovanii i kultov selenginskikh buryat.* Moscow: Nauka.

Anderson, David G. 2000. *Identity and Ecology in Arctic Siberia: The Number One Reindeer Brigade.* Oxford: Oxford University Press.

Anderson, Benedict. 1991. *Imagined Communities: Reflections on the Origin and Spread of Nationalism.* London: Verso.

Apte, Mahedev L. 1985. *Humor and Laughter: An Anthropological Approach.* Ithaca: Cornell University Press.

Ashforth, Adam. 2005. *Witchcraft, Violence, and Democracy in South Africa.* Chicago: University of Chicago Press.

Atkinson, Jane M. 1989. *The Art and Politics of Wana Shamanship.* Berkeley: University of California Press.

Atwood, Christopher P. 2004. *Encyclopedia of Mongolia and the Mongol Empire.* New York: Facts on File.

Badamhatan, S. 1962. *Hövsgöliin tsaatan ardyn aj baidlyn toim.* Ulaanbaatar: Academy of Sciences.

———. 1980. *BNMAU-in ündestnii ba ugsaatni högjliin asuuldad.* Ulaanbaatar.

———. 1986. "Les chamanistes du Bouddha vivant." *Études Mongoles… et Sibériennes* 17: 1–208.

Badamhatan, S. and Ch. Banzragch. 1981. *Hövsgöl aimagiin tovch tüüh.* Mörön, Mongolia.

Badiou, Alain. 2000. *Deleuze: The Clamor of Being.* Translated by Louise Burchill. Minneapolis: University of Minnesota Press.

Balzer, Majorie Mandalstam. 2006. "Sustainable Faith? Reconfiguring Shamanic Healing in Siberia." In *Spiritual Transformation and Healing: Anthropological, Theological, Neuroscientific, and Clinical Perspectives,* edited by J. D. Koss-Chiono and Philip Hefner, 78–100. Lanham, Md.: Altamira Press.

———. 2008. "Beyond Belief? Social, Political, and Shamanic Power in Siberia." *Social Analysis* 52 (1): 95–110.

Barbe, Katharina. 1995. *Irony in Context.* Amsterdam: John Benjamin's Publishing Company.

Bareja-Starzynska, Agata, and Hanne Havnevik. 2006. "A Preliminary Study of Buddhism in Present-Day Mongolia." In *Mongols from Country to City: Floating Boundaries, Pastoralism and City Life in the Mongol Lands,* edited by Ole Bruun and Li Narangoa, 212–36. Copenhagen: NIAS Press.

Barkmann, Udo B. 1997. "The Revival of Lamaism in Mongolia." *Central Asian Survey* 16 (1): 69–79.

Barth, Fredrik, ed. 1969. *Ethnic Groups and Boundaries.* Boston: Little Brown.

Bateson, Gregory. 2000 [1972]. *Steps to an Ecology of Mind.* Chicago: University of Chicago Press.

Bawden, Charles R. 1958. "Two Mongol Texts Concerning *Obo* Worship." *Oriens Extremus* 1: 23–41.

———. 1986. *The Modern History of Mongolia.* London: Kegan Paul International.

Berdahl, Daphne, Matti Bunzl, and Martha Lampland, eds. 2000. *Altering States: Ethnographies of Transition in Eastern Europe and the Former Soviet Union.* Ann Arbor: University of Michigan Press.

Berger, Peter L. 1997. *Redeeming Laughter: The Comic Dimension of Human Experience.* Berlin: Walter De Gruyter.

Bergmann, Jorg R. 1993. *Discreet Indiscretions: The Social Organization of Gossip.* New York: Aldine de Gruyter.

Bergson, Henri. 1999 [1911]. *Laughter: An Essay on the Meaning of the Comic.* Copenhagen: Green Integer.

Blondeau, Anne-Marie, and Ernst Steinkellner, eds. 1996. *Reflections on the Mountain: Essays on the History and Social Meaning of the Mountain Cult in Tibet and the Himalaya.* Vienna: Verlag der Österreichishen Akademia der Wissenschaften.

Bogoraz, Vladimir. 1909. *The Chukchee, The Jesup North Pacific Expedition, Memoir of the American Museum of Natural History,* Vol. VII. New York: G. E. Stechert.

Boyer, Pascal. 1994. *The Naturalness of Religious Ideas: A Cognitive Theory of Religion.* Berkeley: University of California Press.

Broz, L. 2007. "Pastoral Perspectivism: A View from Altai." Special issue on Inner Asian perspectivism, edited by M. A. Pedersen, Rebecca Empson, and Caroline Humphrey. *Inner Asia* 9 (2): 291–310.

Bruun, Ole. 2006. *Precious Steppe: Mongolian Nomadic Pastoralists in Pursuit of the Market.* Oxford: Lexington Books.

Bruun, Ole, and Li Narangoa, eds. 2006. *Mongols from Country to City: Floating Boundaries, Pastoralism and City Life in the Mongol Lands.* Copenhagen: NIAS Press.

Bruun, Ole, and Ole Odgaard, eds. 1996. *Mongolia in Transition: Old Patterns, New Challenges.* Surrey: Curzon.

Bubandt, Nils. 2006. "Sorcery, Corruption, and the Dangers of Democracy in Indonesia." *Journal of the Royal Anthropological Institute* 12: 413–31.

Buchli, Victor. 2000. *An Archaeology of Socialism.* Oxford: Berg.

Bulag, Uradyn E. 1998. *Nationalism and Hybridity in Mongolia.* Oxford: Clarendon.

———. 2002. *The Mongols at China's Edge: History and the Politics of National Unity.* Lanham, Md.: Rowman and Littlefield.

Burawoy, Michael, and Katherine Verdery, eds. 1999. *Uncertain Transition: Ethnographies of Change in the Postsocialist World.* Oxford: Rowman and Littlefield.

Buyandelger(iyn), Manduhai. 1999. "Who 'Makes' the Shaman? The Politics of Shamanic Practices among the Buryats in Mongolia." *Inner Asia* 1 (2): 221–44.

——. 2007. "Dealing with Uncertainty: Shamans, Marginal Capitalism, and the Remaking of History in Postsocialist Mongolia. *American Ethnologist* 34 (1): 127–47.

——. Forthcoming. *Tragic Spirits: Shamanism, Postsocialism, and the Neo-liberal State in Mongolia*. Chicago: University of Chicago Press.

Carty, John, and Yasmine Musharbash. 2008. "You've Got to Be Joking: Asserting the Analytical Value of Humour and Laughter in Contemporary Anthropology." *Anthropological Forum* 18 (3): 209–17.

Charleux, Isabelle. 2002. "Padmasambhava's Travel to the North: The Pilgrimage to the Monastery of the Caves and the Old Schools of Tibetan Buddhism in Mongolia." *Central Asiatic Journal* 46 (2): 168–232.

Christian, David. 1998. *A History of Russia, Central Asia and Mongolia, Volume 1: Inner Eurasia from Prehistory to the Mongolian Empire*. Oxford. Blackwell.

Clark, Herbert M., and Richard J. Gerrig. 1984. "On the Pretence Theory of Irony." *Journal of Experimental Psychology: General* 113 (1): 121–26.

Cleaves, Francis W. 1982. *The Secret History of the Mongols*. Translated with commentary by F. W. Cleaves. Cambridge: Harvard University Press.

Comaroff, Jean, and John Comaroff. 1999. "Occult Economies and the Violence of Abstraction: Notes from the South African Postcolony." *American Ethnologist* 26 (3): 279–301.

Corsín-Jiménez, Alberto. 2003. "On Space as a Capacity." *Journal of the Royal Anthropological Institute* (n.s.) 9: 137–53.

——. 2007. "Well-Being in Anthropological Balance: Remarks on Proportionality as Political Imagination." In *Culture and Well-Being: Anthropological Approaches to Freedom and Political Ethics*, edited by Alberto Corsín-Jiménez, 180–200. London: Pluto Press.

Corsín-Jiménez, Alberto, and Rane Willerslev. 2007. "An Anthropological Concept of the Concept: Reversability among the Siberian Yukaghirs." *Journal of the Royal Anthropological Institute* (n.s.) 13: 527–44.

Das, Veena, and Deborah Poole, eds. 2004. *Anthropology on the Margins of the State*. Santa Fe: School of American Research Press.

Dashpürev, D., and S. K. Soni. 1992. *Reign of Terror in Mongolia, 1920–1990*. New Delhi: South Asian Publishers.

Delaplace, Gregory. 2009. "A Sheep Herder's Rage: Silence and Grief in Contemporary Mongolia. *Ethnos* 74 (4): 514–34.

Deleuze, Gilles. 1990. *The Logic of Sense*. London: Athlone.

——. 1994. *Difference and Repetition*. London: Athlone.

——. 1999. *A Thousand Plateaus: Capitalism and Schizophrenia*. London: Athlone.

Deleuze, Gilles, and Félix Guattari. 2004. *What is Philosophy?* London: Verso.

Descola, Philip. 1996. "Constructing Natures: Symbolic Ecology and Social Practice." In *Nature and Society: Anthropological Perspectives*, edited by Philip Descola and Gisli Pálsson, 82–102. London: Routledge.

Diószegi, László. 1961. "Problems of Mongolian Shamanism." *Acta Ethnographica* 10 (1–2): 195–206.

——. 1963. "Ethnogenic Aspects of Darkhat Shamanism." *Acta Orientalia Hungaria* 16: 55–81.

Douglas, Mary. 1968. "The Social Control of Cognition: Some Factors in Joke Perception." *Man* 3: 361–76.

——. 1993. "Jokes." In *Implicit Meanings: Essays in Anthropology*, 90–114. London: Routledge.

Dulam, Sedenjav. 1992. *Darhad böögiin ulamjlal.* Ulaanbaatar: MUIS-iin Hevlel.

Dulam, Sedenjav, and Marie-Dominique Even. 1994. "Animalité et humanité dans le chamanisme des Darkhates de Mongolie." *Études Mongoles…et Sibériennes* 25: 131–44.

Dumont, Louis. 1980. *Homo Hierarchicus: The Caste System and Its Implications.* Chicago: University of Chicago Press.

Eliade, Mircea. 1964. *Shamanism: Archaic Techniques of Ecstasy.* London: Routledge.

Empson, Rebecca, ed. 2006. *Time, Causality and Prophecy in the Mongolian Cultural Region.* Folkestone, Kent: Global Oriental.

——. 2007. "Separating and Containing People and Things in Mongolia." In *Thinking through Things: Theorising Artefacts Ethnographically,* edited by Amira Henare, Martin Holbraad, and Sari Wastell, 113–40. London: University College London Press.

——. 2011. *Harnessing Fortune: Personhood, Memory and Place in Northeast Mongolia.* Oxford: Oxford University Press.

Englund, Harri, and James Leach. 2000. "Ethnography and the Meta-narratives of Modernity." *Current Anthropology* 41 (2): 225–39.

Enhbat, Badarchyn. 1993. *Local Government Strengthening in Mongolia: Fact-Finding Study at Bulgan um, Dornod Aimag and Alag-Erdene Sum, Hovsgol Aimag.* Ulaanbaatar: Research and Consultancy Center, IAMD.

Enhkbat, Badarchyn, and Ole Odgaard. 1996. "Decentralization and Local Governance." In *Mongolia in Transition: Old Patterns, New Challenges,* edited by Ole Bruun and Ole Odgaard, 165–89. Richmond, Surrey: Curzon Press.

Evans-Pritchard, E. E. 1976 [1937]. *Witchcraft, Oracles, and Magic among the Azande.* Oxford: Clarendon Press.

Even, Marie-Dominique. 1988–89. "Chants de chamanes de mongols." *Études Mongoles…et Sibériennes.* Vols. 19–20.

——. 1991. "The Shamanism of the Mongols." In *Mongolia Today,* edited by Shirin Akiner, 183–205. London: Kegan Paul International.

Ewing, Thomas E. 1981. "The Forgotten Frontier: South Siberia (Tuva) in Chinese and Russian History, 1600–1920." *Central Asiatic Survey* 15 (3–4): 174–212.

Fausto, Carlos, 2007. "Feasting on People: Eating Animals and Humans in Amazonia." *Current Anthropology* 48 (4): 497–530.

Fehérváry, Krisztina. 2002. "American Kitchens, Luxury Bathrooms, and the Search for a 'Normal' Life in Postsocialist Hungary." *Ethnos* 67 (3): 369–400.

Ferguson, James. 1999. *Expectations of Modernity: Myths and Meanings of Urban Life on the Zambian Copperbelt.* Berkeley: University of California Press.

Fernandez, James, and Mary T. Huber, eds. 2001. *Irony in Action: Anthropology, Practice, and the Moral Imagination.* Chicago: University of Chicago Press.

Finlay, Marike. 1988. *The Romantic Irony of Semiotics: Friedrich Schlegel and the Crisis of Representation.* Berlin: Mouton de Gruyter.

Fisher, William F. 2001. *Fluid Boundaries: Forming and Transforming Identity in Nepal.* New York: Columbia University Press.

Forsyth, James. 1992. *History of the Peoples of Siberia: Russia's North Asian Colony 1581–1990.* Cambridge: Cambridge University Press.

Freud, Sigmund. 1991 [1905]. *Jokes and Their Relation to the Unconscious.* London: Penguin Books.

Galdanova, Galina R. 1997. *Dolamaistskiye verovaniia buryat.* Novosibirsk: Nauka.

Gell, Alfred. 1998. *Art and Agency: An Anthropological Theory.* Oxford: Clarendon Press.

Geschiere, Peter. 1997. *The Modernity of Witchcraft: Politics and the Occult in Postcolonial Africa.* Charlottesville: University Press of Virginia.

Gilhus, Ingvild S. 1997. *Laughing Gods, Weeping Virgins: Laughter in the History of Religion.* London: Routledge.

Godelier, Maurice. 1986. *The Making of Great Men: Male Domination and Power among the New Guinea Baruya.* Cambridge: Cambridge University Press.

Godelier, Maurice, and Marilyn Strathern, eds. 1991. *Big Men and Great Men: Personifications of Power in Melanesia.* Cambridge: Cambridge University Press.

Gordon, Linda. 1983. *Cossack Rebellions: Social Turmoil in the Sixteenth-Century Ukraine.* Albany: State University of New York Press.

Grant, Bruce. 1995. *In the Soviet House of Culture: A Century of Perestroikas.* Princeton: Princeton University Press.

Green, Sarah F. 2005. *Notes from the Balkans: Locating Marginality and Ambiguity on the Greek-Albanian Border.* Princeton: Princeton University Press.

Gupta, Akhil, and James Ferguson, eds. 1997. *Culture, Power, Place: Explorations in Critical Anthropology.* Durham: Duke University Press.

Halemba, Agnieszka. 2006. *The Telengits of Southern Siberia: Landscape, Religion and Knowledge in Motion.* London: Routledge.

Hamayon, Roberte. 1984. "Is There a Typically Female Exercise of Shamanism in Patrilinear Societies Such as the Buryat?" In *Shamanism in Eurasia,* part 2, edited by Mihály Hoppál, 307–18. Göttingen: Herodot.

———. 1990. *La chasse à l'âme: Esquisse d'une théorie du chamanisme sibérien.* Nanterre: Société d'ethnologie.

———. 1992. "Game and Games, Fortune and Dualism in Siberian Shamanism." In *Northern Religions and Shamanism,* edited by Mihály Hoppál and Juha Pentikainen, 134–37. Budapest: Akademiai Kiado.

———. 1993. "Are 'Trance,' 'Ecstasy' and Similar Concepts Appropriate in the Study of Shamanism?" *Shaman* 1 (2): 3–25.

———. 1994. "Shamanism in Siberia: From Partnership in Supernature to Counter-power in Society." In *Shamanism, History, and the State,* edited by Nicholas Thomas and Caroline Humphrey, 76–89. Ann Arbor: University of Michigan Press.

Handelman, Don. 1990. *Models and Mirrors: Towards an Anthropology of Public Events.* Cambridge: Cambridge University Press.

Hangalov, M. N. 1958. *Sobranie sochinenij.* Vol. 1. Ulaan-Ude: BION.

Hangartner, Judith. 2006. "The Resurgence of Darhad Shamanism: Legitimisation Strategies of Rural Practitioners in Mongolia. *Tsantsa* (11): 111–14.

———. 2011. *The Constitution and Contestation of Darhad Shaman's Power in Contemporary Mongolia.* Leiden: Brill.

———. In press. "Darhad Shamanism and the Constitution of the Mongolian Nation-State." Forthcoming in *Inner Asia* 12 (2).

Hangin, Gombojav, et al. 1986. *A Modern Mongolian-English Dictionary.* Bloomington: Research Institute for Inner Asian Studies.

Hansen, Thomas B., and Finn Stepputat, eds. 2001. *States of Imagination: Ethnographic Explorations of the Postcolonial State.* Durham: Duke University Press.

Heissig, Walter. 1980. *The Religions of Mongolia.* London: Routledge and Kegan Paul.

Henare, Amira, Martin Holbraad, and Sari Wastell, 2007. "Introduction: Thinking through Things." In *Thinking through Things: Theorising Artefacts Ethnographically,* edited by Amira Henare, Martin Holbraad, and Sari Wastell, 1–31. London: Routledge.

Herzfeld, Michael. 1985. *The Poetics of Manhood: Contest and Identity in a Cretan Mountain Village*. Princeton: Princeton University Press.

Hirsch, Francine. 2005. *Empire of Nations: Ethnographic Knowledge and the Making of the Soviet Union*. Ithaca: Cornell University Press.

Hobsbawm, Eric. 1959. *Primitive Rebels: Studies in Archaic Forms of Social Movements in the Nineteenth and Twentieth Centuries*. New York: W. W. Norton & Company.

Hodges, Matt. 2008. "Rethinking Time's Arrow: Bergson, Deleuze and the Anthropology of Time." *Anthropological Theory* 8 (4): 399–429.

Højer, Lars. 2004. "The Anti-social Contract: Enmity and Suspicion in Northern Mongolia." *Cambridge Anthropology* 24: 41–63.

——. 2009. "Absent Powers: Magic and Loss in Postsocialist Mongolia." *Journal of the Royal Anthropological Institute* (n.s.) 15 (3): 575–91.

Holbraad, Martin. 2003. "Estmando a nessesidade: Os oraculos de Ifa e a verdade em Havana." *Mana* 9 (2): 39–77.

——. 2007. "The Power of Powder: Multiplicity and Motion in the Divinatory Cosmology of Cuban Ifá (or Mana, Again)." In *Thinking through Things: Theorising Artefacts Ethnographically*, edited by Amira Henare, Martin Holbraad, and Sari Wastell, 189–225. London: Routledge.

——. 2008. "Definitive Evidence, from Cuban Gods." *Journal of the Royal Anthropological Institute* 14 (1), 93–109.

——. 2010. "'Ontology is just another word for culture': Against the Motion." Special issue of *Critique of Anthropology*, edited by Soumhya Venkatesen: 30 (2), 179–84.

——. n.d. "Can the Thing Speak?" Paper presented at the Things and Spirits Conference, Lisbon, September 15–17, 2010.

Holbraad, Martin, and Morten Axel Pedersen, eds. 2009a. Special issue, "Technologies of the Imagination." *Ethnos* 74 (1).

——. 2009b. "Planet M: The Intense Abstraction of Marilyn Strathern." *Anthropological Theory* 9 (4), 371–94.

Holbraad, Martin, and Rane Willerslev. 2007. "Transcendental Perspectivism: Anonymous Viewpoints from Inner Asia." Special issue on Inner Asian perspectivism, edited by M. A. Pedersen, Rebecca Empson, and Caroline Humphrey. *Inner Asia* 10 (1): 329–45.

Holmberg, David H. 1989. *Order in Paradox: Myth, Ritual, and Exchange among Nepal's Tamang*. Ithaca: Cornell University Press.

Honderich, Ted, ed. 1995. *The Oxford Companion to Philosophy*. Oxford: Oxford University Press.

Houseman, Michael, and Carlo Severi. 1998. *Naven or the Other Self: A Relational Approach to Ritual Action*. Leiden: Brill.

Huizinga, Johan. 1970. *Homo Ludens: A Study of the Play Element in Culture*. London: Temple Smith.

Humphrey, Caroline. 1985. "Barter and Economic Disintegration." *Man* (n.s.) 20 (1), 48–72.

——. 1991. "'Icebergs,' Barter, and the Mafia in Provincial Russia." *Anthropology Today* 2 (7): 8–13.

——. 1994a. "Shamanic Practices and the State in Northern Asia: Views from the Centre and Periphery." In *Shamanism, History, and the State*, edited by Nicholas Thomas and Caroline Humphrey, 191–228. Ann Arbor: University of Michigan Press.

———. 1994b. "Remembering an Enemy: The Bogd Khaan in Twentieth Century Mongolia." In *Memory, History, and Opposition under State Socialism,* edited by Rubie S. Watson, 21–44. Santa Fe: School of American Research.

———. 1995. "Chiefly and Shamanic Landscapes in Mongolia." In *The Anthropology of Landscape: Perspectives on Place and Space,* edited by Eric Hirsch and Michael O'Hanlon, 135–62. Oxford: Clarendon Press.

———(with Urgunge Onon). 1996. *Shamans and Elders: Experience, Knowledge, and Power among the Daur Mongols.* Oxford: Clarendon Press.

———. 1997. "The Host and the Guest: One Hundred Rules of Good Behavior in Rural Mongolia." *Journal of the Anglo-Mongolian Society* 10 (1): 42–54.

———. 1998. *Marx Went Away—But Karl Stayed Behind.* Ann Arbor: University of Michigan Press.

———. 2002. *The Unmaking of Soviet Life: Everyday Economies after Socialism.* Ithaca: Cornell University Press.

———. 2005. "Ideology in Infrastructure: Architecture and Soviet Imagination." *Journal of the Royal Anthropological Institute* 11 (1): 39–58.

———. 2007. "Inside and Outside the Mirror: Mongolian Shamans' Mirrors as Optical Instruments of Perspectivism." *Inner Asia* 10 (1): 153–72.

———. 2008. "Reassembling Individual Subjects: Events and Decisions in Troubled Times." *Anthropological Theory* 8 (4): 357–80.

Humphrey, Caroline, and David Sneath. 1999. *The End of Nomadism? Society, State, and the Environment in Inner Asia.* Durham: Duke University Press.

Hutcheon, Linda. 1995. *Irony's Edge: The Theory and Politics of Irony.* London: Routledge.

Hyer, Paul, and Segchin Jagchid. 1983. *A Mongolian Living Buddha: Biography of the Kanjurwa Khutughtu.* Albany: State University of New York Press.

Hymes, David. 1974. "Ways of Speaking." In *Explorations in the Ethnography of Speaking,* edited by Richard Bauman and Joel Sherzer, 433–52. Cambridge: Cambridge University Press.

Ingold, Tim. 1986. *The Appropriation of Nature: Essays on Human Ecology and Social Relations.* Manchester: Manchester University Press.

———. 2000. *The Perception of the Environment: Essays in Livelihood, Dwelling and Skill.* London: Routledge.

Jagchid, Sechin, and Paul Hyer. 1979. *Mongolia's Culture and Society.* Boulder: Westview.

Jensen, Casper Bruun, and Kjetil Rödje, eds. 2009. *Deleuzian Intersections in Science, Technology and Anthropology.* Oxford: Berghahn.

Kapferer, Bruce. 1991. *A Celebration of Demons: Exorcism and the Aesthetics of Healing in Sri Lanka.* Oxford: Berg.

Kaplonski, Christopher. 1999. "Blame, Guilt and Avoidance: The Struggle to Control the Past in Postsocialist Mongolia." *History and Memory* 11 (2): 99–114.

———. 2004. *Truth, History and Politics in Mongolia: The Memory of Heroes.* London: Routledge.

Kelly, Sean D. 2005. "Seeing Things in Merleau-Ponty." In *Cambridge Companion to Merleau-Ponty,* edited by Taylor Carman and Mark B. N. Hansen, 74–110. Cambridge: Cambridge University Press.

Kendall, Laurel. 1985. *Shamans, Housewives, and Other Restless Spirits: Women in Korean Ritual Life.* Honolulu: University of Hawaii Press.

Kierkegaard, Søren. 1963 [1846]. *Afsluttende uvidenskabelig Efterskrift* (Andet Halvbind). Copenhagen: Gyldendal.

——. 1989 [1841]. *The Concept of Irony—With Continual Reference to Socrates.* Princeton: Princeton University Press.

Koestler, Arthur. 1964. *The Act of Creation.* London: Arkana.

Kornblatt, Judith. 1992. *The Cossack Hero in Russian Literature: A Study in Cultural Mythology.* Madison: The University of Wisconsin Press

Kristensen, Benedikte. 2007. "The Human Perspective. *Inner Asia* 10 (1): 275–90.

Lacaze, Gaëlle. 1996. "Thoughts about the Effectiveness of the Shamanism Speech: Preliminary Data to the Study of Today's Uses of Maledictions by the Darxad of the Xovsgol." In *Tsentral'no–azyatskii shamaanizm,* 149–50. Ulan-Ude: Akademiia nauk.

——. 2000. "Représentations et techniques du corps chez les peuples mongols." Ph.D. dissertation, University of Paris–X.

Latour, Bruno. 1993. *We Have Never Been Modern.* London: Harvester Wheatsheaf.

——. 2002. *War of the Worlds: What About Peace?* Chicago: Prickly Paradigm Press.

——. 2005. *Reassembling the Social: An Introduction to Actor-Network-Theory.* Oxford: Oxford University Press.

Law, John, and Annemarie Mol, eds. 2002. *Complexities: Social Studies of Knowledge Practices.* Durham: Duke University Press.

Leach, James. 2003. *Creative Land: Place and Procreation on the Rai Coast of Papua New Guinea.* Oxford: Berghahn.

Legrand, Jacques. 1976. *L'administration dans la domination Sino-Mandchoue en Mongolie Qalq-a.* Paris: Collège de France.

Legrain, Laurent. 2001. *Chants du peuple Darxad.* Collection musiques populaires. Col CD 111, Colophon Editions.

——. 2007. "Au bon vieux temps de la coopérative: À propos de la nostalgie dans un district rural de la Mongolie contemporaine." *Civilisations* 56 (1–2): 103–20.

——. 2008a. "Chants longs, rivières et mémoire." *Communication du 3ème congrès du Réseau Asie.* Paris: CNRS.

——. 2008b. "Que sont les perceptions esthétiques en contexte mongol?" *Communication du 3ème congrès du Réseau Asie.* Paris: CNRS.

Lévi-Strauss, Claude. 1962. *The Savage Mind.* Chicago: Chicago University Press.

Lindquist, Galina. 2005. *Conjuring Hope: Healing and Magic in Contemporary Russia.* Oxford: Berghahn.

Macdonald, Alexander W., ed. 1997. *Mandala and Landscape.* New Delhi: D.K. Printworld.

Maidar, D. 1971. *Architektura: Gorodostroiltel´stvo Mongolii.* Moscow.

Marsh, Peter. 2006. *The Horse-Head Fiddle and the Cosmopolitan Reimagination of Mongolia.* London: Routledge.

Maurer, Bill. 2005. *Mutual Life, Limited: Islamic Banking, Alternative Currencies, Lateral Reason.* Princeton: Princeton University Press.

Mbembe, Achille. 1992. "Provisional Notes on the Postcolony." *Africa* 62 (1): 3–37.

McKinnon, Susan. 1991. *From a Shattered Sun: Hierarchy, Gender, and Alliance in the Tanimbar Islands.* Madison: University of Wisconsin Press.

Merleau-Ponty, Maurice. 2002 [1945]. *Phenomenology of Perception.* London: Routledge.

Merli, Latetia. 2000. *Call for Grace.* Manchester: Granada Centre for Visual Anthropology.

——. 2006. "Shamanism in Transition: From the Shadow to the Light." In *Mongols from Country to City: Floating Boundaries, Pastoralism and City Life in the Mongol Lands,* edited by Ole Bruun and Li Narangoa, 254–71. Copenhagen: NIAS Press.

Meyer, David, and Peter Pels, eds. 2003. *Magic and Modernity: Interfaces of Revelation and Concealment.* Stanford: Stanford University Press.

Moore, Henrietta L., and Todd Sanders. 2001. *Magical Interpretations, Material Realities: Modernity, Witchcraft and the Occult in Postcolonial Africa.* London: Routledge.

Morgan, David. 1986. *The Mongols.* Oxford: Blackwell.

Morreall, John. 1983. *Taking Laughter Seriously.* Albany: State University of New York Press.

———. 1999. *Comedy, Tragedy, and Religion.* Albany: State University of New York Press.

Morris, Elizabeth. 2001. *The Informal Sector in Mongolia: Profiles, Needs and Strategies.* Bangkok: International Labour Office.

Mosko, Mark. 1985. *Quadripartite Structures: Categories, Relations, and Homologies in Bush Mekeo Culture.* Cambridge: Cambridge University Press.

Mueggler, Erik. 2001. *The Age of Wild Ghosts: Memory, Violence, and Place in Southwest China.* Berkeley: University of California Press.

Mumford, Stan R. 1989. *Himalayan Dialogue: Tibetan Lamas and Gurung Shamans in Nepal.* Madison: University of Wisconsin Press.

Navaro-Yashin, Yael. 2002. *Faces of the State: Secularism and Public Life in Turkey.* Princeton: Princeton University Press.

Nazpary, Joma. 2002. *Post-Soviet Chaos: Violence and Dispossession in Kazakhstan.* London: Pluto Press.

Niehaus, Isak. "Witches and Zombies of the South African Lowveld: Discourse, Accusations and Subjective Reality." *Journal of the Royal Anthropological Institute* (n.s.) 11: 191–210.

Nielsen, Morten. 2009. "In the Vicinity of the State: House Construction, Personhood and the State in Maputo, Mozambique." Ph.D. dissertation, University of Copenhagen.

Oosten, J. 2001. "Ritual Play in an Inuit Winter Feast". *Journal of North Atlantic Studies* 4.

Park, Hwan-Young. 1997. "Kinship in Postsocialist Mongolia: Its Revival and Reinvention." Ph.D. dissertation, University of Cambridge.

Pedersen, Morten A. 2001. "Totemism, Animism and North Asian Indigenous Ontologies." *Journal of the Royal Anthropological Institute* 7 (3): 411–27.

———. 2006a. "Where Is the Centre? The Spatial Distribution of Power in Postsocialist Rural Mongolia." In *Mongols from Country to City: Floating Boundaries, Pastoralism and City Life in the Mongol Lands,* edited by Ole Bruun and Li Narangoa, 82–109. Copenhagen: NIAS Press.

———. 2006b. "Tarrying with Repression: Political Anecdotes and Social Memory in Northern Mongolia." *Inner Asia* 8 (2): 163–82.

———. 2007a. "Talismans of Thought: Shamanic Ontology and Situated Cognition in Northern Mongolia." In *Thinking through Things: Theorising Artefacts Ethnographically,* edited by Amira Henare, Martin Holbraad, and Sari Wastell, 141–66. London: University College London Press.

———. 2007b. "From 'Public' to 'Private' Markets in Postsocialist Mongolia." *Anthropology of East Europe Review* 25 (1): 64–72.

———. 2007c. "Multitude Minus Myth: Theorizing Darhad Mongolian Perspectivism." *Inner Asia* 10 (1): 311–28.

———. 2009. "At Home Away from Homes: Navigating the Taiga in Northern Mongolia." In *Boundless Worlds: An Anthropological Approach to Movement,* edited by Peter Wynn Kirby, 135–52. Oxford: Berghahn.

———. 2011. "The Virtual Temple: The Imaginary Power of Relics in Darhad Mongolian Buddhism." In *Representing Power in Asia*, edited by Roberte Hamayon, Isabelle Challeux, and Gregory Delaplace. Bellingham: Western Washington University Press.

Pedersen, Morten Axel, Rebecca Empson, and Caroline Humphrey, eds. 2007. Special issue on Inner Asian perspectivism. *Inner Asia* 10 (1).

Pedersen, Morten Axel, and Lars Højer. 2008. "Lost in Transition: Fuzzy Property and Leaky Selves in Ulaanbaatar." *Ethnos* 73 (1): 73–96.

Pedersen, Morten Axel, and Rane Willerslev. 2010. "Proportional Holism: Joking the Cosmos into the Right Shape in Northern Asia." In *Experiments in Holism*, edited by Nils Bubandt and Ton Otto, 262–78. London: Blackwell.

Pegg, Caroline. 2001. *Mongolian Music, Dance, and Oral Narrative.* Seattle: University of Washington Press.

Pelkmans, Mathijs. 2009. *Conversion after Socialism: Disruptions, Modernisms and Technologies of Faith in the Former Soviet Union.* Oxford: Berghahn.

Peterson, Nicolas. 1993. "Demand Sharing: Reciprocity and the Pressure for Generosity among Foragers." *American Anthropologist* 95 (4): 860–73.

Potanin, Grigorij N. 1883. *Ocherki severo-zapadnoi Mongolii, vyp. 4 (materialy ethnograficheskie).* St. Petersburg: Imperial Russian Geographical Society.

Potapov, L. P. 1964. "The Tuvans." In *The Peoples of Siberia*, edited by M. G. Levin and L. P. Potapov 381–422. Chicago: University of Chicago Press.

Potkanski, Thomasz. 1993. "Decollectivisation of the Mongolian Pastoral Economy (1991–92): Some Economic and Social Consequences." *Nomadic Peoples* 33: 123–35.

Pozdneyev, Alexei M. 1971 [1892]. *Mongolia and the Mongols.* Vol. 1. Richmond, Surrey: Curzon.

Pürev, Otgony. 1980. *Hövsgöl aimgiin ulaan-uul sum, 'jargalant-am'dral negdel' (Tüüxen nairuulal).* Mörön, Mongolia.

———. 1993. "The Problem of Knots of Mongolian Shamans' Garment." In *International Symposium of Mongolian Culture*, edited by J. Zhang), 85–108. Taipei.

———. 1999. *Mongol böögiin shashin.* Ulaanbaatar: Mongolian Academy of Science.

———. 2004. *Mongolian Shamanism.* Ulaanbaatar: Admon.

———. 2008. *Har darhadyn hyraaneyi tüühees.* Ulaanbaatar: Mongolian Academy of Science.

Radcliffe-Brown, A. R. 1968. "'On Joking Relationships' and 'A Further Note on Joking Relationships.'" In *Structure and Function in Primitive Society.* London: Cohen & West.

Ramble, Charles. 1997. "The Creation of the Bon Mountain Kongpo." In *Mandala and Landscape*, edited by A. W. Macdonald, 133–232. New Delhi: D.K. Printworld.

Ratchnevsky, Paul. 1991. *Genghis Khan: His Life and Legacy.* Oxford: Blackwell.

Rethmann, Petra. 2000. *Tundra Passages: History and Gender in the Russian Far East.* University Park: Pennsylvania State University Press.

Ries, Nancy. 1997. *Russian Talk: Culture and Conversation during Perestroika.* Ithaca: Cornell University Press.

———. 2002. "'Honest Bandits' and 'Warped People': Russian Narratives about Money, Corruption, and Moral Decay." In *Ethnography in Unstable Places: Everyday Lives in Contexts of Dramatic Political Change*, edited by C. J. Greenhouse, Elizabeth Mertz, and K. B. Warren, 276–315. Durham: Duke University Press.

Riles, Annelise, 1998. "Infinity within the Brackets." *American Ethnologist* 25 (3): 378–98.

Rinchen, Barsbold. 1979. *Atlas ethnologique et linguistique de la République Populaire de Mongolie.* Ulaanbaatar.

Rossabi, Morris. 2005. *Modern Mongolia: From Khans to Commissars to Capitalists.* Berkeley: University of California Press.

Sahlins, Marshall. 1963. "Poor Man, Rich Man, Big Man, Chief: Political Types in Melanesia and Polynesia." *Comparative Studies in Society and History* 5: 285–303.

——. 1985. *Islands of History.* Chicago: University of Chicago Press.

Samuel, Geoffrey 1993. *Civilized Shamans: Buddhism in Tibetan Societies.* Washington, D.C.: Smithsonian Institution Press.

Sandschejew, Garma D. 1930. *Darkhaty.* Leningrad: Akademiia nauk.

——. 1931. Darkhatskii govor i fol'klor: *Materialy kommisii po issled ovanii mongol'skoi narodnoi respubliki* 15: 1–113.

Sanjdorj, M. 1980. *Colonial Rule in Northern Mongolia.* Translated by Urgunge Onon. London: C. Hurst.

Schechner, Richard. 1985. *Between Theatre and Anthropology.* Philadelphia: University of Pennsylvania Press.

Scott, James. 1990. *Domination and the Art of Resistance: Hidden Transcripts.* New Haven: Yale University Press.

——. 1998. *Seeing Like a State: How Certain Schemes to Improve the Human Condition Have Failed.* New Haven: Yale University Press.

Seizer, Susan. 1997. "Jokes, Gender, and Discursive Distance on the Tamil Popular Stage." *American Ethnologist* 24 (1): 62–90.

Shagdarsüren, Ts. 1994. "Quelques aspects du chamanisme des Doukhas (Tsaatanes) de Mongolie." *Études Mongoles…et Sibériennes* 25: 145–66.

Sherzer, Joel. 1983. *Kuna Ways of Speaking: An Ethnographic Perspective.* Austin: University of Texas Press.

Siklos, Bulcus. 1991. "Mongolian Buddhism: A Defensive Account." In *Mongolia Today,* edited by Shirin Akiner, 155–82. London: Kegan Paul International.

Sinor, Denis, ed. 1990. *The Cambridge History of Early Inner Asia.* Cambridge: Cambridge University Press.

Sneath, David. 1993. "Social Relations, Networks and Social Organisation in Postsocialist Rural Mongolia." *Nomadic Peoples* 33: 193–207.

——. 2000. *Changing Inner Mongolia: Pastoral Mongolian Society and the Chinese State.* Oxford: Oxford University Press.

——. 2002. "Pastoral Adaptation and Subsistence in Mongolia's 'Age of the Market.'" In *Rethinking Development in East Asia: From Illusory Miracle to Economic Crisis,* edited by Pietro Masina. London: Curzon Press.

——. 2007. *The Headless State: Aristocratic Orders, Kinship Society, and Misrepresentations of Nomadic Inner Asia.* New York: Columbia University Press.

——. 2009. "Reading the Signs by Lenin's Light: Development, Divination and Metonymic Fields in Mongolia." Special issue, "Technologies of the Imagination," edited by Martin Holbraad and Morten Axel Pedersen. *Ethnos* 74 (1): 72–90.

Snellgrove. David L. 1997. *Indo-Tibetan Buddhism: Indian Buddhists and Their Tibetan Successors.* London: Serindia.

Sperber, Dan. 1985. *On Anthropological Knowledge.* Cambridge: Cambridge University Press.

——. 1996. *Explaining Culture: A Naturalistic Approach.* Oxford: Blackwell.

Sperber, Dan, and Deirdre Wilson. 1981. "Irony and the Use-Mention Distinction." In *Radical Pragmatics,* edited by Peter Cole, 295–318. New York: Academic Press.

Ssorin-Chaikov, Nikolai. 2003. *The Social Life of the State in Subarctic Siberia.* Stanford: Stanford University Press.

Stewart, Michael. 1997. *The Time of the Gypsies*. Oxford: Westview.

Strathern, Marilyn. 1988. *The Gender of the Gift: Problems with Women and Problems with Society in Melanesia*. Berkeley: University of California Press.

———. 1992. "Qualified Value: the Perspective of Gift Exchange." In *Barter, Exchange and Value: An Anthropological Approach*, edited by Caroline Humphrey and Stephen Hugh-Jones, 169–91. Cambridge: Cambridge University Press.

———. 1999. *Property, Substance and Effect: Anthropological Essays on Persons and Things*. London: Athlone Press.

———. 2004. *Partial Connections*. Updated edition. Walnut Creek, Calif.: Altamira.

Sürenjav, D. 1998. *Hövsgöl aimgiin hödöö aj ahui, 1957, 1961–1977*. Mörön, Mongolia: Möngön Üseg Kompani.

Swancutt, Katherine. 2006. "Representational vs. Conjectural Divination: Innovating Out of Nothing in Mongolia." *Journal of the Royal Anthropological Institute* 12 (2): 331–54.

———. 2007. "The Ontological Spiral: Virtuosity and Transparency in Mongolian Games." *Inner Asia* 9 (2): 237–60.

Tambiah, Stanley J. 1985. "The Galactic Polity in Southeast Asia." In *Culture, Thought, and Social Action: An Anthropological Perspective*, 252–86. Cambridge: Harvard University Press.

Taussig, Michael. 1987. *Shamanism, Colonialism, and the Wild Man: A Study in Terror and Healing*. Chicago: University of Chicago Press.

———. 1992. *The Nervous System*. London: Routledge.

———. 1997. *The Magic of the State*. London: Routledge.

Taylor, A. C. 1993. "The Soul's Body and Its States: An Amazonian Perspective on the Nature of Being Human." *Journal of the Royal Anthropological Institute* (n.s.) 2: 201–15.

Tsegmed, Namdagiin. 1992. *Alag shishgediin uyanga: darhad ardyn duunuud*. Mörön, Mongolia: Möngön Üseg Kompani.

Tsing, Anna L. 1993. *In the Realm of the Diamond Queen: Marginality in an Out-of-the-Way Place*. Princeton: Princeton University Press.

Turner, Terence. n.d. "Cosmology, Objectification and Animism in Indigenous Amazonia." Presented to the first meeting of the Nordic Network for Amerindian Studies, Copenhagen, November 9, 2008.

Tylor, Edward Burnett 1958 [1871]. *Primitive Culture: Researches into the Development of Mythology, Philosophy, Religion, Language, Art, and Custom*. Vol. 1. London: John Murray, Albemarle Street.

Vainshtein, Seyan. 1980. *Nomads of South Siberia: The Pastoral Economies of Tuva*. Edited by and with an introduction by Caroline Humphrey. Cambridge: Cambridge University Press.

Vaté, Virginia. 2009. "Redefining Chukchi Practices in Contexts of Conversion to Pentecostalism." In *Conversion after Socialism: Disruptions, Modernisms and Technologies of Faith in the Former Soviet Union*, edited by Mathijis Pelkmans, 39–58. Oxford: Berghahn.

Venkatesen, Soumhya, ed. 2010. "Ontology Is Just Another Word for Culture." Special issue, *Critique of Anthropology* 30 (2).

Verdery, Katherine. 1996. *What Was Socialism and What Comes Next?* Princeton: Princeton University Press.

———. 2003. *The Vanishing Hectare: Property and Value in Postsocialist Transylvania*. Ithaca: Cornell University Press.

Vigh, Henrik. 2006. *Navigating Terrains of War: Youth and Soldiering in Guinea-Bissau.* Oxford: Berghahn.

Vitebsky, Piers. 1993. *Dialogues with the Dead: The Discussion of Mortality among the Sora of Eastern India.* Cambridge: Cambridge University Press.

——. 2005. *Reindeer People: Living with Animals and Spirits in Siberia.* London: Harper-Collins.

Viveiros de Castro, Eduardo. 1998a. "Cosmological Deixis and Amerindian Perspectivism." *Journal of the Royal Anthropological Institute* 4 (3): 469–88.

——. 1998b. "Cosmological Perspectivism in Amazonia and Elsewhere." Four lectures delivered February 17–March 10 at the Department of Social Anthropology, University of Cambridge.

——. 2004. "Exchanging Perspectives: The Transformation of Objects into Subjects in Amerindian Ontologies." *Common Knowledge* 10 (3): 463–84.

——. 2007. "The Crystal Forest." *Inner Asia* 10 (1): 153–72.

——. 2011. "The Nazis and the Amazonians, but Then Again, Zeno." Special issue on Comparative Relativism, edited by Casper Bruun Jensen, Morten Axel Pedersen and Britt Ross Wintereik. *Common Knowledge* 17 (1).

Volkov, Vadim. 2002. *Violent Entrepreneurs: The Use of Force in the Making of Russian Capitalism.* Ithaca: Cornell University Press.

Vreeland, Herbert H. 1962. *Mongol Community and Kinship Structure.* New Haven: Human Relations Area Files.

Wagner, Roy. 1977. "Analogic Kinship: A Daribi Example." *American Ethnologist* 4 (4): 623–42.

——. 1981. *The Invention of Culture.* Chicago: University of Chicago Press.

——. 1986. *Symbols That Stand for Themselves.* Chicago: University of Chicago Press.

——. 1991. "The Fractal Person." In *Big Men and Great Men: Personifications of Power in Melanesia,* edited by Maurice Godelier and Marilyn Strathern, 159–73. Cambridge: Cambridge University Press.

West, Harry G. 2005. *Kupilikula: Governance and the Invisible Realm in Mozambique.* Chicago: University of Chicago Press.

——. 2007. *Ethnographic Sorcery.* Chicago: University of Chicago Press.

Wheeler, Alan. 1999. "The Dukha: Mongolia's Reindeer Herders." *Mongolia Survey* 6: 58–66.

——. 2000. "Lords of the Mongolian Taiga: An Ethnohistory of the Dukha Reindeer Herders." MA thesis, Indiana University.

——. 2004. "Moralities of the Mongolian 'Market': A Genealogy of Trade Relations and the Zah Zeel." *Inner Asia* 6 (2): 215–38.

Whitehead, Neil L., and Robin Wright, eds. 2004. *In Darkness and Secrecy: The Anthropology of Assault Sorcery and Witchcraft in Amazonia.* Durham: Duke University Press.

Willerslev, Rane. 2004. "Not Animal, Not Not-animal: Hunting, Imitation and Empathetic Knowledge among the Siberian Yukaghirs." *Journal of the Royal Anthropological Institute* 10: 629–52.

——. 2007. *Soul Hunters: Hunting, Animism, and Personhood among the Siberian Yukaghirs.* Berkeley: University of California Press.

——. 2009. "The Optimal Sacrifice: A Study of Involuntary Death among the Siberian Chukchi." *American Ethnologist* 36 (4): 693–704.

Yurchak, Alexei, 1997. "The Cynical Reason of Late Socialism: Power, Pretence, and the Anekdot." *Public Culture* 9 (2): 161–88.

——. 2006. *Everything Was Forever, Until It Was No More: The Last Soviet Generation.* Princeton: Princeton University Press.

Zhamtsarano, Tsyben. 1979 [1934]. "Ethnography and Geography of the Darkhat and Other Mongolian Minorities." *The Mongolia Society: Special Papers* (8): 1–166.

Žižek, Slavoj. 1993. *Tarrying with the Negative: Kant, Hegel and the Critique of Ideology.* London: Verso.

Glossary

agsan   violent rage, ferocious horse

ail   household

aimag   regional province (highest administrative level below state)

ataman   leader, strongman

badagshin   half-person

bag   subdistrict (smallest administrative level, comprising around one hundred households)

bandi   novice lama receiving monastic education

Bogd Khan   the eighth and last Jebtsundamba Khutuktu (1870–1924)

böö   shaman

darga   leader, boss

Darhad Ih Shav'   the Great Darhad Ecclesiastical Estate (1757–1921)

deel   traditional Mongolian garment *ezen* (pl. *ezed*): master, owner

ferm   socialist cattle farm consisting of several nomadic *ails*

ger   yurt (nomadic tent)

hadag   ceremonial silk scarf

haraal   curse, malediction

hel am   evil tongue, malicious gossip

hoimor   honored space in the northern corner of the *ger*

horlol   poison, evil, doing harm

hoshuu   "banner," the smallest administrative unit in Manchu Mongolia

hudal   a lie

huvilgaan   metamorphosis, reincarnation

hüree   monastery

Jebtsundamba Khutuktu   highest-ranking reincarnation in presocialist Outer Mongolia

lama   Buddhist monk

lus savdag   water and earth spirits

manjig   tassel (on shamanic gown)

negdel   collective farm

nutag   homeland

ongon (**pl.** *ongod*)   shamanic spirit/spirit talisman

ovog   clan

ovoo   stone (or wooden) cairn

shabi(nar)   ecclesiastical subjects, Buddhist disciples

shav'   ecclesiastical estate

sum   district (intermediate administrative level above *bag* and below *aimag*)

süns   soul

taiga   alpine forest

tanil   acquaintance

tenger   sky, skies

tögrög (**Tg.**)   Mongolian currency (In 1999, $1 U.S. equals approximately 1,000 Tg.)

Tsagaan Sar   lunar New Year

udgan   female shaman

udha   shamanic capacity

yas ündes   patrilines

yos   custom, tradition

zaarin   male shaman

zasal   shamanic curing

Index

Page numbers followed by letter *f* indicate figures.

241